Dramatic Black and White Photography

Shooting and Darkroom Techniques

J. D. Hayward

Amherst Media, Inc. ■ Buffalo, NY

ACKNOWLEDGEMENTS

This book is dedicated to the three most significant people in my life whom I love very much – Jimmy, Christopher and Ginny. Without you, photography is an unknown factor in my life.

Additionally, the tabulation of names and people and friends who have assisted my photographic endeavors are too numerous to list individually. However, I would like to pay special appreciation to:

Dexter and Jean Russ for showing me the basics of darkroom work, and loaning me their darkroom into the wee hours of the morning way back in 1968.

Frank Hardy, Sr., one of Florida's finest portrait photographers, who took me under his wing by giving me equipment for my first studio, and basically serving as my mentor.

Ray Malinowski, for all of his patience in listening to countless hours of questioning regarding commercial photography, and ably correcting my mistakes.

—JDH

Published by:
Amherst Media, Inc.
P.O. Box 586
Buffalo, N.Y. 14226
Fax: 716-874-4508
www.AmherstMediaInc.com

Publisher: Craig Alesse
Senior Editor/Project Manager: Michelle Perkins
Assistant Editor: Paul Grant

ISBN: 1-58428-027-1
Library of Congress Control Number: 99-76254

Printed in Korea.
10 9 8 7 6 5 4 3 2 1

Table of Contents

Introduction

by Michael B. DeMaria, Ph.D.

A boat lies empty, begging the viewer to climb aboard and take a ride, careening through a lake of dream imagery. Light, dark, tombstones, rays of sunlight... shapes from some distant land casting shadows that envelop the viewer. Life, death, chaos, order. One minute straight clean lines, the next, rounded curves—sensuality and logic dance together in this scene. Sexuality becomes spirituality. Do you dare get in the boat and begin the adventure of your life? Welcome. You have just stepped into the world of J.D. Hayward.

It is said that images are the food of the soul. If so, Hayward's images are a feast. Words too easily reinforce our habitual ways of thinking, knowing and understanding the world; images have the power to open us to the unknown vastness that lies beyond the categories of logic and reason. There is always something more in the image, that which cannot be reduced to a theory. J.D. Hayward has spent his life photographing that "something more."

I first met Jimmy back in 1996, collaborating with him on a calendar that he had been commissioned to do for the University of West Florida. He did not know me, nor did he have any idea that I was a clinical psychologist. I was just sent to his studio to be photographed, and the University had given him artistic license to do the job as he saw fit. What was to follow was the beginning of a great friendship and a heck of a good time. Before I knew it, he was photographing me with black veils, to make my head "float" in space. That was nothing compared to what happened in the darkroom where his creative juices really cut loose. Between the vines growing out of my head and the darkness enveloping my body, I knew I had stepped into an altered reality upon viewing the finished prints. They were fantastic.

What I love most about Jimmy is his willingness to let the "little kid" come out whenever he is immersed in the creative process, whether photographing his subject, endlessly playing with light and shadow, or sculpting and painting the "perfect" image in his endless explorations in the darkroom. I say sculpting and painting because that is the attention to detail he brings to his printing. Although he is the consummate professional who knows the process inside and out, he is also the playful artist always ready and willing to be surprised by the unknown. This is the gift he also gives his fortunate viewer.

It is this sense of mystery that is pregnant in all of his work. It is no wonder he holds his cards close when he talks about his work as well. He gives very little away. He takes great pleasure in bantering with those who want to "dissect" his thinking or psychoanalyze his images. His usual response: "Heck if I know. I just have a demented mind, I guess. Why, what do you think it means?" Little do they know that the mischievous J.D. Hayward is still at work, joking at his own admission of having a "demented mind" while forcing the viewer to challenge her own thoughts and seducing her into putting her own perspective on the line. Many a viewer has become totally naked by having to tell Jimmy what she sees in his pictures. Perhaps that is why this collection is such a rare gift. It is truly a glimpse into Jimmy, "behind the scenes." The background he provides to these masterful prints is as intriguing and impish as the pictures themselves, something to be cherished for decades to come.

To the uninitiated, here is a brief sketch of some of the most prevalent and evocative themes in Jimmy's work. Hayward is always on a journey of the imagination, so it is no wonder that in every picture in some way he is incessantly and shamelessly enticing the viewer to take a succulent journey to never-never land. Many have had this experience in viewing Jimmy's work. The inner dialogue goes something like this: the logical mind is saying, "No, no, this makes no sense...you never put that with that." Yet something deep down inside is intrigued, even spellbound and somehow feels at home in this altered reality. A dream comes back from childhood. You cannot quite put your finger on it, but the shadows in the picture feel oddly familiar. Before you know it, there you are immersed, hypnotized, "lost in space"—Hayward style. Of course, whenever someone asks Jimmy why he put "this with that," he usually responds with a profound answer like, "Why not?"

Of course, his journeys take a seemingly infinite variety of directions. Some of his favorites: the winding staircase, a railroad track, a canal... sure enough, he's luring you right into his demented mind again. Sometimes I imagine that if his photographs could talk they would say something like, "Come on in, the water's fine, look out, or you'll loose your mind." Of course, you won't lose your sanity, or at least I haven't found anyone yet who has. What you will lose are your assumptions and expectations of what reality is. This is to me the most profound and important aspect of his work. By dislodging the logical mind's hold on reality, these surrealistic images open the windows of feeling and imagination in a way that invites the viewer to behold the greater mystery of being alive. So often we walk through life feeling everything has been discovered and known. We arrogantly believe we know what a tree is, what a lake is, and how the world works. How sad. What we lose when we assume that we know is the ability to see with the fresh and innocent eyes of the child. This is the place where wonder, awe and mystery lace the outer edges of our everyday lives. Jimmy's pictures ask us, beg us, to wake up to that awe, wonder and mystery again! By making the extraordinary ordinary, Hayward brings us face to face with the enigma of being alive. Taunting and tantalizing, one minute, soothing and hypnotizing the next, his images challenge the viewer to see the unexpected all around us in every waking moment.

The other major theme in Jimmy's work is dreams. It seems all great artists and poets unabashedly plagiarize their dreams. Jimmy's no exception. To our ancestors we did not have dreams, but rather were being dreamed by the Creator. This perspective has helped me understand Jimmy. There is no doubt in my mind that something else is dreaming Jimmy Hayward. None of us are sure what—but, something is there, a demon or an angel. Of course, like all of us, it's a little of both.

In the end, underneath these endless dreamy, exotic journeys and at times eerie images lies the heart of a man who is in love with life, with nature, with the mystery of light and shadow. Yes, his mind, eye and heart love to play with reality, like we all did as children, yet he does it every day with his camera and his darkroom. Come in and play a while in the world of J.D. Hayward. You won't see the world quite the same ever again.

Michael B. DeMaria, Ph.D.
Pensacola, FL

The Concepts

The idea of creating photo-montages or printing more than two negatives on the same sheet of paper is almost as old as photography itself. Photographers have used this process since before the turn of the last century. One of the main purposes of this book is to help the student and beginning professional accomplish this with as little complication as possible. Multiple image printing, montages, and overlay prints all have the same thing in common: it's a creative reinvention of the original scene to a new visualization of something that has never existed. Also, I would like to emphasize that this is not a complicated task, but something that should be an enjoyable darkroom experience. For the sake of simplification, I will go through the basics of the techniques here for those who are new to the process.

Dodging the Print

"Dodging" is nothing more than simply withholding light from the photographic paper in your enlarger, thereby printing select portions of your negative lighter than they would otherwise be. To withhold light from exposing designated areas of the print, you can use tools as simple as your hand or a spoon for small areas. Some photographers simply use a stiff wire with cardboard shapes that are cut to their specifications taped to it.

As an example, if you wanted to create a portrait print with "no face," only hair and ears, it would be as simple as making a tight fist with your right hand and holding this hand under the enlarger to block out the eyes, nose and mouth while exposing the portrait negative on the paper. The resulting print would be a well-sculpted face with forehead, hair, chin, ears, etc., but a voided white space where the eyes, nose and mouth were. A section where your wrist was blocking light would also be blank. To avoid this, you could have used the aforementioned wire technique. Cut out a circular piece of cardboard, tape this to a wire, and use the wire to place the circle of cardboard over the area you wish to have missing from the print.

Part of the trick to getting a smooth edge to your missing section is to keep your hand several inches above the paper, and to keep your hand (or cardboard piece) moving gently back and forth, or in a small circular fashion. By keeping the object blocking the light in motion, the edge of the area you are dodging is kept soft and subtle. Leaving your hand still or too near the paper will result in a much harder and visible edge. Now the fun begins, and all you need is one enlarger!

Repeat the above process of your friend's portrait on a new sheet of paper (dodge the face to remove the eyes, nose and mouth), and then return this exposed but undeveloped paper to your light-tight paper box. Now, using a pencil (which will erase from the easel that holds your paper), lightly trace an approximation of your friend's head and face directly on the easel. Don't be too detail-oriented in this, but merely try to get an idea of the size of his head.

The next step will be for you to remove the first negative from the enlarger and replace it with one of a cat or a dog who is looking in the same general direction as your friend from the first negative. Project this second negative of the animal's face directly onto the same easel that you have traced your friend's face.

Now, using your pencil tracing as a guide, adjust the size of the animal's face until it is approximately the same size and in the same location as the "empty" section of your friend's portrait. Remove the paper you had already exposed and put it back into the easel. Be careful not to move the easel, and be sure that the side of the paper that was the top before is still the top this time. Also be sure your enlarger is turned off when moving the paper to the box and back again.

Next, print the animal's face onto the paper, dodging the opposite areas of the print this time. In other words, use your hands or a piece of cardboard to block out all of the print except for the area that you had previously dodged (the face of your friend). There is also a piece of equipment you can purchase called a vignetter, which is available at most photo supply stores. This device works along the same lines as cutting a hole in a piece of black cardboard, only with it you can change the size and shape of the hole through which you are printing. What you are doing this time is blocking the image of the cat from appearing on the paper in any area except for the area that you had left blank when doing this process the first time, with the portrait of your friend. When you run this print through the developing process, you will find that your friend's face has been replaced with that of an animal! It may take a few practice runs for you to get experience with aligning the negatives correctly, and to find the proper exposures, but the concept itself is very easy. It will merely take a little practice before you begin making prints that are quite satisfying artistically.

Burning the Print

The process of "burning" or "burning in" the print is very simple as well. Simply stated, you are making one area of the print darker than the rest.

Let's assume you have a landscape negative that has been properly exposed and compositionally meets your satisfaction. The only problem is that the sky isn't dark enough to make the print feel balanced; your clouds are too light. You can correct this problem through burning in. To do this, determine the correct exposure time for the remainder of the print (ignoring the sky values at this time). For the sake of this example, let's say the exposure time for your foreground is fifteen seconds. With this information, make another test print of only the sky area, and determine the correct exposure, which in this case we'll say is twenty-five seconds. Now get a fresh sheet of paper and expose the entire image for fifteen seconds, the proper time to assure that your foreground area is properly exposed. DO NOT turn off the enlarger, however, when you reach the fifteen second mark, but rather block all of the print except for the sky with your hand or a piece of cardboard (just as you did when dodging in the previous example). Allow the sky area by itself to be exposed an extra ten seconds (making a total of twenty-five seconds of exposure for the sky, as opposed to only fifteen for the rest of the print).

All that's left to do is develop your print. When you do, you will find that where there was a washed-out sky and properly printed landscape, now the sky is darker, and there is more of a sense of balance to the overall image.

Masking the Print

Masking a print is basically the same principle as dodging, only in this case you need to have sharp lines to completely remove an area of the print, as opposed to the fuzzier and less-defined edges you'll get from using your hand. For example, let's say you have a negative of three adjoining townhouses, all connected to one another, and you wish to removed the house on the left end. What you must do is cut out a black paper mask which exactly matches the size, shape and location of the area of the print you wish to remove.

This is easily done. First, project the negative of the houses onto your easel, and enlarge it to the size that you wish your final print to be. When everything is arranged, place a black sheet of paper or cardboard into the easel and draw the outline of the house you wish to have removed, being careful that your drawing matches exactly the size of the house. Remove the paper (being careful not to move the easel), and cut out the shape of the house. Now place an unexposed sheet of photographic paper into the easel, and carefully place the mask on top of it.

Expose the image correctly, and there you are; you have successfully blocked out the end building and are now free to print another negative, such as clouds, in this area. Masking is somewhat more time consuming, but with practice it can produce some interesting results.

Once you feel comfortable with these basic printing techniques, it will vastly enhance your creative thought process. Furthermore, if you can perfect these tasks, it will improve your print quality beyond your wildest dreams. I highly recommend going through this discipline in the traditional darkroom techniques for two reasons. First, it will enhance your printing skills. Second, it will make you more aware of negatives that are compatible for multiple image printing. No matter how great the creative thought process might be, dissimilar negatives sometimes cannot be forced together to make a cohesive print. One of Ansel Adams' greatest quotes goes something like this: "There is nothing worse than a sharp image of a fuzzy concept." Amen.

Good luck and have fun.

J.D. Hayward

Interview with J.D. Hayward

Why don't you use computer/digital imaging in your prints?

Probably it has something to do with being born in 1949. It wasn't until three years ago that I acquired my first computer. It's a PC, not a Macintosh, and I mainly use it for word processing and bookkeeping. Computers and digital imaging are now at the forefront of commercial illustrative photography, and they are without a doubt here to stay. In my commercial and architectural work for magazines, I will occasionally use a computer guru adept at Adobe® Photoshop® to remove obvious distractions from scenes (overhead power lines, street markers, etc.) But I will emphasize that this work is craft work, and not a creative task exercised by this photographer.

With regards to my black and white art photography, which has been referred to as photo-montages, photo-overlays, image manipulation, and a long litany of other descriptive terms, it is simply creative darkroom work of combining several images (negatives) into a final print. This is done through the traditional channels of printing on fiberbase paper (although RC can be substituted), using three enlargers in the darkroom, and moving the paper from one enlarger to the next, printing each subsequent image over the previous ones.

The computer removes and replaces this discipline, and basically makes the process of photo manipulation and visual representation into something more akin to child's play. A lot of this work is now being accepted as art, but from my mindset, it is infantile with limited interpretations. By my standards (or those of photographers better known than I am), I have yet to see a computer-based photo image that surpassed the quality of a traditional silver-based image, archivally printed and mounted in the style of the masters.

Which camera formats do you work in?

Since the late 1980s, I have stayed with the medium (6x7cm) and large (4x5in.) format, due to the quality and tonal scale afforded by the larger negative. I also shoot 35mm when it is requested by a client. For my personal use, however, I stick mostly with the larger cameras.

What sort of equipment do you use?

Today, all camera lenses are of extremely high quality, so I really don't think it makes a great deal of difference what camera you use. Presently in my studio, I'm using the Mamiya RB 6x7, Pentax 6x7, Hasselblad 500CM, Anba 4x5 Wooden Field Camera (with Schneider lenses), and a Corfield 6x7 Architectural camera made in England. This is a unique camera in having a front shift, but using a Mamiya RB back. With its Schneider 47mm lens, I can achieve quality I've only seen on a 4x5 camera. As for 35mm cameras, I have two Nikon Fs and one FTN, twenty years old. Quote me on this: "Who needs new equipment to produce fine photographs?"

And your darkroom equipment?

As I've mentioned, I am presently using three enlargers in the darkroom. The two primary enlargers are Bessler 4x5s, with the third enlarger being a Bessler 22C (largest format is 6x7cm). The chemistry is very straightforward. I use Kodak Dektol Developer for the prints, plain water for the stop bath, and Ilford Universal Fixer before the final washing. The print washer is a 16x20 Zone VI. As for paper, I alternate between Kodak and Ilford. They are both suitable for fine art printing. However, they each dry down differently.

What about lighting?

I am basically resistant to exertion when it comes to moving heavy equipment and having power cords all over the place, so I've opted for the White Lightning 1800s. In these electronic flash units, the power source is self-contained, and they have proven to be powerful and reliable, and especially lightweight. They work well in both studio and location applications.

Do you have a system for choosing which objects or locations you are going to photograph?

In regards to my surreal images, I never know in advance precisely what I will photograph. When I am in the field or on location, I hope that I will come across something that essentially interests me. When times are favorable, and I happen across scenes that have potential (in my eye), after taking a light reading, I will make the exposure. The negatives are promptly developed and then proofed as contact sheets and cataloged. Ironically, the images which I have made might not be incorporated into a future art print until a year or so later, or maybe not at all. My negative file is a true graveyard of ideas, some that are great, and other negatives that are totally unsatisfactory in regards to blending in with other negatives for the final surrealistic print.

The Zone System

I make mention later in this book of how my prints didn't really begin to stand out until I learned how to control the range of tones in my images. The method for doing this is called the Zone System. It's a method, designed by Ansel Adams, that allows for very accurate measurement of tonal values—and even allows for altering them from reality to make a more pleasing artistic outcome. While using this system isn't a requirement for making satisfying prints, you will have more control over your images and better results with your final prints if you learn and put into practice the Zone System. There are numerous books which are dedicated to this system, including one from Ansel Adams himself entitled *The Negative*, so I will not attempt to provide an exhaustive explanation of the process here. Rather, I will give you a quick overview so that you, as a reader and photographer, have a better sense of what I am discussing when I talk of tonal contrast.

The system is based on the idea that there is an eleven-step tonal range to every image you photograph. Zone 0 is totally black, Zone X is totally white, and Zone V is middle gray (18% gray). Zones IV down to 0 get progressively darker, while Zones VI up to X become progressively lighter. On a superficial level, this system can give you a very accurate indication of how your image will look tonally when it is photographed.

You, as the photographer, choose which area will record as middle gray by metering from that area of the scene or subject. All of the other areas of the negative will then fall automatically into the Zone scale. All areas that would be in Zones VI to 0 become progressively darker, and those from Zone VI through X get lighter. Once you have measured Zone V, you can meter any other area of the print. By measuring the difference in stops between your chosen middle gray and the other areas, you can evaluate the tonal range of your image before tripping the shutter.

For example, imagine you take a meter reading (say, f16 at 1/125) from an area of craggy boulders. Those boulders will record as middle gray in your negative. A reading of the sky that gives an exposure reading of f16 at 1/500 will record as Zone VII (two stops difference in the meter readings means two Zones of difference). Your rocks will be recorded as middle gray, and the sky will be two stops lighter. If an exposure reading is taken from trees in the foreground of your image, and the meter suggests an exposure of f16 at 1/30th, then that tree-line will record as Zone III (two stops darker than Zone V), and your trees will record as a very dark gray. Each reading (in relation to the initial Zone V reading) will give you a corresponding Zone on the Zone scale. From this you can tell where each area will fall tonally when the negative is exposed.

While this is useful in and of itself, the Zone System also allows you to alter where these tonal areas fall, giving you the power to record a scene not only as it actually appears, but also how you would rather it had appeared. For example, you can choose to place any particular area of your image into Zone V when you are metering at the scene. Then, by altering the development time of your negative (either longer or shorter than is suggested by the manufacturer) you can compress or expand the tonal range of the image. This enables you to bring detail to areas that would otherwise have recorded as either too bright or too dark.

You can also, through development, deliberately choose which zones you wish to shift, and how far you wish them to go. For example, you could bring the washed-out highlight area of Zone IX down into Zone VII. This will put details into your highlights. Bear in mind that rest of the negative will also shift, so your Zone III (in this example) would then become Zone I, with a resulting loss in detail in the shadow areas.

Again, this is a very superficial explanation of the Zone System, and I highly recommend you read up on it to fully realize your potential as a creative photographer. Mastering this process will put at your fingertips a powerful tool for increasing the quality of your negatives and the power of your creative expression.

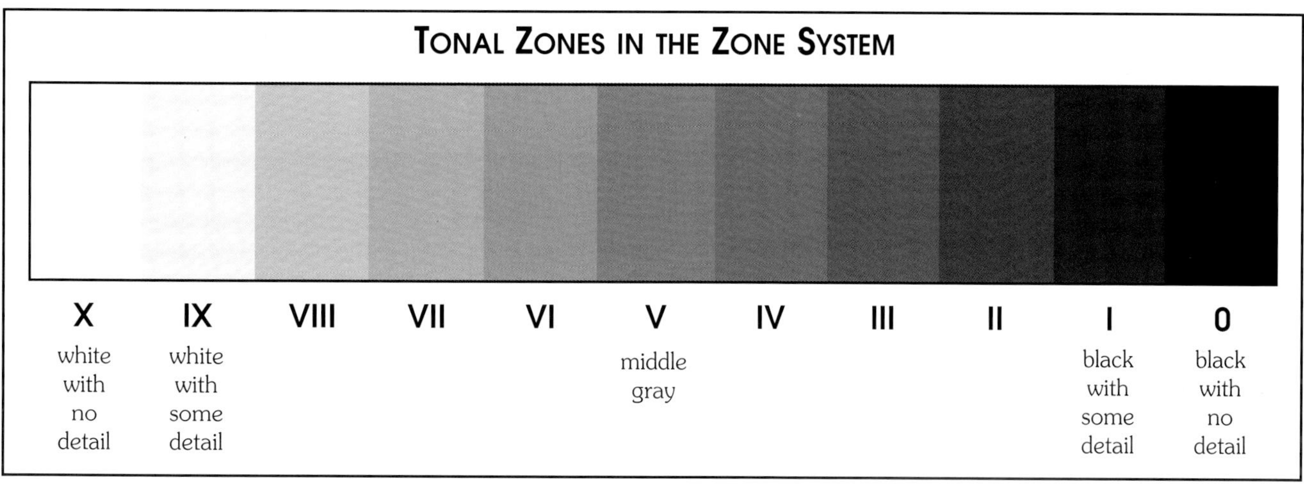

Plantation Upper Gallery

The plantations of the Deep South, especially around Louisiana and close to New Orleans, have always held a great deal of mystique, fantasy and mystery to me, not to mention a feeling of nostalgia. This is somewhat like peering into a time capsule of Southern hospitality and grace that has long since faded from our society. This photograph from the upper gallery (balcony), with the forgotten rocking chair, symbolizes in my mind the vision of the person who rocked away countless hours, commiserating on the agony of the plantation system, not to mention defeat in the Civil War.

This photograph was made on my first trip to Ashland Plantation in Louisiana, which at the time belonged to distant relatives of mine. I had allocated only three hours to document the grounds as well as the interior and exterior of the remains of this old home. After a cursory survey of the mansion, I decided that the early morning light giving the long shadows from the columns lent itself to the concept which I have mentioned above regarding the rocking chair. This was my first negative made at this location, and my favorite exterior image of this magnificent old home. I had pre-visualized a ghost-like figure walking away from the rocking chair towards the rear center of the print. However, after several attempts in the darkroom to incorporate an additional image from the existing negative file (ghost image), I gave into the realization that this scene needed no manipulation; it stood on its own as a straight print. With this in mind, the only corrections made were to dodge the ceiling and burn in (darken) the edges and floor below the rocking chair.

There is a tendency when an artist learns a new technique to perhaps overuse it, often to the detriment of the final piece of art. When first creating images in your darkroom using the negative manipulation techniques you'll learn about in this book, don't overdo your efforts and make your final prints too busy or noisy.

My first lesson for you is that it isn't the equipment that makes the photograph, it's the photographer. This image was taken with a twenty year-old camera, but it looks as good as if it were shot with a brand new expensive one. What makes a great photograph is the eye of the photographer. Certainly there are technical issues as well (film speed, negative size, lens quality), but what it really all boils down to is how well, as a photographer, you are able to envision what you want your final image to look like, and how best you complete that goal! I'll talk about this more later on in the book.

EQUIPMENT

Camera: Mamiya C33 Twin Lens Reflex (6x6 format)
Lighting: Early morning sun
Film: Kodak Tri-X ASA 400 (rated at 250)
Development: Kodak HC 110
Print: 11x14 Ilford Variable Contrast (Fiberbase), #2-1/2 filter, Dektol Developer

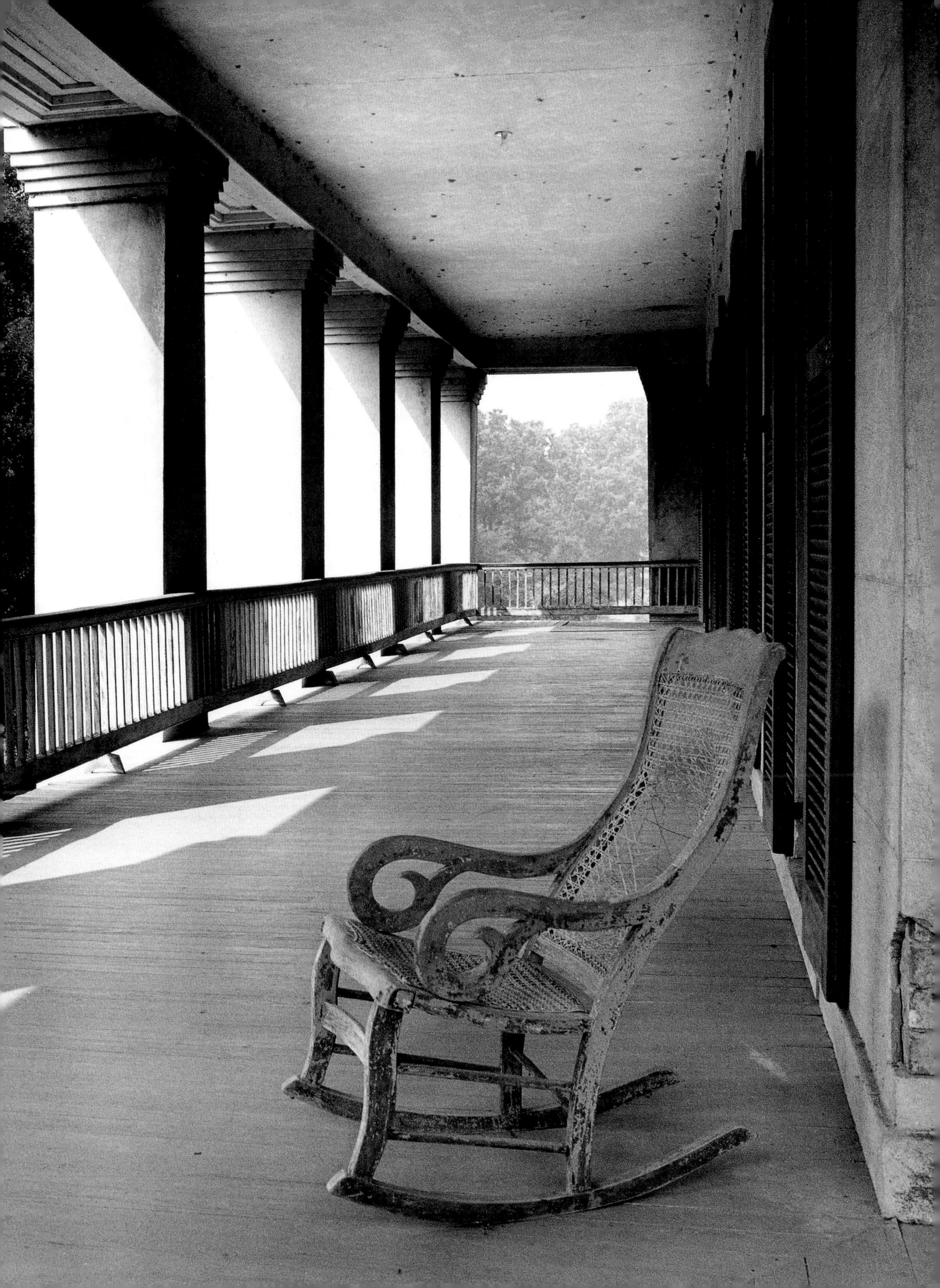

Street Car New Orleans

Since the majority of my work, either editorial or advertising, requires a medium or large format camera, the 35mm format is the least used tool in my studio or for location photography. However, there are great possibilities for extreme grain and tonal shifts in the final print through the use of infrared film on 35mm. Infrared was originally designed for aerial photographers to spot the blight or decay in farmers' crops in specific areas of the field (infrared film "sees" the infrared spectrum of light, and healthy leaves record as ghostly white in the final print). It did not take long for creative photographers to identify the possibilities of this film as an artistic expression in black and white imaging.

I had photographed the main street car line in New Orleans on St. Charles Avenue on numerous occasions in my traditional manner. Nonetheless, my ideas of this old romantic Southern city were not mirrored in the images I shot. The 4x5 negatives, and likewise 6x7 negatives of the street car (trolley car) yielded perfect craftsmanship, but gave the appeal more afforded to a calender or brochure image, rather than the haunting views I had imagined. I finally decided that to achieve the previsualized image in my mind, the "offbeat" black and white tones and the heavy grain pattern would be best achieved with infrared 35mm film. I bracketed several exposures from speeds as long as four seconds (note the movement of the subject boarding the car) to as short as 1/2 second.

There are a few things you should know about infrared film before you buy a dozen rolls and go out to shoot. Firstly, infrared film is especially sensitive to light, and as such should only be loaded into your camera in complete darkness. You must also use a red filter on your lens in order to give the film the inimitable "infrared" look, either a standard #25A red filter or the #87 filter (which appears totally opaque to the eye, but which in reality only blocks visible light from passing through it while allowing the infrared spectrum to pass unhindered). Also, infrared light focuses slightly behind the film plane, which means that if you focus your lens as you would for normal film, the image will be out of focus when shot. To correct this, many lenses have a small red dot on the lens barrel to help you with focusing. First, focus as normal, and then rotate the focus ring until the focal distance lines up with the red dot instead of the standard marking on the lens. Many books are available on infrared photography, and it may be helpful for you to consult them for more tips and suggestions if you wish to explore this facet of photography further. Some truly haunting images can be made by a talented photographer with a working knowledge of this different medium.

EQUIPMENT

Camera: Nikon FTN
Lens: 55mm
Accessories: Red filter
Lighting: Late morning sun
Film: Kodak 35mm infrared
Print: Ilford Fiberbase VC, 0 filter, Dektol Developer

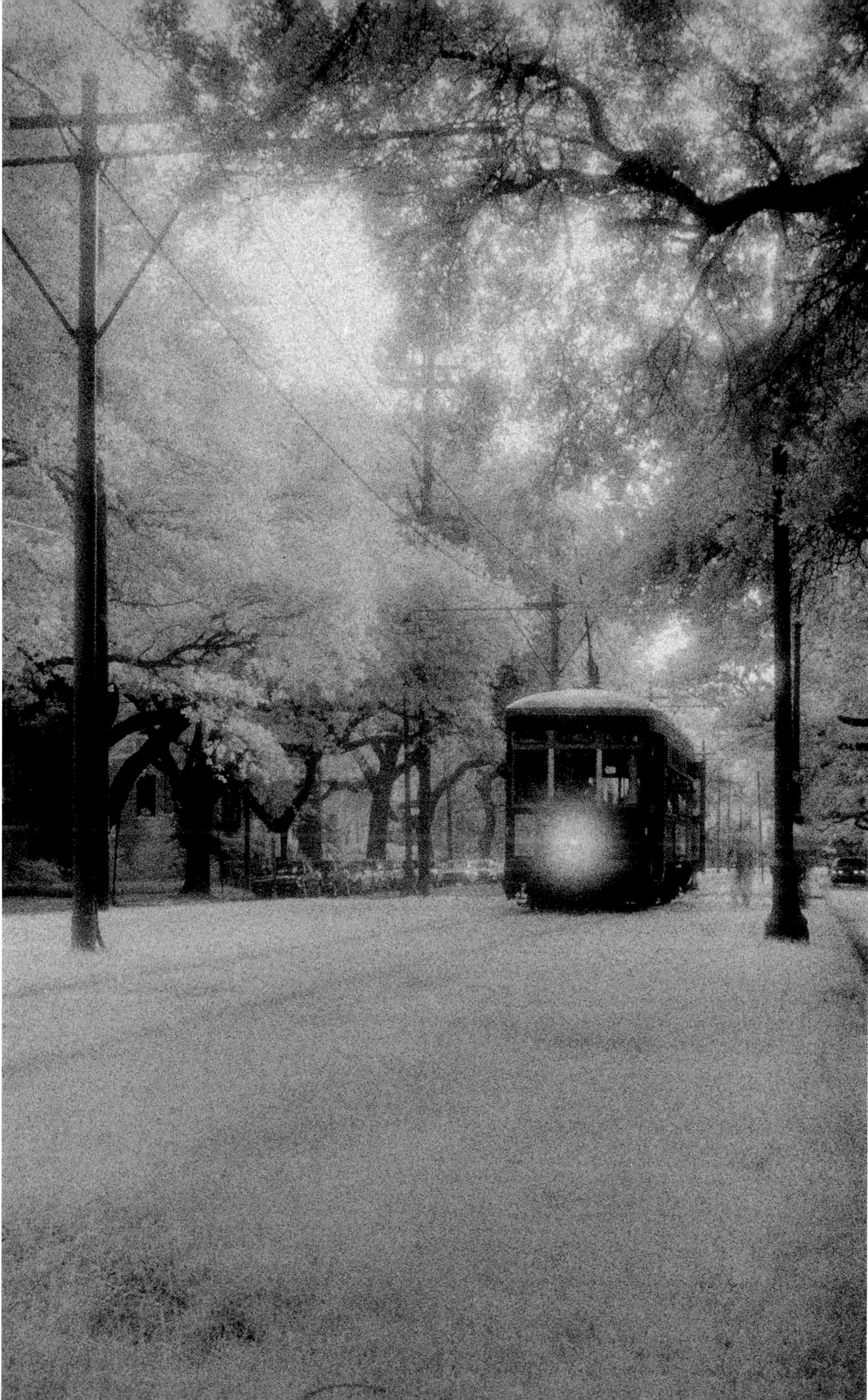

The Cherubs

The old Southern graveyards, with stately oak trees laced with Spanish moss, have always been an inspiration for photographers. If you are fortunate enough to find such a cemetery, possibly that has been neglected but not abandoned, you will find enough images to keep you occupied for most of the day. The most fascinating cemeteries are to be found in New Orleans and Paris, where the natives refer to them as "Cities of the Dead." However, this image was made only sixty miles from my studio, in Mobile, Alabama.

One of the problems with taking on an assignment such as this, if you are a history buff of any note, is that you have an inclination to spend far too much time reading inscriptions on these old tombs, as opposed to setting up the camera. All the same, after walking through Mobile's oldest burial ground, I noticed the grave of twin sisters who died a hundred years ago in childhood. Their parents had commissioned the artisan to craft a pair of 2-1/2 foot tall angels (or cherubs) in their memory. The look on the faces of the statues was well executed by the sculptor: each had a very quiet, faintly serene smile.

Initially, I made several exposures from various angles looking directly at the cherubs, as this appeared to be the best composition. One greatly helpful aid in composing a scene such as this is a viewing filter, such as a Wratten #90 or the viewing filter offered by Zone VI through Calumet Photo. This type of filter is held in front of the eye (not used on the camera lens) so that its amber color will somewhat neutralize the color in the scene, and give you an idea of how the tonal scale or print values will look in the finished black and white print. After you have completed this step, the making of the exposure is purely a mechanical execution.

The lesson here is to never assume that you have exhausted every possibility for a subject just because you've snapped a few shots of it, no matter how well-composed or planned out. The image you see here was taken just after I had decided to pack it in and call it a day. I had taken the head-on shots of the cherubs and was satisfied with them, and began to walk back to my car to leave. I gave one last look over my shoulder to make sure that I had left no equipment behind, and as I did so I caught a glance of the cherubs. I saw immediately something that I had missed before. I had totally failed to look at the cherubs from the rear view, and in doing so had missed the best composition. The light was fading, but there was still enough to make another exposure. The cross in the background lined up perfectly between the statues and I knew then that this image was the one that would be selected for the final print. Remember to look at a subject from as many angles as possible before finishing your shoot. Even old pros can be amazed at what they find when they take the time to really look.

The darkroom work proved to be very straightforward; one exposure with slight dodging of the middle of the print, and a few additional seconds of burning in the edges to darken the sky and foreground.

EQUIPMENT

Camera: Pentax 6x7
Lens: 90mm
Accessories: Yellow filter
Lighting: Very late afternoon, setting sun
Film: Ilford HP5
Print: Ilford Fiberbase VC, #2-1/2 filter, Dektol Developer

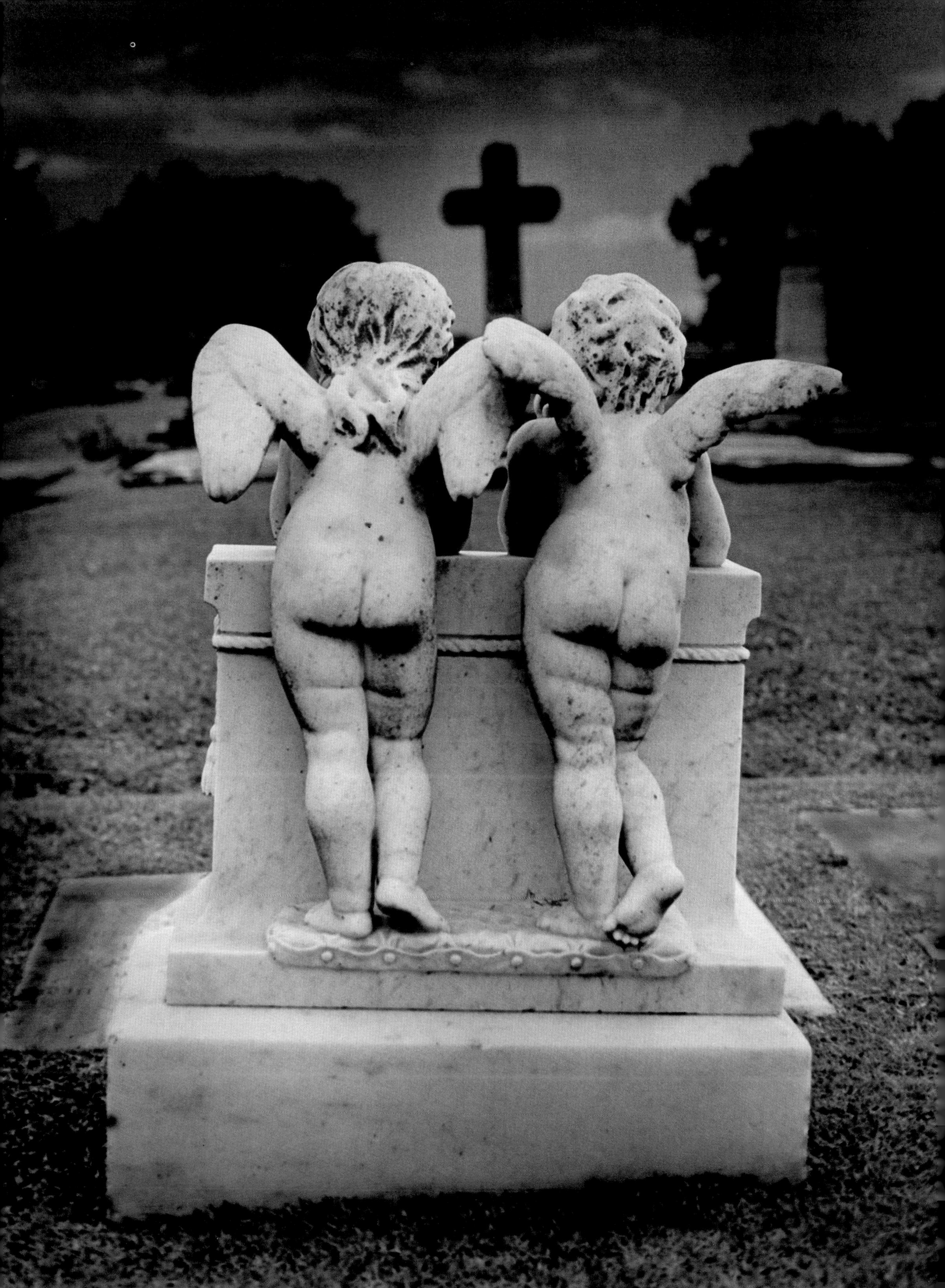

Iron Fence

Creative art photographers have a great deal in common with the journalists who produce your newspaper on a daily basis. We both are looking for something new to either report or photograph. Although I am not a photojournalist, I have a great deal of respect for those who can see the commonplace out of the corner of their eye, and turn it into a great editorial piece or a powerful photograph that sends a message. To be remembered, you need to make the viewer look twice, stop and think. This weathered iron fence, which is in my home town of Pensacola, Florida, caught my attention in 1968. In that same year, I exposed the original negative. The print has sold countless time to natives of this city, who ironically, driving by at approximately 45 miles per hour, have never noticed, much less acknowledged, the simplistic beauty of the fence. The statement being made here is that the "piece de resistance" is often right in your own backyard—but you have to look for it.

After seeing the subject for a great photograph, and having camera in hand, I realized that I had one of the most basic and elementary problems to beginning photographers: recording total sharpness in the negative. I needed complete depth of field to properly maintain sharpness throughout all of the pickets, from the foremost post at the left to the last one at the right side of the image. At the beginning stage of my photography, Kodak Plus-X was the film of choice of many black and white photographers, who as a rule rated the film at ASA 100. The light reading from a Weston meter indicated an exposure of 125th at f5.6. If the camera were to be hand-held, the f5.6 lens aperture would not suffice for the needed sharpness. To maintain complete sharpness and depth of field, the lens needed to be stopped all the way down to its smallest aperture.

I placed the camera on a tripod and used a cable release, which allowed me to use an exposure of 1/8th second at f22 (which explains the obvious motion of Spanish moss in the trees). I would strongly suggest you invest in a sturdy tripod and use it whenever you are in doubt as to your ability to hold the camera steady enough to ensure a crisp image (again, definitely at any shutter speed of 1/30th second or longer). Tripods are available in a very wide range of prices, from twenty dollars on up to hundreds of dollars. When shopping for one, I would suggest taking your camera with you, and trying it out on the tripod you are considering buying to get a sense of how it feels when in use. Be sure that your tripod is solid enough for your camera, and doesn't feel flimsy. There are also table-top tripods and monopods (which, obviously, only have one leg) which might suit your purposes as well. No matter which you choose to begin with, all of these devices will aid you in the creation of a good, crisp negative.

Remember, creating a good print in the darkroom begins with taking a good negative in the field, and no amount of darkroom work can correct a blurry negative.

EQUIPMENT

Camera: Mamiya C3 Twin Lens Reflex
Lens: 80mm
Accessories: Yellow filter
Lighting: Late afternoon hazy sky
Film: Kodak Plus-X ASA 100
Print: Kodak Ektalure-X (no longer manufactured)

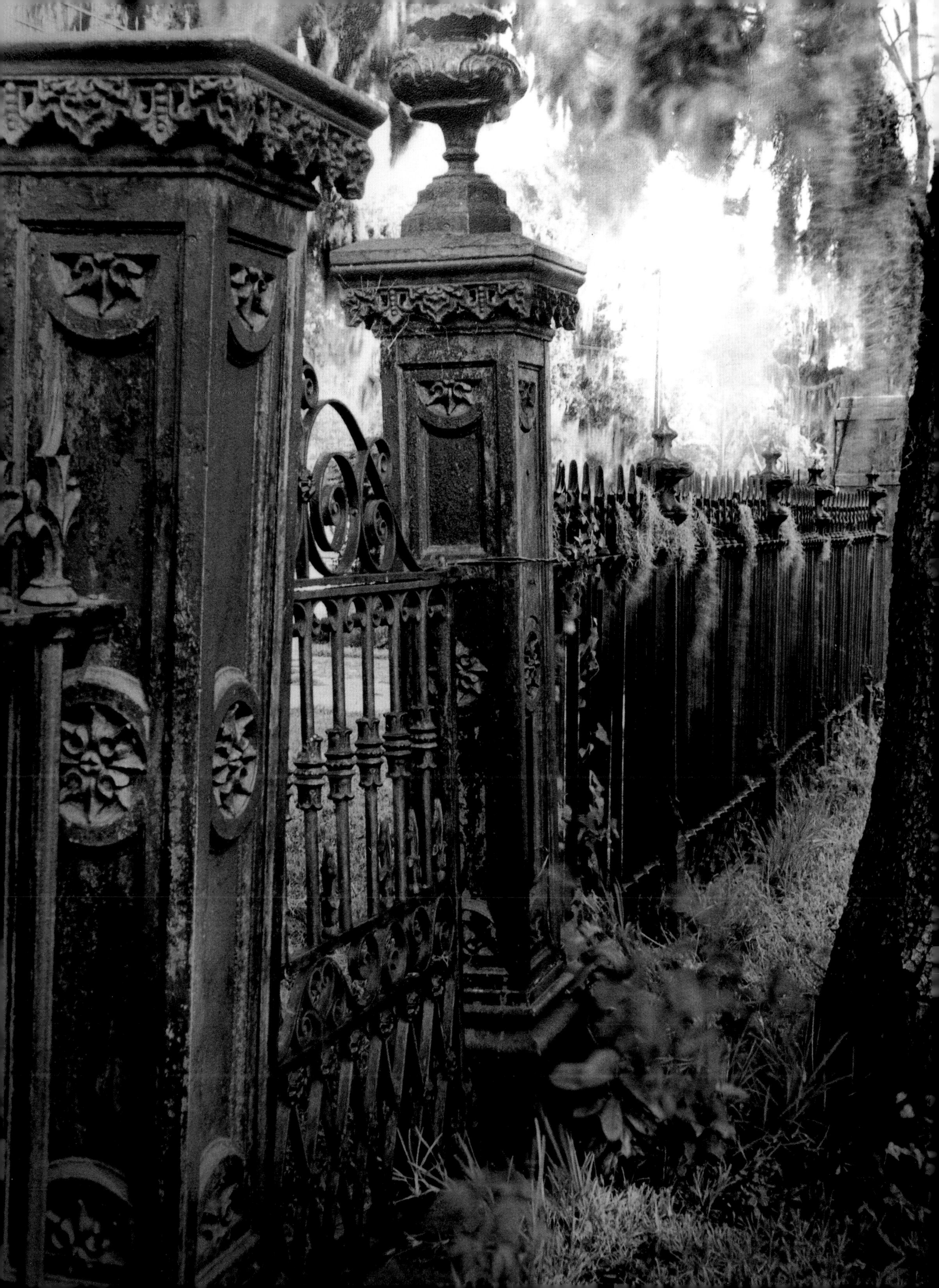

Piano Hands

I was commissioned three years ago to collaborate on and photograph the annual calender for The University of West Florida. The University, after much bantering with staff, made the decision to produce not the traditional color calender, but an art calender with all black and white photography featuring "hands at work." Although the majority of my studio work is in color, I was quite pleased to have an assignment working totally with monochrome film. An added bonus to me was that I had complete freedom to work on the design and conception of each photograph, without having to follow an artist's layout or sketch. The concept was verbal, and we started from there.

Joy Ward was the art director on this project, and quite a saint. By this I mean that she was extremely tolerant of some of my wacky ideas, not to mention my somewhat demented sense of humor while working on this project. We were approximately halfway through a sequence of photos, when a substitution was made to show the elegance of hands on a piano keyboard. The idea was to have a dramatic angle to the photograph, and at the same time have a third tonal scale to contrast with the starkness of the solid black and white piano keys. To accomplish the "third tonal scale" we didn't want the hands on the piano to be those of a Caucasian, but rather those of a fair-skinned black person with graceful hands. Since my connections with the musicians were somewhat limited, I put Joy in charge of finding this person.

We made arrangements to use the piano in the music room of Christ Episcopal Church, as opposed to renting a piano to shoot in the studio. I put my portable White Lightning strobe lights in place, and suspended a roll of black seamless paper at the end of the piano to remove any distracting background. Joy Ward's piano man arrived, and after brief introductions, I asked him to sit down and play a few tunes to get warmed up. He looked me straight in the eye and replied, "Warm up what? I don't play the piano, I'm a model." I was now panic-stricken, sure that every musician who saw this calender would see it as a hoax if the fingers were not properly positioned as those of a pianist. Luckily, Ken Karadin, director of music for the church, was in the building, and came to the rescue. He deftly placed the model's fingers at the precise angle and on the proper keys so that there would be no doubt that we had captured a virtuoso at work.

Despite the fact we didn't have a noted pianist's hands in this image, our intentions came through. The image depicts lithe and graceful hands that show an amazing elegance, with an angle that allows you to fall into the picture as if you are hearing that one sublime chord he is playing.

As a photographer, be aware that the angle at which you photograph your subject can have a big influence on the success of the image. Would this photo be as interesting if it were shot from above, with the keys at a ninety degree angle with the borders of the frame? Hardly. Always be on the lookout for interesting camera angles, and don't be afraid to try something that you aren't sure will work. After all, you'll never know until you give it a try.

EQUIPMENT

Camera: Hasselblad 500CM

Lighting: Two White Lightning 1800 Strobes (one behind hands, second as fill light with white umbrella)

Film: Kodak Tri-X

Print: Ilford Multi-Grade RC, #2-1/2 filter

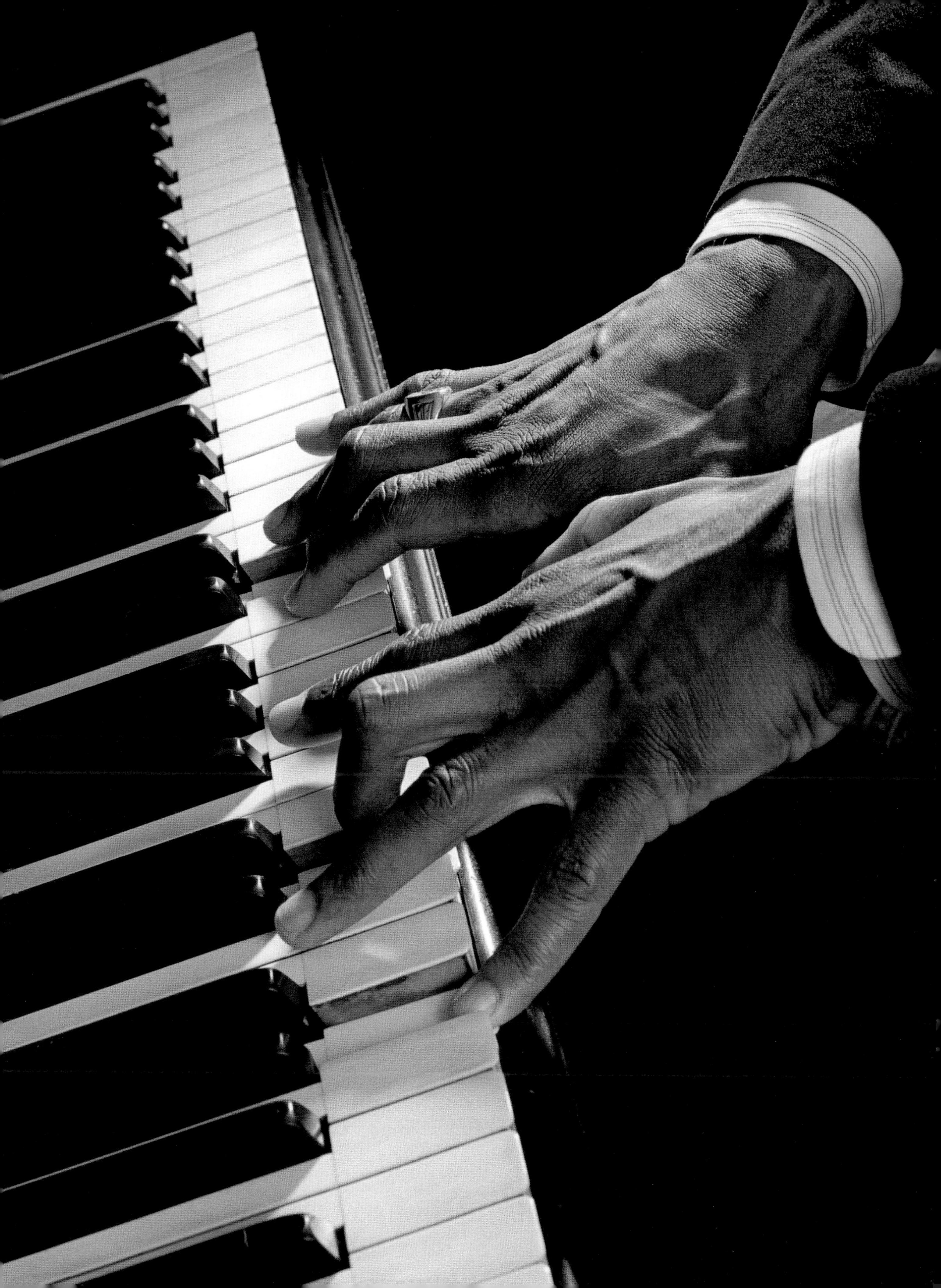

The Bridesmaid

What began as a favor to a young lady (who happened to be a personal friend getting married) became an image that has generated more attention than I ever anticipated. The sales of this print have surpassed my wildest imagination. I do not claim to be a traditional wedding photographer in any sense of the word, and I conveyed this same message to Tina when she asked if I would be her wedding photographer. As politely as possible, I asked her to look to other photographers who specialize in weddings, and let me enjoy her wedding day as a guest and not as the photographer. I did, however, offer to do the formal bridal portrait sitting in the studio as a wedding present. She was most pleased and accepted the offer.

When it comes to formal bridal sittings, I have seen more than my share of prospective brides who were in need of either a tranquilizer or a double gin martini to settle their nerves in front of the camera. This was not the case with Tina. She wheeled into the parking lot of the studio in her red sports car with the top down and the wedding dress buckled into the passenger seat so that it wouldn't blow away. She walked into the studio with her dress over her shoulder, and informed me that she needed only five minutes to slip into it and put on lipstick. My friends, the personality of this type of person is what every photographer needs to make his day fly by.

Tina was striking in front of the camera and it certainly made my job very easy. Every lighting combination was flattering to her. We finished the portrait session in thirty minutes (a normal shoot for brides is about one hour), including the full length and traditional head-and-shoulder poses.

Since I assumed the photo session was over, I began the task of shutting the studio lights down and unloading the Hasselblad film backs. Tina remarked, "Hey, let's do a fun shot for Greg (the future husband)!" We tried a few high kicking "can-can" shots, but the effect wasn't quite what she wanted. Finally, with two frames left in the camera I suggested the pose seen in this print. I shot one frame, and then had her hold the flower bouquet in her toes. What you see here is the final frame from that session.

It's very important that you are open and receptive while shooting portraits to ideas put forth by the model. Very often these ideas are something that will provide you with an exciting final print. At the very least, collaboration with the model can help to relax her and make your job as a photographer that much easier. Don't be afraid to try something simply on a whim, because that whim might unexpectedly produce the best image of the entire shoot.

EQUIPMENT

Camera: Hasselblad 500CM
Lens: 80mm
Lighting: Two Ultra White Lightning 1200 with umbrellas (black seamless paper background)
Film: Kodak T-Max ASA 100
Print: Kodak 11x14 Polymax Fine Art (Fiberbase)

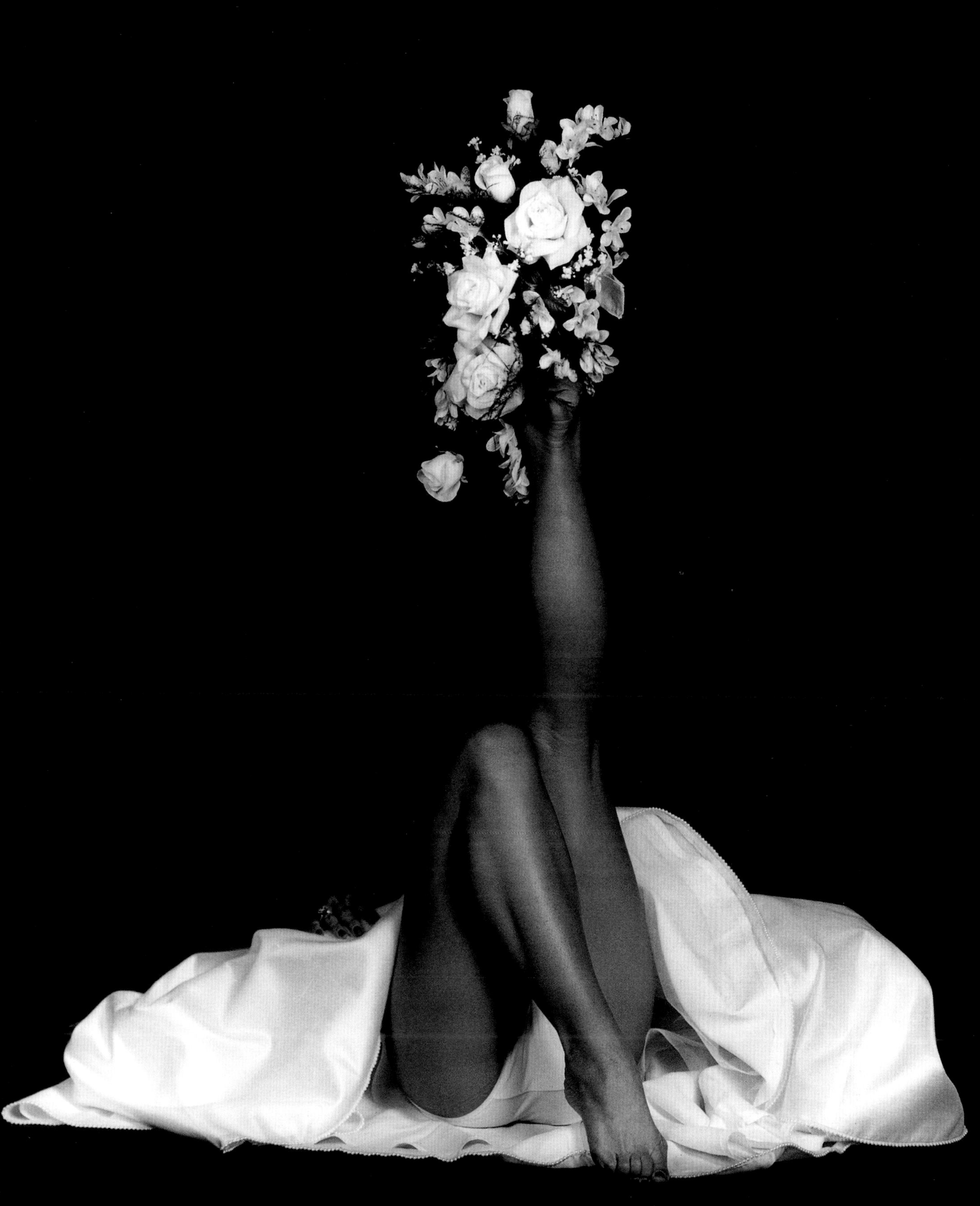

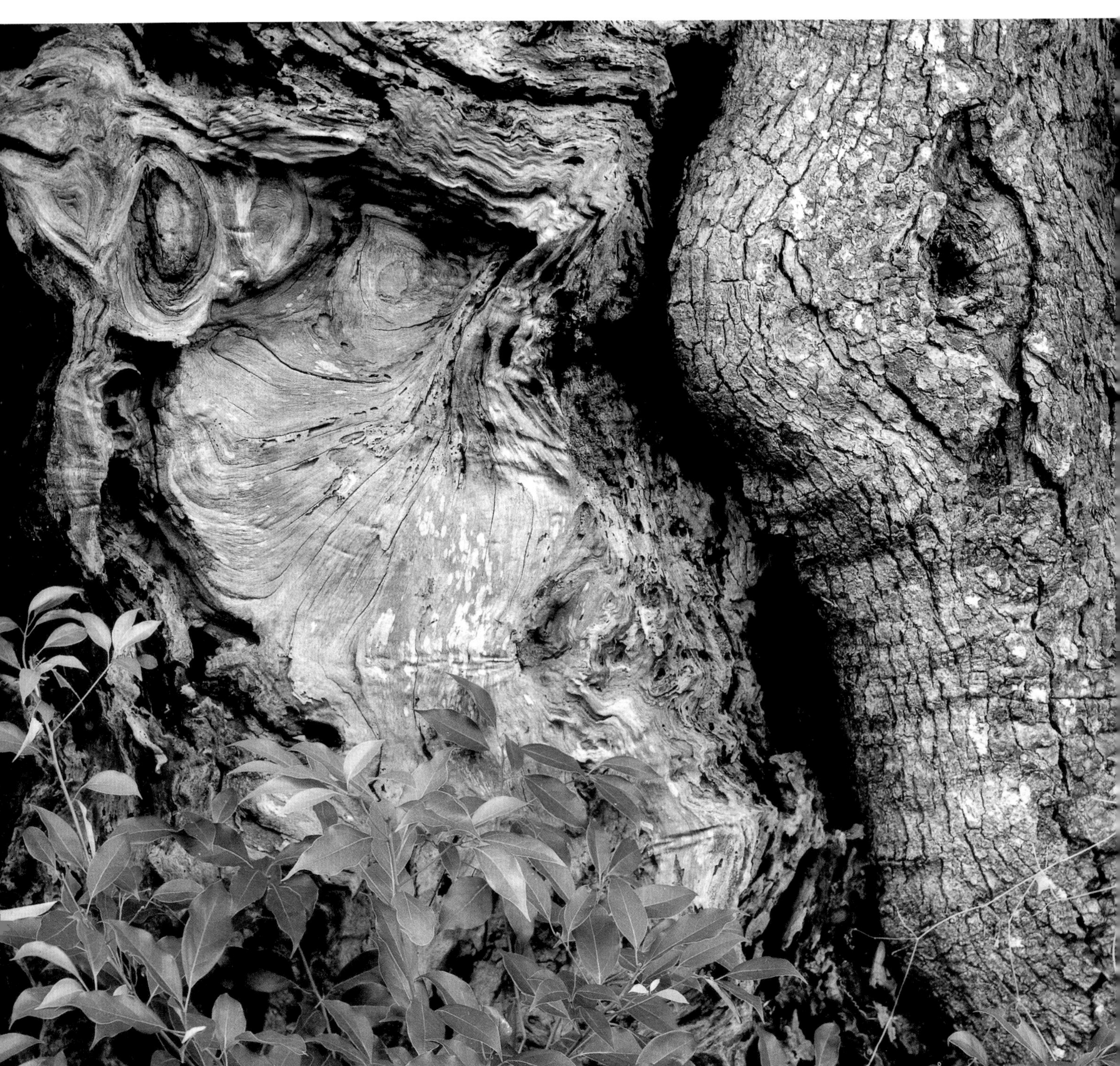

The Bird and Elephant

I love the texture of old oak trees almost as much as old faces... there is an uncanny parallel. Gorgeous gnarled bark holds infinite wonders for the eye and camera to play with, each in sync with the other.

This abstract design, made on Tri-X film, came about merely as a test for a new 4x5 field camera that I had recently purchased. While it is possible to make very pleasing images like this with 35mm film, I prefer to use one with the largest negative possible to record the greatest amount of detail (the beauty and splendor of Ansel Adams and Edward Weston's prints—the tonal scale, depth of field, and sharpness—were not the result of a hand-held 35mm camera). An 8x10 negative and camera would be the ultimate, but very impractical for most of today's photographers, including the professionals. For this type of work, my next choice would be a 4x5 wooden field camera, coupled with a lens of the most acceptable quality that you can afford.

The 35mm camera has opened the world for us, as photographers, to be very speedy and efficient, to use our little cameras to fire off negatives like a machine gun. Then we cross our fingers and hope that one negative might be a Pulitzer-winning, front-page photo. However, large format (4x5) cameras force us to slow down, and have other rewards above the greater tonal quality mentioned above. The image you see in the viewfinder is upside down on ground glass, and this forces you to become more aware of the scene you are shooting. It is a little disconcerting at first to see the world this way, but it forces you to develop a selective eye in viewing the image that you would like to make. You are made to previsualize—to stop, think and then re-compose the image in your mind before inserting the film holder. This style of photography is for the purists, but leads to great rewards in the quality of the finished print.

This is not to say that you can't create a textural study such as this one with a 35mm camera, and I don't want to give the impression that you must purchase a large format camera in order to put forth images such as this. What I am saying is that the larger negatives give you a greater range of clarity and tonal control than you can have with 35mm film. This has nothing to do with composition. As I've said before, it's not the equipment that makes the photographer, it's the photographer herself. You are only limited in composition by your own imagination. A good photographer with poor equipment can make some truly remarkable images. Conversely, a poor photographer with fantastic equipment can still create very poor images as well. Which would you prefer to be?

Finally, what have my eyes seen in this primitive cross section of an old decaying oak tree? Leonardo Da Vinci would draw upon his students to think, and have them find figures in clouds and bark... a true exercise for the imagination. As for me, I claim that there are truly a bird and elephant in this image—if your imagination is up to the task of finding them.

EQUIPMENT

Camera: Anba 4x5 Wooden Field Camera
Lens: 150mm Schneider
Lighting: Diffuse overcast sunlight
Film: Kodak Tri-X (4x5)
Development: Kodak HC-110-B
Print: Kodak Polymax Fine Art VC, #3 filter

The Shell

The creation of the negative for this print began simply as test of a new lens for my 4x5 camera. Additionally, I wanted to test a different film/developer combination with Kodak's HC-110, to boost the highlights on this otherwise gray and mundane clamshell. At the time of this testing, I had no conception that this project would end with the finished print being recognized as "erotic and sensual."

Before we begin to print in the darkroom, we have to remember the most elementary rule in photography: you cannot make a fine print from a marginal negative. By marginal, I'm not referring to subject matter, but mistakes made by either under-/overexposure in the camera, or improper development techniques through not being familiar with exact time and temperature combinations. I have witnessed students who are so enamored with a poorly exposed negative, that they sometimes devote hours of darkroom time trying to make a great print; it's not worth the time. If at all possible, it would be better to reshoot the scene and duplicate the lighting conditions. You must consider the negative for its intended purpose, as the source of the material required for the creation of a fine print, and look for one that has been properly exposed and developed.

I made a 4x5 Kodak Tri-X negative of this tiny 2-1/2 inch tall clam shell. The shell was placed on black velvet cloth, which does not reflect any light sources. Normally, I make contact proofs or prints of all negatives prior to starting to work on the finished print, but this was not the case here. Seeing that the values and tonal scale were to my satisfaction in the negative, I made an 11x14 as my first test print. This is when I saw the sensual and erotic feeling of this image, which I failed to recognize in the initial testing stage of the shoot. With select dodging of the curves of the shell on both sides, and a slight burning in on the edges, I had achieved a very provocative print—talk about hindsight!

Who would have considered a minuscule clam shell found on Pensacola Beach to be erotic? The curving nature of this shell and the play of lighting, as though it is suspended in darkness, give an erotic and almost earthly spirituality. Like Georgia O'Keefe's detailed flower paintings that are so sensuous, this shell gives hints of more than seafood.

Keep in mind when shooting a subject in extreme close-up that your depth of field is very, very shallow, and you will need to be as exact as possible in your focusing to avoid any fuzziness. In fact, it will probably be easy once you are in close to adjust your focus by moving the entire camera, rather than simply adjusting the lens.

EQUIPMENT

Camera: Anba 4x5 Wooden Field Camera
Lens: 150 Schneider
Lighting: 150 watt bulb in silver pan reflector
Film: Kodak Tri-X (4x5)
Print: 11x14 Kodak Fiberbase VC, #3 filter

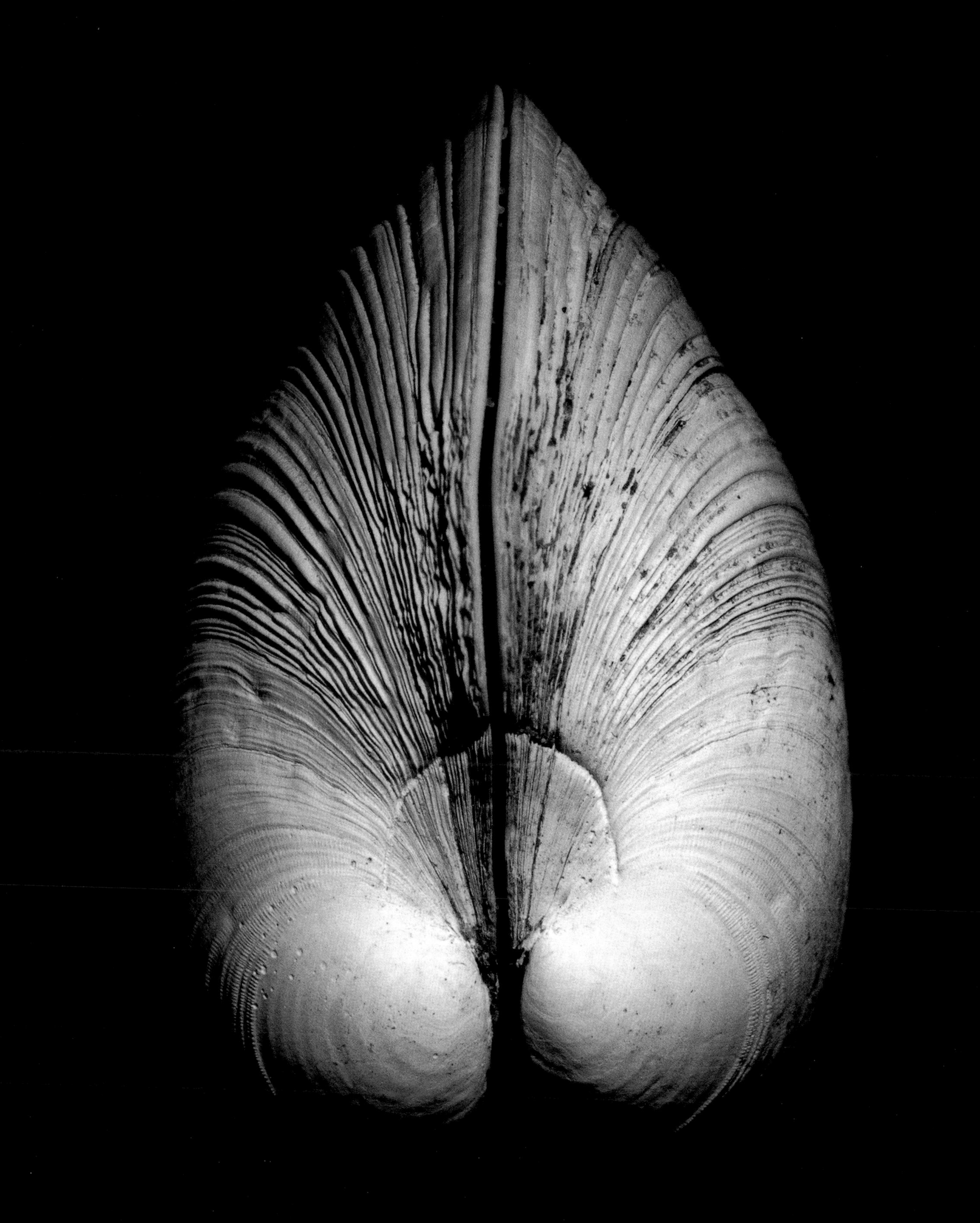

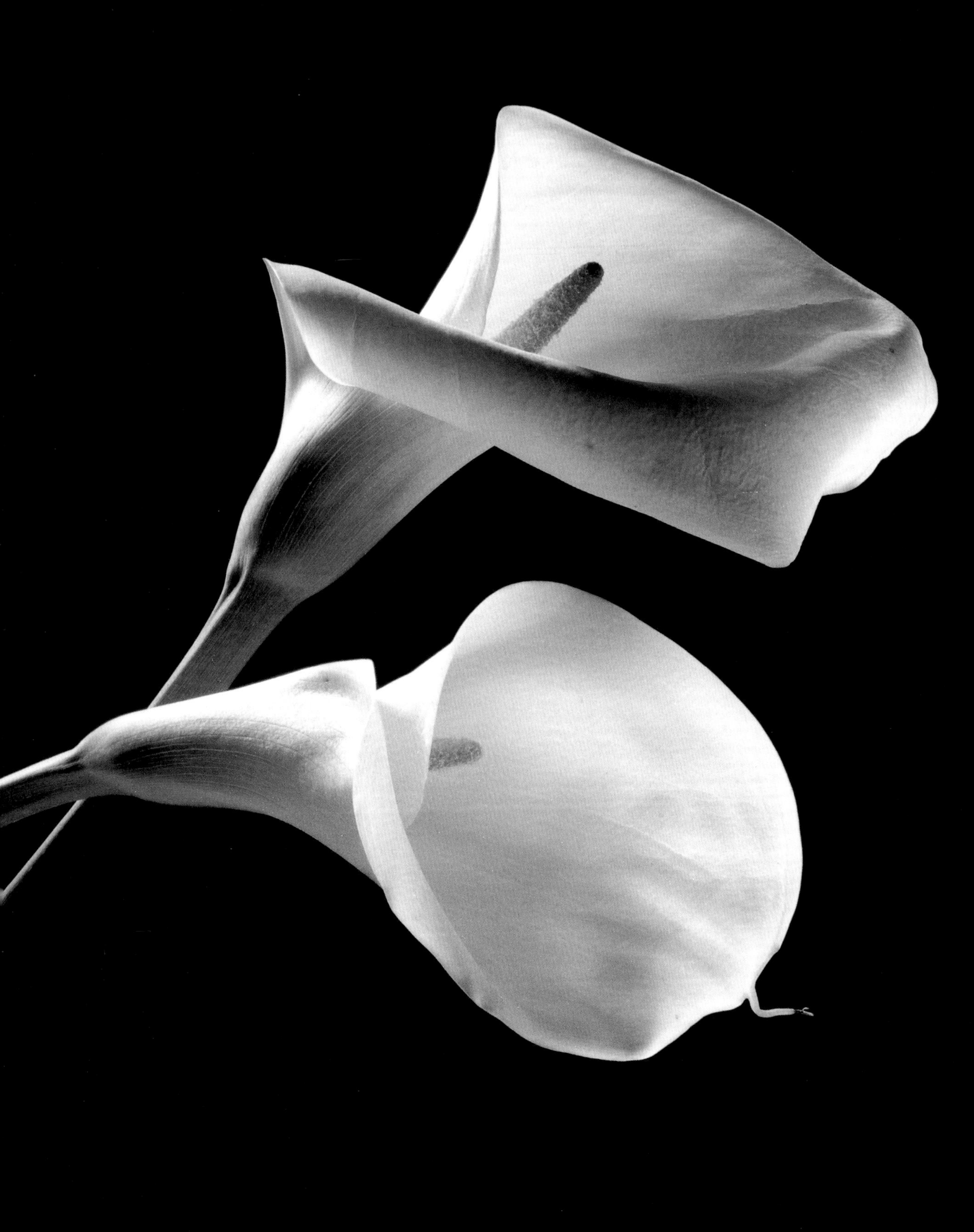

This photograph came about as a "commission assignment" from a very elegant lady who had not only purchased my prints in the past, but was a substantial benefactor to the Northwest Florida arts community. This lovely grand dame asked if I had any flowers in my negative file in black and white that could be enlarged to at least 16x20 and then matted and framed to a minimum of 24x30. She was looking for a very "striking" black and white image for her foyer, that guests arriving at her home would immediately note. Knowing this person's great taste, I did not bother to show what I had on file, but instead asked what she would like, if she could have anything she wanted. She replied, "Calla lilies... large and in full bloom, and with nothing in the background." The commission was set in motion; my problem was finding the perfect flowers for this image.

She had a pre-visualization of this image, and I was striving for the ultimate. The last headache I needed were flowers that are were not as close to perfection as possible. A friend, Debbie Turner, who owns and manages a very upscale florist in this area (called Celebrations) came to my rescue. She stated very directly that there were no Calla lilies in her inventory, and unfortunately, the wholesalers could not offer anything better. However, she had some growing in her backyard, and I was welcome to either cut what I needed, or dig them up. With flowers in hand and a black velvet background, a perfect negative was made. The ensuing print was made to the specified 16x20 proportions, and my client was quite satisfied.

The finished print was most rewarding. There are a few hints and sensuous details to give the viewer plenty to imagine—the silhouette white against the black background, an arabesque dance, pure and simple.

EQUIPMENT

Camera: Hasselblad 500C
Lens: 80mm
Lighting: One White Lightning 1200, pan reflector, black background
Film: Kodak Tri-X
Print: Ilford Fiberbase VC, #3 filter

The Piano Bar

This image was designed to look as though it could have been taken anywhere in the world. The intent is to remind you of those extraordinary evenings spent listening to great, melancholy jazz. This monochrome image could have been made at the acclaimed Hotel Carlisle on the upper east side of New York City or in the side bar of your favorite gin joint in your hometown.

Although I admit to not being able to play a note whatsoever, I have always loved piano music. If you throw in a clarinet to back up the piano, I'll be the last guy to leave for the evening. The inspiration for this print came about in August of 1983, on a trip to San Francisco with my wife, Robin. At about eleven in the evening, in our last night in this great city, I persuaded her to go to the piano bar at the famed Mark Hopkins Hotel, for a final good-night salute to a great trip. Being that she was six months pregnant with our first child, she was not overly keen on the idea, but reluctantly agreed that this would be the last stop for the night.

The piano man was one of the best, and when a friend, a fellow musician, stepped in with his clarinet, it was music made to last all night. Robin, knowing that I would close the place down listening to this music, arranged for a cab to deliver her to our hotel. The Huntington Hotel was a steep six blocks uphill from the Mark Hopkins. When the last set was over from this great jazz trio, I was walking out, and looked over my shoulder at the piano and clarinet. I noticed the white gloves left on top of the piano—strange, since during the jazz set, no one was wearing gloves.

It was now two in the morning. I was looking for a cab to get back to our hotel, but there were no cabs on the street. I walked up the steep hill of Montgomery Street, which at this hour was akin to hiking Mt. Everest. After walking a few more blocks, I spotted a cab, and after hailing him, got into the back seat. "Where to, buddy?" he asked. I told him the Huntington Hotel, and he simply reset his meter and said, "No charge." He points his finger at the front door of the hotel, and said,"You're there."

This trip to the West Coast was not a photo assignment. However, flying home, I had an indelible image in my mind of the dimly lit piano bar, and wanted to recreate this scene. The image was recreated only two blocks from my studio, at Dollarhide's Music Store. I used a roll of black seamless paper behind the piano, and set the props into place: a clarinet, whiskey shot glass and those mysterious white gloves. I was quite pleased that the final print came extremely close to replicating this ultimate night in a great city. I imagine the piano man on break, the clarinetist flirting with a cocktail waitress, while at the piano, the clarinet and gloves wait, playing the most sublime music of all: stillness.

EQUIPMENT

Camera: Hasselblad 500C
Lens: 80mm
Lighting: White Lightning 600 Strobe; Larson Silver Umbrella
Film: Kodak Tri-X ASA 400 (rated at 250)
Print: Ilford VC Fiberbase, #2-1/2 filter

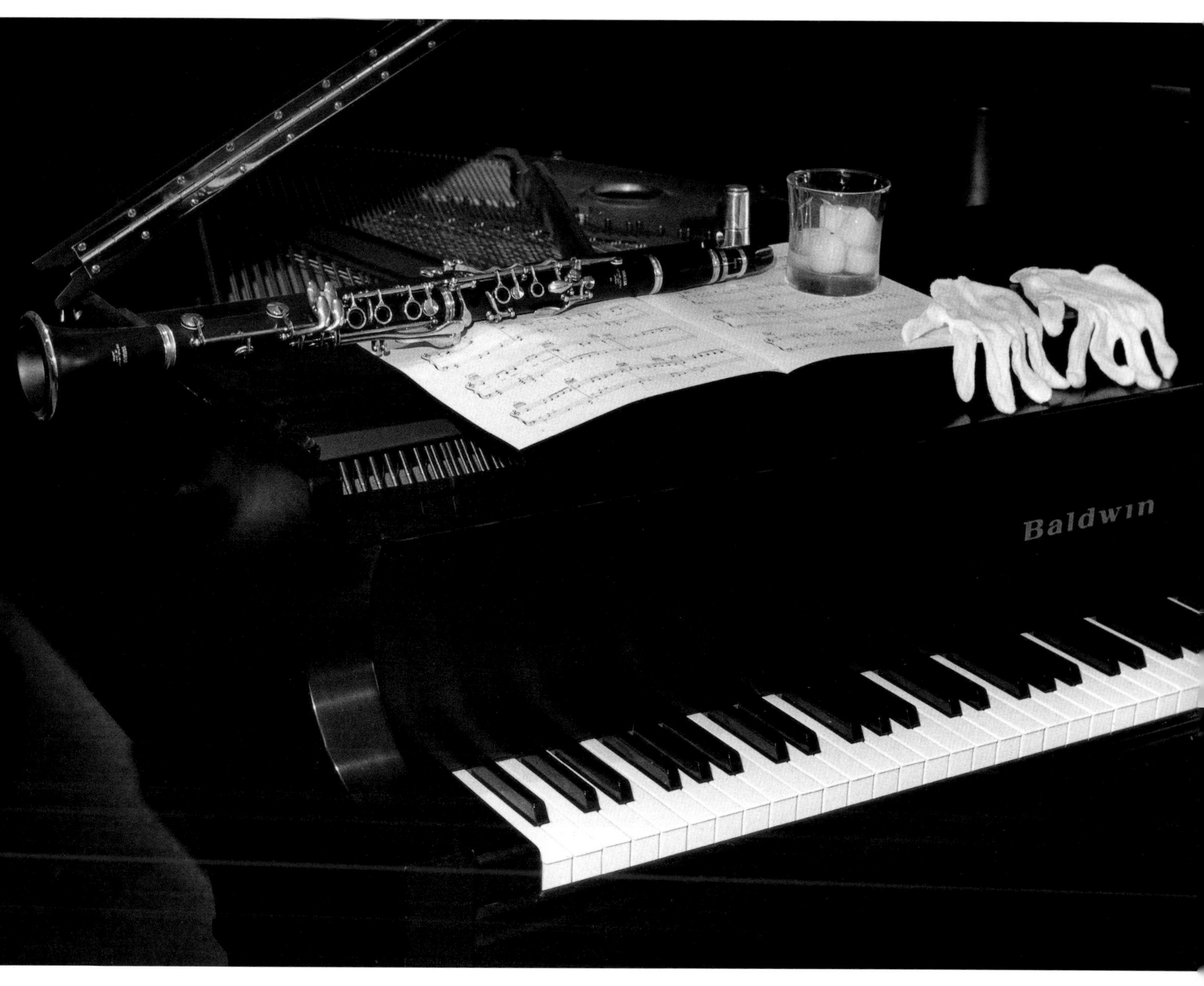
Baldwin

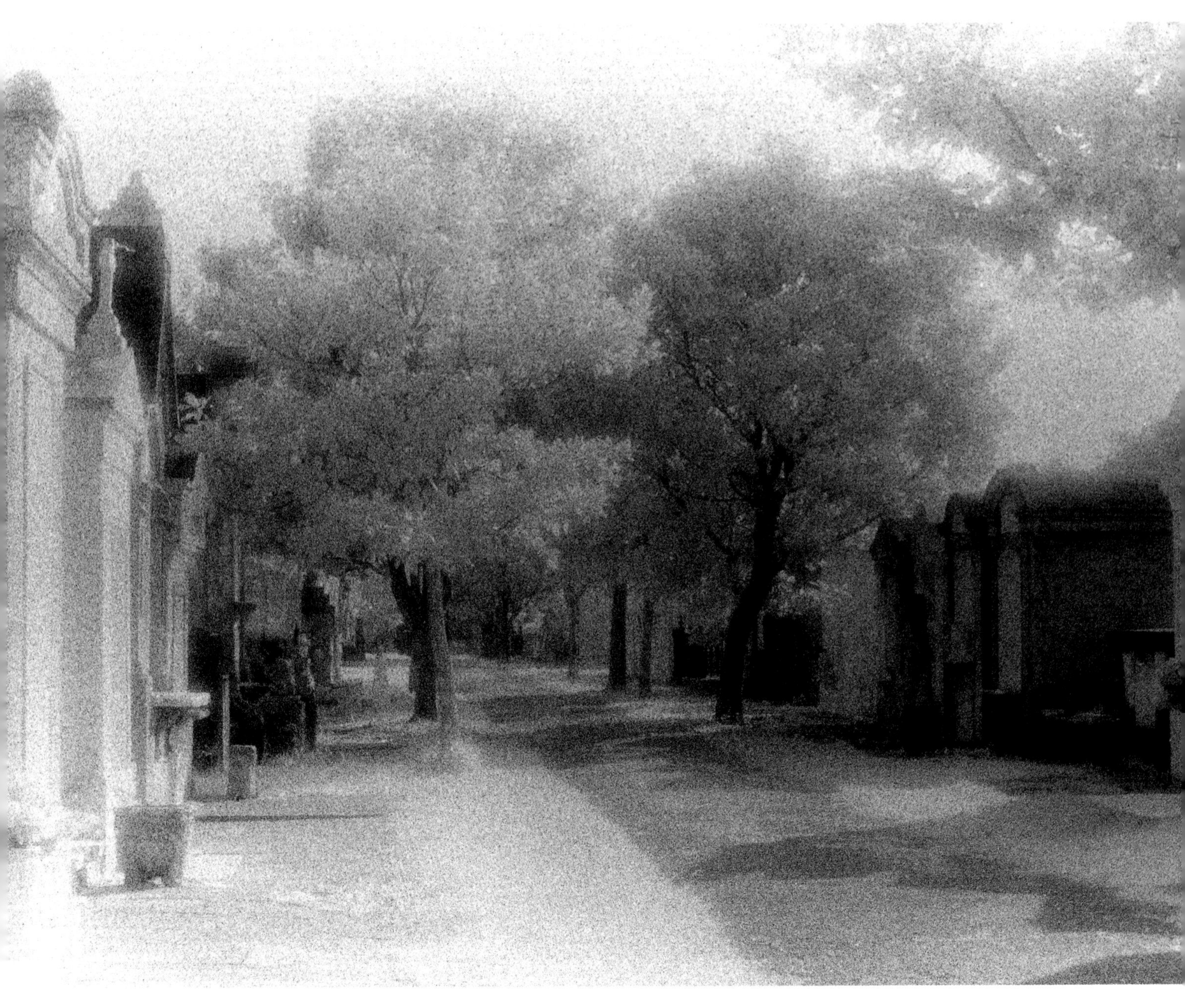

This picture is a dreamy walk through one of the "Cities of the Dead," Lafayette Cemetery, which resides across the street from the legendary restaurant Commander's Palace, on Washington Avenue in the Garden District of New Orleans.

This old burial ground houses many a great person of Irish and German origin who lived in the old city of Lafayette. When Lafayette was annexed to the city of New Orleans in 1852, New Orleans inherited this old churchyard. Some of the tombs are well-designed and well-kept, others were neglected, decaying, or even in ruins as late as the 1970s. A preservation movement shortly afterwards marked the restoration of most of the old vaults and tombs. Today, you can safely walk from Commander's with a Bloody Mary or gin and tonic in hand on All Saint's Day and give a slight "knock on the door" of an ancestor's tomb... hopefully with no response.

The concept of this image was not to be a perception of total sharpness and tonal scale as seen in the 4x5 format. This was to be a dreamy, moody and haunting image: a perfect recollection to be recorded on infrared film on a foggy, gray day.

To execute that impression, I used Kodak's infrared 35mm film in an aging and worn Nikon F-3. This camera looks like hell, and has been dropped more times than I can count, but it's always worked when I needed it (and why I have no faith in the longevity of cameras with plastic bodies). Remember to always use a red filter with infrared film, and to use your light meter only as a starting point. Always bracket your exposures several stops in each direction. Lastly, have patience in the darkroom, as infrared negatives are extremely dense and require an exposure time in the enlarger sometimes triple what a normal negative would dictate.

Putting aside all the pontification on photo technique and history of old graveyards, what's going on in this image? I see it as one of those images that you faintly remember upon waking from a dream. You don't remember the story, you don't remember what happened, you don't remember who was in the dream with you, but this one image lingers in your brain like a cobweb, just hanging there...

EQUIPMENT

Camera: Nikon F-3
Lens: 50mm
Accessories: Red filter
Lighting: Morning sunlight
Film: Kodak Infrared (35mm)
Print: Kodak Polymax Fiberbase, #1 filter

Oak Tree Thibodeaux

One of the most priceless things in the world is the splendor and beauty of a three hundred year-old oak tree garnished with Spanish moss. With all due respect to my Yankee friends, this is indisputably a Southern scene. If the New England landscape had this flavor, there would be no tourists on the Gulf Coast.

At the prodding of my sister Christine, who is a Southerner by birth, but now a converted New Englander, we took a sentimental journey through the lowlands of Louisiana. She drove and I took pictures. We journeyed through the Cajun country, starting at Baton Rouge, and then meandered our way through the small towns and parishes in the delta country. There is a rhythm to the names of the parishes, almost like B.B. King was singing their names himself. The parishes themselves have never had a better christening. You have names such as Ascension, Beauregard, Evangeline and my favorite, Thibodeaux (pronounced "tib-a-doe").

We were driving through Thibodeaux above the designated speed limit when this ancient oak tree caught the corner of my eye. I thought the Spanish moss resembled icicles. Making a U-turn in the middle of the road, we drove back for a closer look. Luckily, two men were working on a fence nearby and gave me permission to enter the field to set up my camera. Most inhabitants of small towns are not accustomed to seeing photographers work with large format cameras, especially with their heads under the dark focusing cloth. My sister, who happened to be within hearing distance of the property owners, overhead one of them comment, "Poor guy must be embarrassed having to use that old camera... 'ya see him hide his face under that blanket when he took his picture?"

I knew that I had captured a fantastic scene, and this proved true after seeing the first test print. However, an August sky, coupled with high heat and humidity, does not produce a cloud formation as seen in this finished image. My stock file yielded the sky negative that I had visualized when taking the original scene. The paper was exposed under the first enlarger with the tree negative, and then moved to the second enlarger where the cloud negative was overprinted onto the bald sky. The only other modification to the print was burning in the foreground to darken the field. The steps above can easily be done with only one enlarger, though it takes a little longer.

The finished print has a surreal look, as if this is a life-size bonsai with Spanish moss, twisting, turning, spreading out wider than it is tall.

Pay attention when composing your image to the framing, either vertical or horizontal. In this print, the obvious choice was to shoot at a horizontal angle, making the tree seem to almost crawl along the horizon. However, not all choices are as obvious. Consider which framing best suits your image. Generally, a vertical frame is best for vertical subjects, and horizontal is best for horizontal subjects. Working in the opposite direction can create a disjointed and jarring print (which might be what you are artistically seeking).

EQUIPMENT

Camera: Anba 4x5 Wooden Field Camera
Lens: 90mm
Lighting: Late afternoon sun
Film: Kodak Tri-X ASA 400 (rated at 250)
Print: Ilford Multigrade Fiberbase

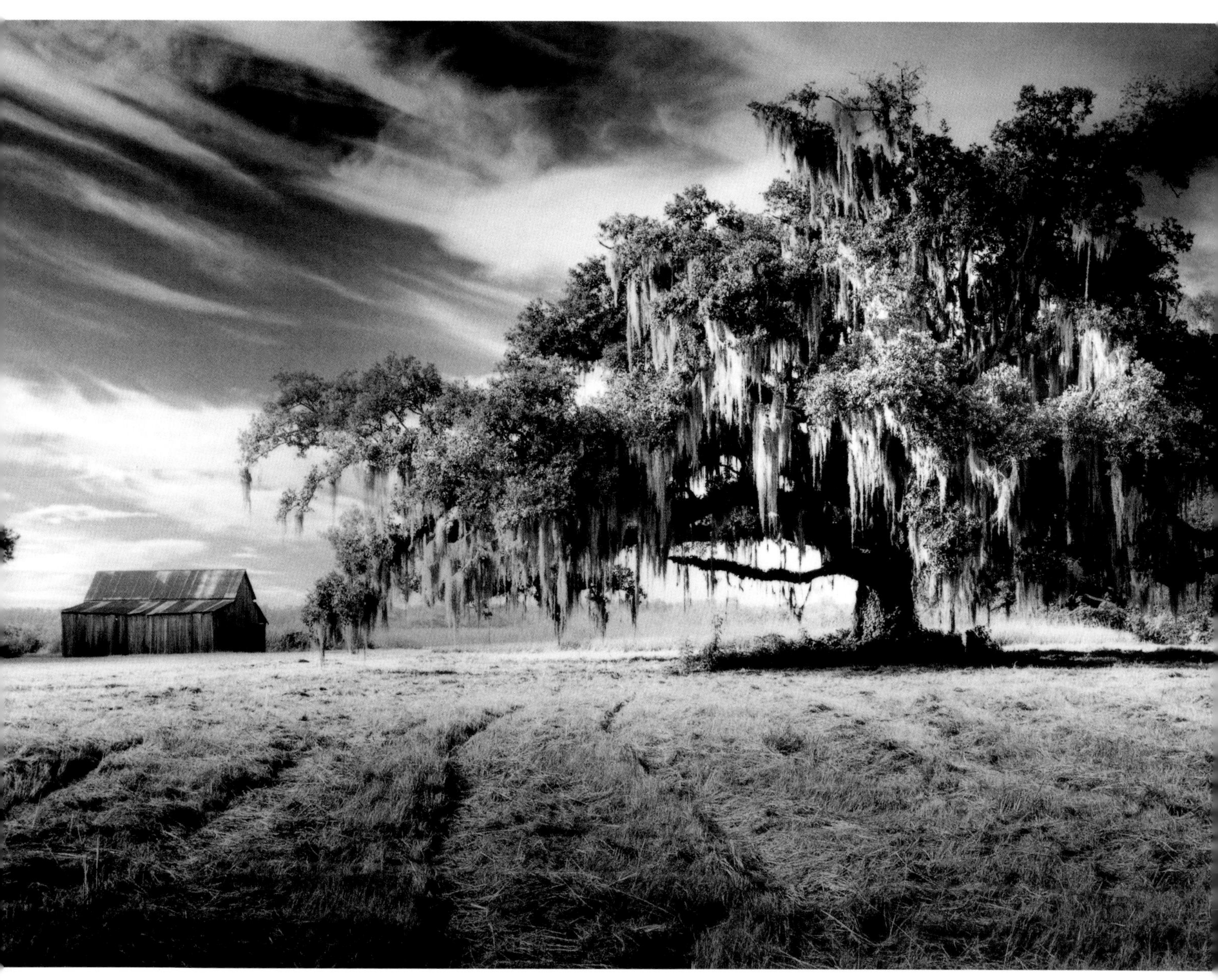

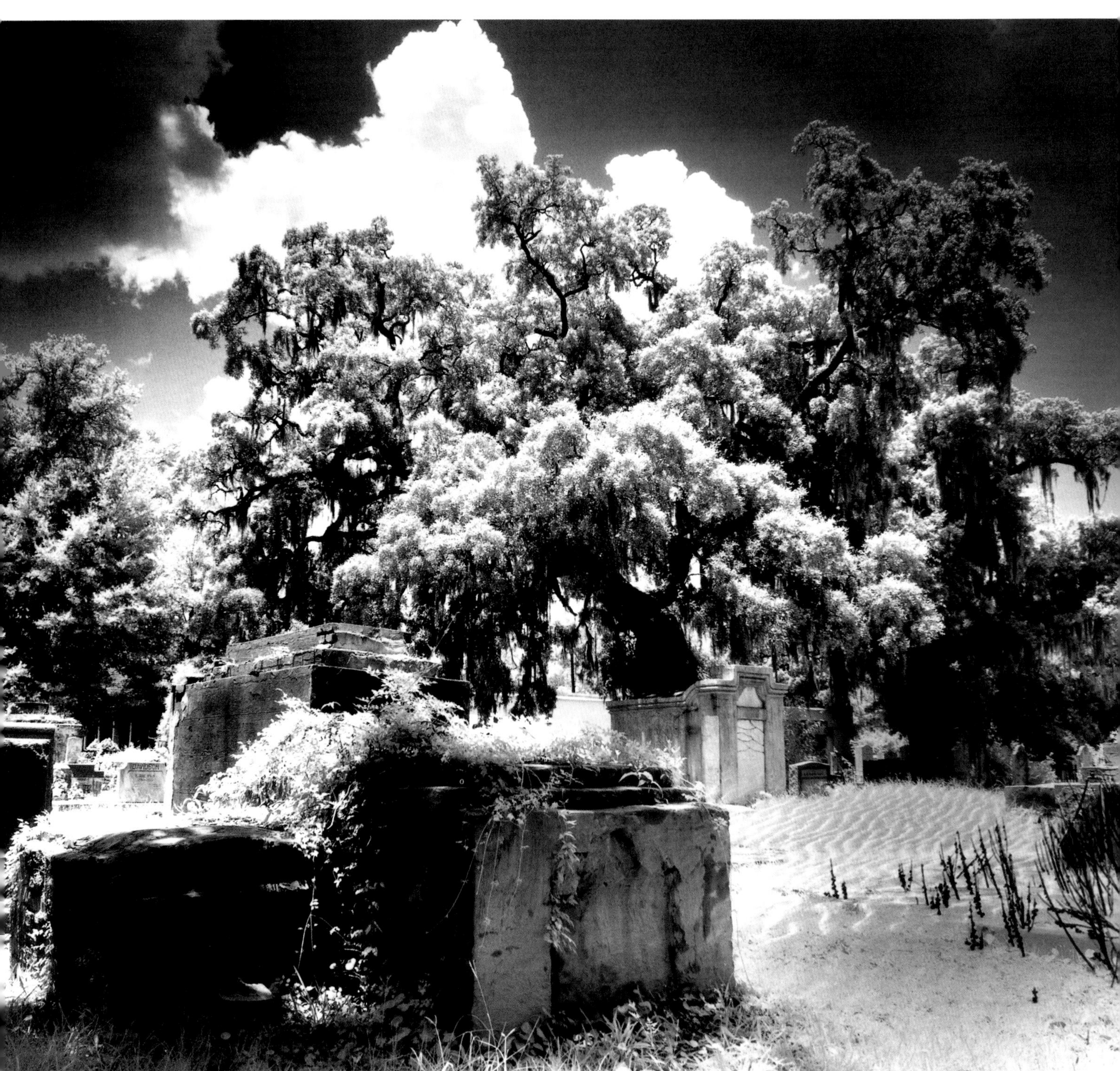

Overgrown, almost buried in the Gulf Coast sand, this mystical place came into my mind as I played with the combination of two dissimilar negatives.

At the turn of the last century, the old Mississippi Gulf Coast was a small piece of paradise. The coast back then was a place of white picket fences, tunnel-like roads of soft powdered gravel, covered by branches of live oak trees and Spanish moss. The natives would give no consideration to living elsewhere. The New Orleans aristocracy, living sixty miles to the west, savored it to the extent of building summer cottages so they could commute by train. The reference to "cottages" can also be synonymous with "mansions." If you had the means, nine months of the year were spent in the city proper of New Orleans, and the summer months on the Gulf Coast, to escape the heat and humidity of the city. It was a distinguished life style, somewhat similar to New Yorkers fleeing Manhattan on the weekends for the Hamptons or Cape Cod.

In 1968, Hurricane Camille, the most devastating storm ever, marched through the Gulf Coast, wreaking havoc and destruction as never seen before in a coastal city. I remember being dumfounded as I flew over the area several days after the storm, taking aerial photographs. It seemed as if the beach was non-existent, and so many of the elegant antebellum mansions were gone. An era of gentile, Southern lifestyle had been flattened in just twelve hours.

Hurricanes destroy most everything in their path, with the mysterious exception of graveyards. Ten years after the storm, I photographed this old burial ground that had been close to eye of Hurricane Camille. Not much had changed. Everybody was still dead, and all the tombs were still intact. In printing this image, I thought of all the sand from the hurricane, and made the decision to merge a negative below the tombs, one of sand dunes. Somehow everything seems so much more beautiful and peaceful for these departed souls to be in this windblown sand, almost like old friends congregating and sharing old times.

EQUIPMENT

Camera: Mamiya RB 6x7
Lens: 90mm
Accessories: Green filter
Lighting: Late afternoon sun
Film: Konica Infrared (120 format)
Print: Ilford Multigrade Fiberbase

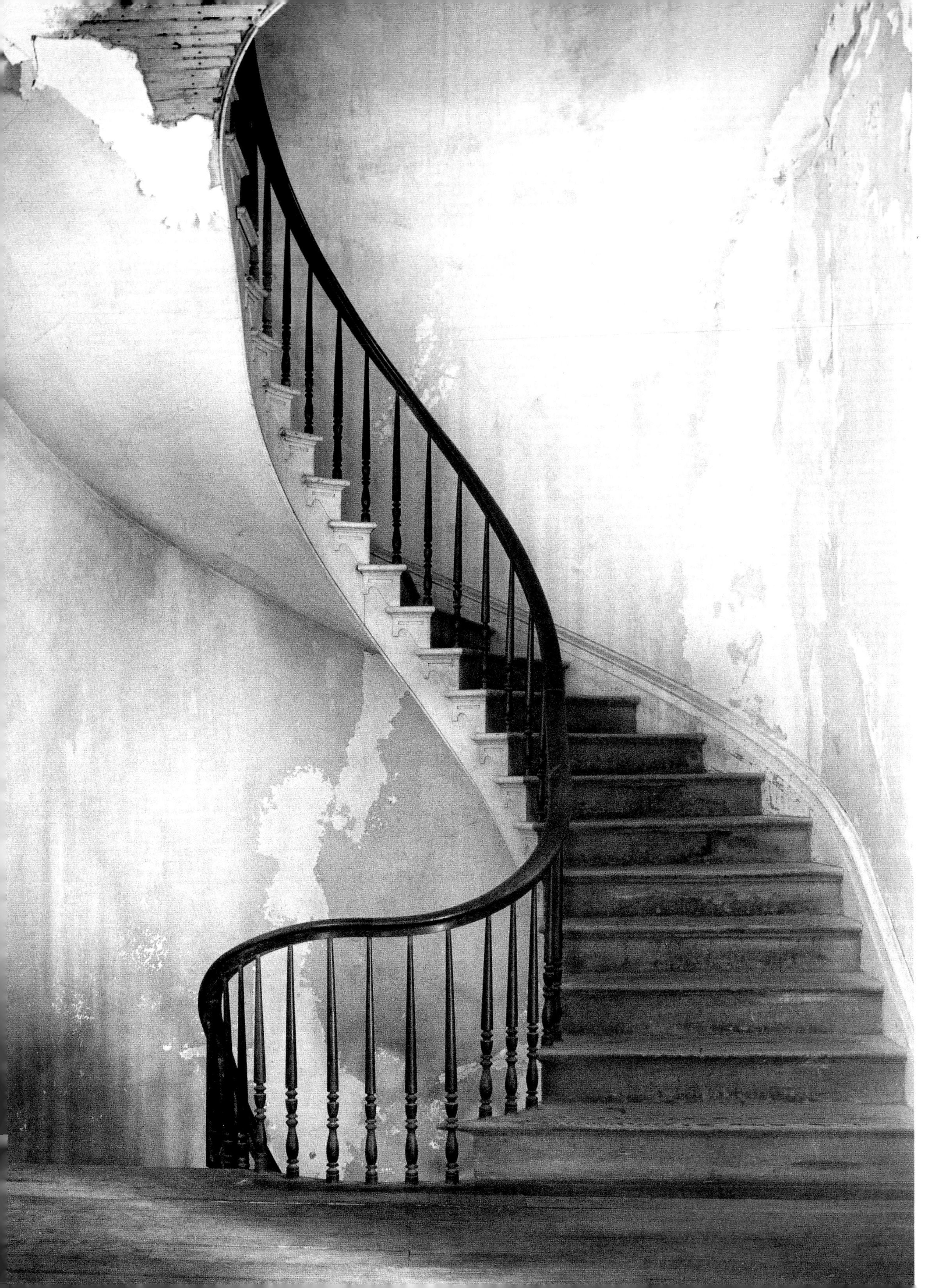

This is the time-honored, well-established "S-curve" recorded by photographers, illustrators, and artists for centuries. There is a definite sex appeal to this alluring staircase—it's the romance of women throughout history who have descended these stairs to encounter the gentlemen of their dreams, who wait for them at the base of these same steps.

I had the good fortune of having a distant relative who still held the title to this fine old mansion in Louisiana. I was reminded of this when a friend of mine, the now-deceased Dave Johnson, told me of a story he had read in the *New Orleans Times Picayune* in 1988. In this story was a profile of the plantation, and it prompted me to contact a cousin of mine that I had never met, Joanne McKee. After talking with me, she agreed to take me to the plantation, specifically to take pictures.

We were met at the entrance to this patriarchal estate by Joanne's uncle, William Hayward, my third cousin, whom I had never met. With his red suspenders and jaundiced eyes peering at me, he was a character to behold. He confused me for a time with the Las Vegas entertainer, Wayne Newton, which struck me as odd, since I look nothing like him, can't sing the first note, and our financial statements are light years apart. Nevertheless, the fact that I am not Wayne Newton didn't prevent William from giving me clearance to enter the property to take a few snapshots.

This seasoned, old mansion had more photo opportunities than the average photographer could absorb in several days. I had a time frame of only three hours, since Joanne had to be back in New Orleans by early afternoon. I made some hurried exterior views, and then immediately moved to documenting the interior views. The spiral staircase proved to be the dominating theme, and best exemplified the mood of this old Southern dwelling.

Architects who have commissioned me to photograph the interior of their buildings sometimes complain about the use of artificial light. Some say it's too flat and takes away from the mood of the place. This wasn't the case here. The total available light was one bare bulb at the top of the third floor, and a whimper of light coming in through the door. This could be the stairway to heaven—at this second floor landing we can go up, or we can go down. Perhaps it's merely purgatory, which would explain the chipping of plaster and stains on the wall.

Compositionally, try to decide what your photograph is actually about before you shoot it. Previsualize, and carefully select the portion of the area you are in that will best suit the message you are trying to present through your photo. Check that there is no extraneous information in the image, and that the edges of the frame do not work against you, either cutting into your subject or allowing too much space around it. Decide if the background is too busy, which will detract attention from your main subject. Are there any areas of the image that are distracting in their tonal values, and can this be worked around through the Zone System? There is a lot to think about in the previsualization stage. With time and practice, most of this will become second nature, but when you are first starting out, try to think of these things purposely in order to train your brain.

EQUIPMENT

Camera: Mamiya C33 Twin Lens Reflex
Lens: 55mm
Lighting: Available light
Film: Kodak Tri-X
Print: Kodak Polymax Fiberbase

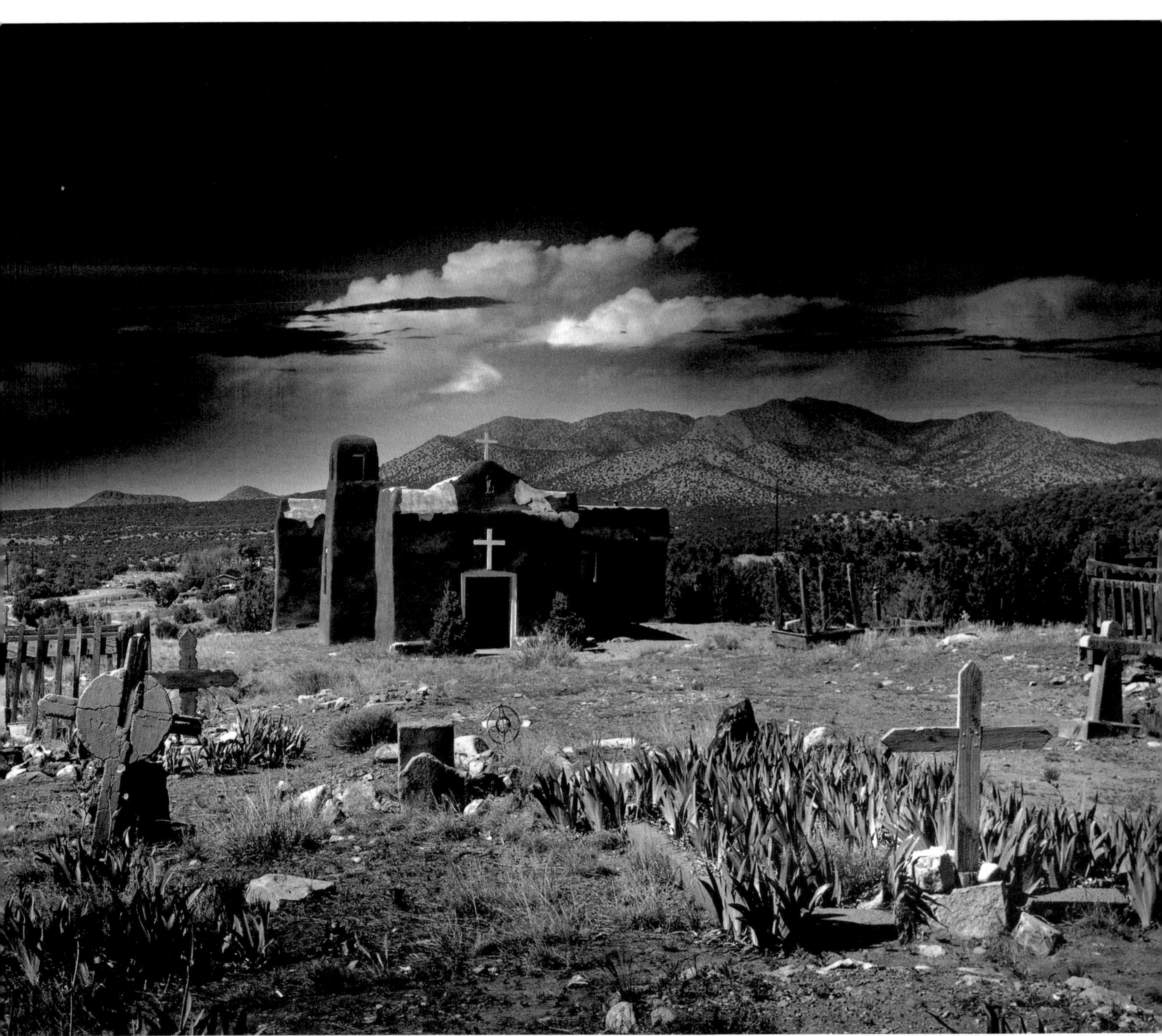

Churchyard New Mexico

The darkness that is framing the sky and creeping in from the lower left seems to be made of the same blackness that sits at the entrance of this small adobe chapel.

As readers of this book will notice, the majority of my work has a predominately Southern flavor. I have a great deal of respect for the large format landscapes of the West Coast photographers, and if I were not living on the Gulf Coast, I could easily be at home in California, Oregon or inland in New Mexico.

After visiting a friend in Taos, New Mexico, I was driving to Albuquerque for my flight home. Time did not permit a stop in Santa Fe, where there are more fine artists per square mile then any place in the country. Mistakenly, I made a wrong turn on the interstate, to the old highway which delivered me to the almost deserted town of Golden, New Mexico. This proved to be good fortune. This old adobe chapel at the top of a hill was waiting to be photographed. Seeing the light changing by seconds, I gathered my 4x5 equipment from the car.

I scaled a little three foot chain link fence, and my first concern was being bitten by a snake. Fortunately, there appeared to be no snakes in the area, although as my foot hit the ground, I spooked two dogs (I first though they were wolves) who had been frolicking in some nearby bushes. There was a horrible howl—from the dogs or from me, I couldn't say which.

I gathered my nerves about me again, and settled down to the original mission, which was to make the best negative possible of this great, western landscape without missing my scheduled flight. I exposed only four negatives, two each from different angles. The values of the third negative best reflected the original scene. There was almost a complete lack of detail in the sky, thus the cloud formation seen in this print was added in the darkroom, with heavy burning of the top of the print to get the black sky.

EQUIPMENT

Camera: Anba 4x5 Wooden Field Camera
Lens: 90mm Caltar
Accessories: Green filter
Lighting: Daylight, late afternoon
Film: Kodak Tri-X
Print: Kodak Polymax Fiberbase, #3 filter

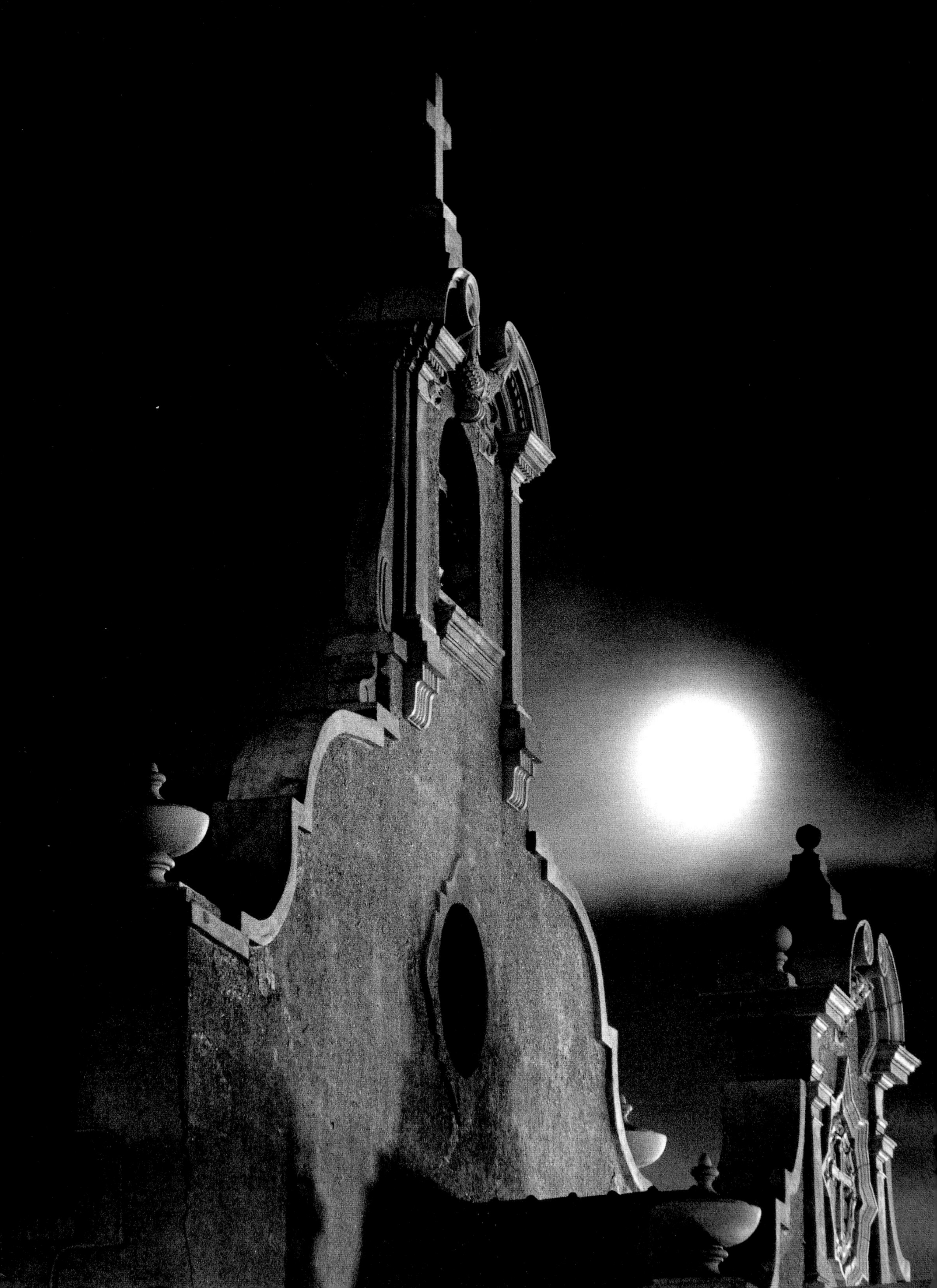

Christ Church/Full Moon

Shadows and shadows—this is moonlight at its best. The diffused light of the moon adds to the beauty and splendor of this gorgeous old church of Spanish design and architecture.

Normally, I will refer to my calender or appointment book to recall the exact date that I photographed a specific location. However, this is one I remember well. It was Thanksgiving night of 1987. As a rule, I'm not the type of photographer who always has a camera within arm's reach, as a policeman always has his gun. I try to plan what I will be shooting, and have a blueprint in my mind of all equipment needed. This image was pure luck regarding the timing of the shot.

After a large-scale Thanksgiving dinner at my sister's home, I remembered an unmailed letter in my car. I decided to mail this letter at the closest drop box in downtown Pensacola. With the mail delivered, and driving home, I caught a glimpse of this gorgeous moon, just beginning to rise. I mentioned luck—well, my well-used Nikon 35mm, with a 135mm lens, and sturdy Bogan tripod were in the backseat of my car, from taking outdoor portraits of nieces and nephews earlier in the day. Knowing there was very little time to scout locations, I made the decision to drive only two blocks, and position Christ Episcopal Church in the foreground for this enigmatic nighttime scene.

With the camera on the tripod, I found the perfect composition, placing the moon to the right of the bell tower of the church. I did not have a light meter, so this was a classic case of bracketing the exposure across the board. The aperture was placed at f22 to ensure complete depth of field, and I then started exposing film. Starting with an initial exposure of thirty seconds, I then made subsequent exposures in five second increments, i.e. twenty-five seconds, twenty seconds, with the last exposure being 1/2 second. I never recorded the best negative, but I would deem the one used for the final print was approximately ten seconds.

The irony of this image is that when we contemplate that the moon was the pagan goddess, who watched over the patriarchy of the fatherly image of the church, you truly realize that man is not the ruler in this picture.

EQUIPMENT

Camera: Nikon FTN
Lens: 135mm
Accessories: Bogen tripod
Lighting: Moon and fill from street lights on opposite side of church
Film: Kodak Plus-X ASA 100
Print: Ilford VC Fiberbase

Trader Jon's / Morning Fog

Foggy mornings and grey skies are reminiscent of evocative cityscapes such as those seen in Seattle. This is not Seattle, though. In fact, it's a scene in front of one of the most noted bars in America, Trader Jon's— a spot well known to every Naval aviator passing through flight training in Pensacola. Although the fog was hanging in the downtown area like a wet blanket, the bicycle which had been left in front of this ancient watering hole suggests that the last patron leaving for the evening knew he wouldn't be able to trust his legs.

You will have noted from the majority of the images in this book that I favor the medium and large format cameras. However, for this scene I used a 35mm camera in order to emphasize the grain and enhance the grey tones in the heavy fog. The majority of buyers of this print are photography collectors and assume that the heavy grain pattern of this image means that it was exposed on infrared film. However, this is not the case.

The negative was exposed on Tri-X 35mm ASA 400 film. Instead of developing in a traditional developer, such as D-76 or HC-110, I developed it in Kodak's paper developer, Dektol. To the best of my memory, it was processed for two minutes straight in Dektol at 75°F. If you want golf ball-sized grain, this is the way to go. Although it is somewhat unconventional and unpredictable, the results (through testing) can produce some interesting negatives.

Trader Jon, the grand old man who owned this saloon and whose given name was Martin Weismann, died this year at the age of 84. I gave him a copy of the original print a few years earlier, and only last year gave him the altered version to which I had added the vines at the bottom and a dramatic new sky at the top. With his goofy smile and Bronx accent, he gave me the ultimate compliment, "J.D., only you could take such a picture... It's beeeeautiful."

EQUIPMENT

Camera: Nikon FTN
Lens: 50mm
Lighting: Available light
Film: Kodak Tri-X ASA 400, developed in Dektol developer
Print: Polymax Fine Art, #2-1/2 filter

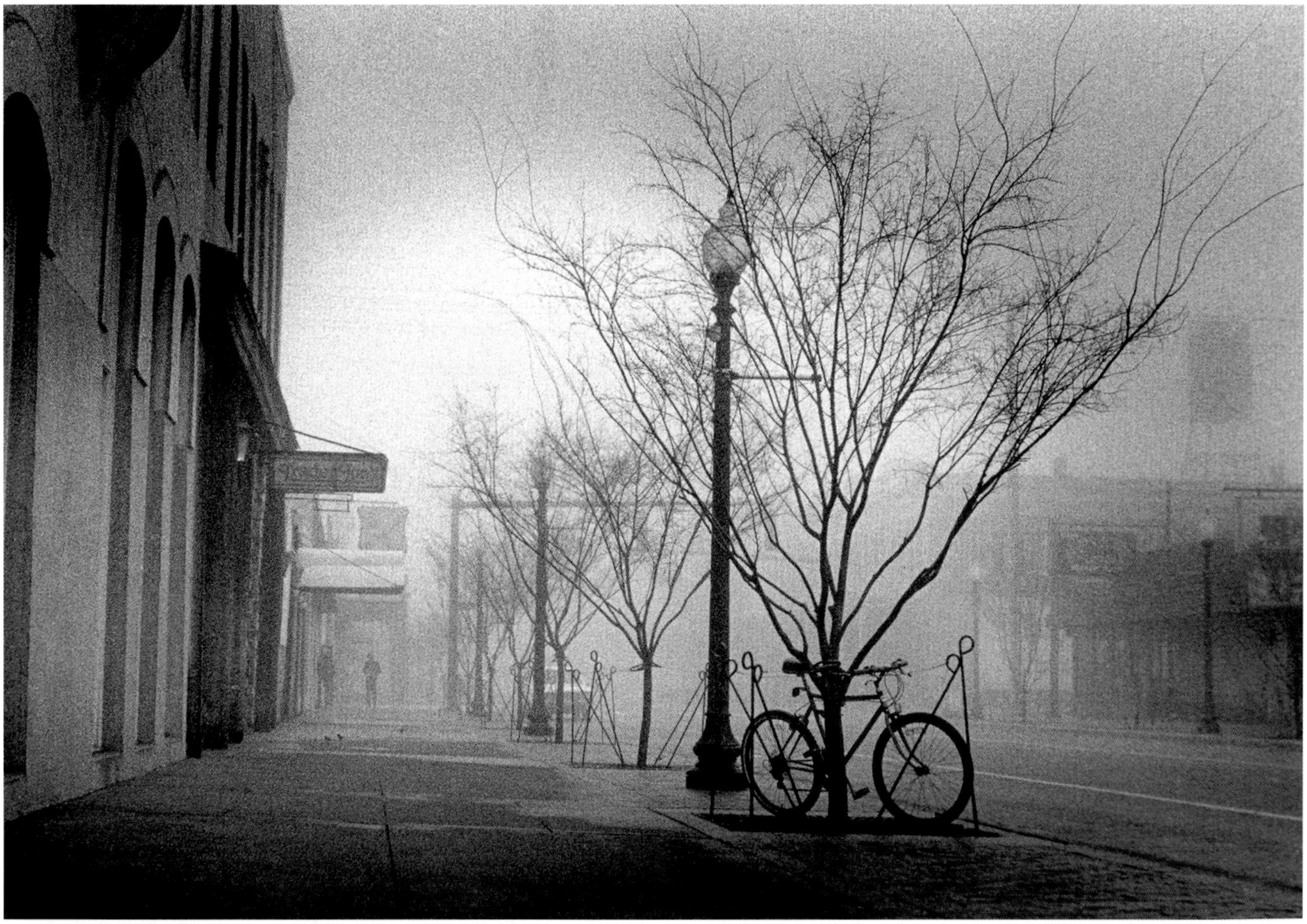

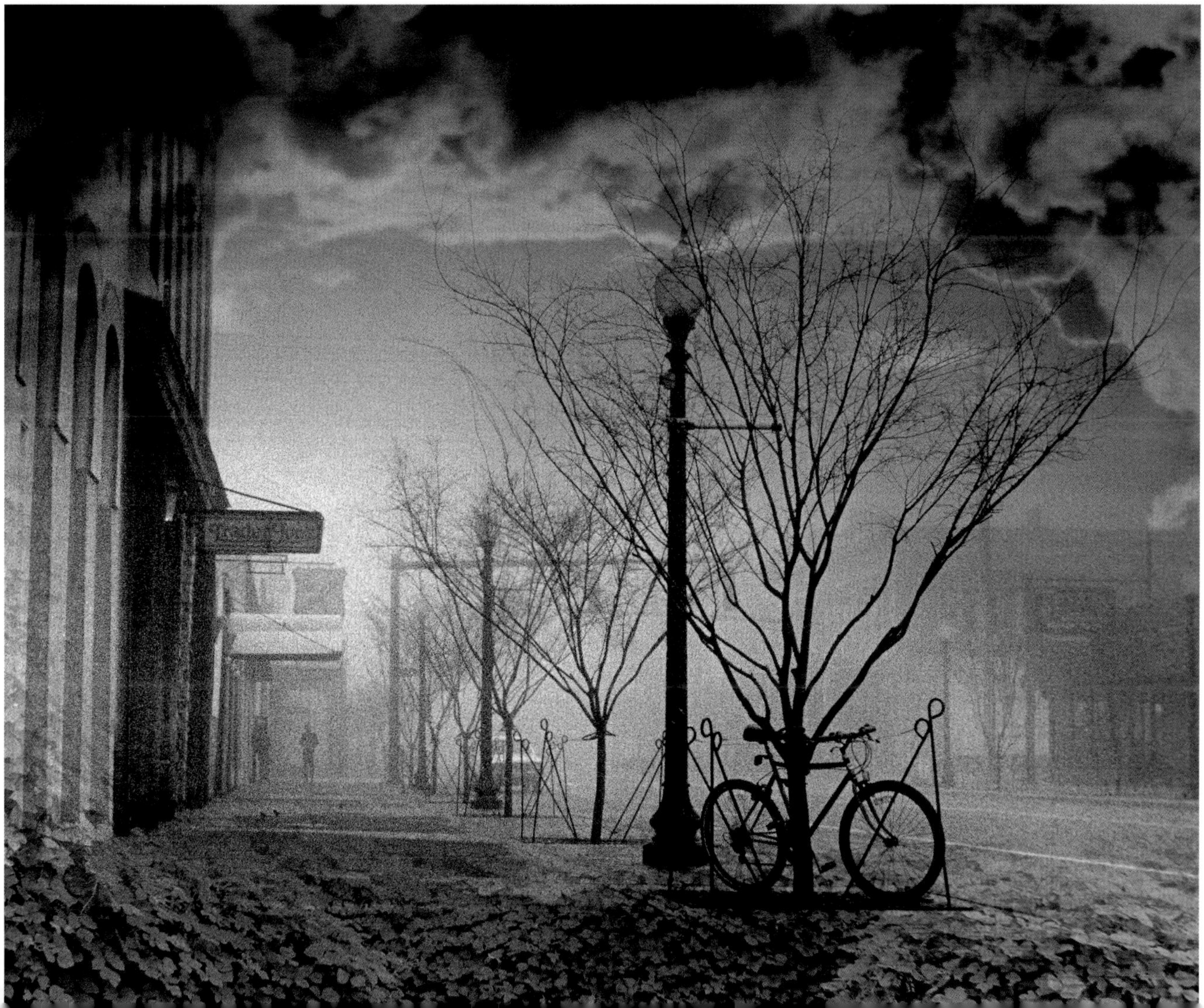

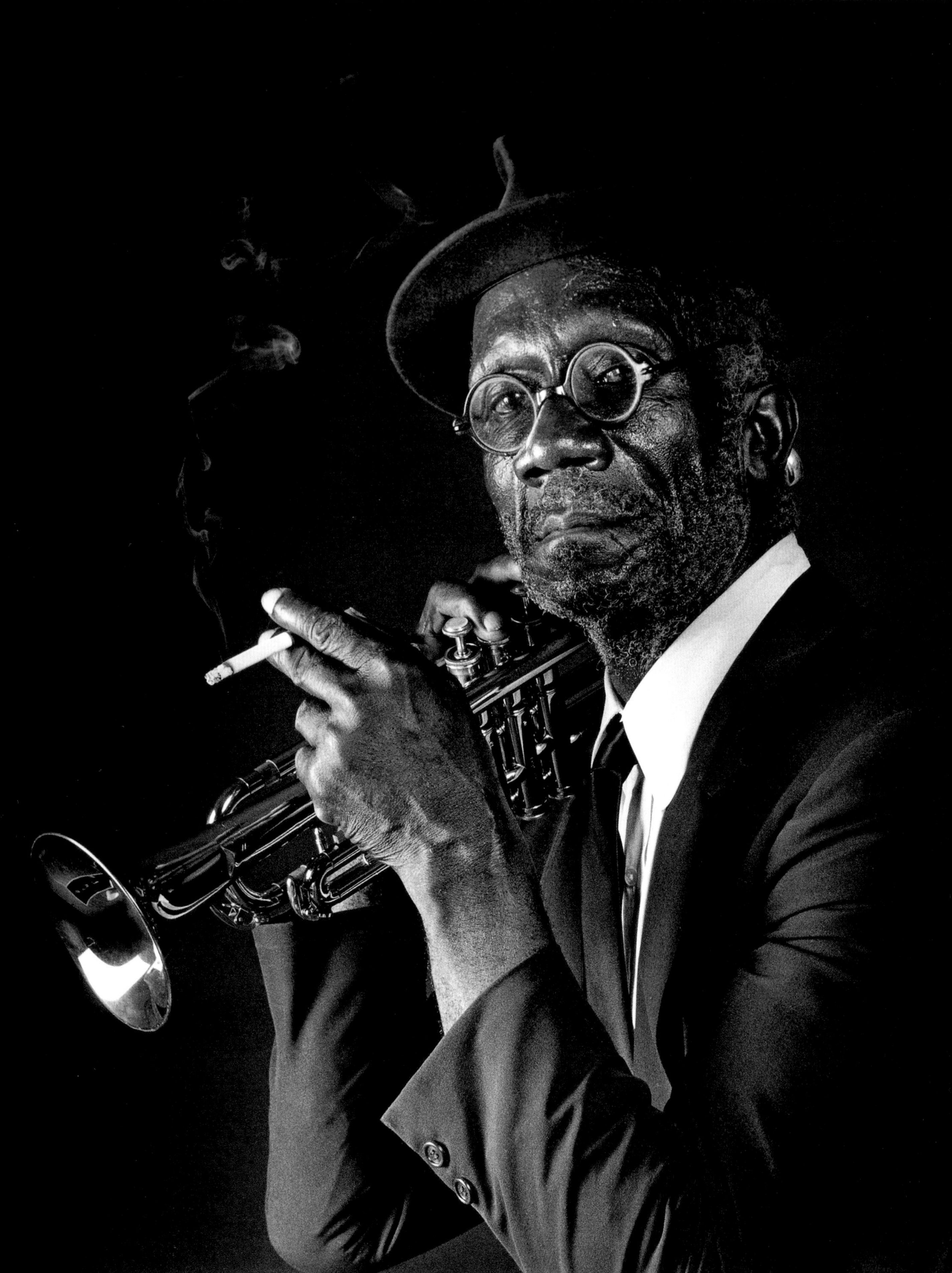

This print is quintessential Jazz—the dark, rich heritage shows that this man's got soul, and he knows it.

I was a weekend guest of a friend who kept an apartment as a retreat in the lower section of the French Quarter in New Orleans, close to Esplanade Avenue. On a balmy summer night, we walked into this musician's gig for the night, in a small, dark jazz joint, very close to the apartment. The great thing about going to local jazz clubs, as opposed to Bourbon Street "grind joints," is that you have the opportunity to mix with the natives—as opposed to tourists, such as myself. Additionally, you will hear jam sessions and improvisations of Dixieland Jazz that truly reflect a legacy passed down from one old black musician to another.

I love all forms of Dixieland Jazz, especially when the clarinetist hits the high notes, and really makes the instrument sing. However, on this evening, the man with the trumpet was the stellar performer. He wasn't Al Hirt; he was Jack Butler, playing his own style, and it seemed that he was playing to himself, not the audience. Seeing this man with his trumpet made an indelible image in my mind. I did not want to miss the opportunity to photograph this jazz man on this very night. My host for the evening happened to be friends with the owner of this jazz club, and mentioned to him that I, as a photographer, would like to photograph the trumpet player, not with flash on camera during the performance, but as a character study. "No problem," said the proprietor, "On the next break have your camera ready."

If you have thought, as a great number of people just getting their toes into the water of photography have, that you must have an expensive studio set-up with dozens of lights and backdrops and an army of assistants on hand in order to get quality portrait work done, then think again. This photo proves that you don't need much more than a camera and your imagination in order to get a very good portrait. My studio for this image was the back alley behind the bar. My subject was seated on a chrome bar stool (not shown in the print) and my assistant (the friend who had accompanied me to the bar) hand-held a Lumedyne portable strobe at a 45-degree angle. I only made two exposures, and both of them were great! There was no need for a black background. With the camera shutter set at 1/500th of a second, the dark alley would not record any detail. For more information on this technique, see the section on the Zone System earlier in this book.

EQUIPMENT

Camera: Hasselblad 500CM
Lens: 150mm
Lighting: Lumedyne Portable Strobe
Film: Tri-X ASA 400 (rated at 250)
Print: Kodak 11x14 Polymax FB, #3 filter

Pops

The great weathered face of this ancient mariner belongs to a man I knew (but knew nothing about) when I was eighteen.

As kids in our high school days, there were several popular hangouts in our hometown of Pensacola, Florida. The Union Pool Hall, with no exception, was hailed as the finest establishment in town "for the boys." The hall was at the bottom floor of a flophouse formerly known as the Gilbert Hotel on Wright Street, in the downtown corridor. It was truly a seedy joint, one whose plaster ceiling might give out at any moment. This added to the ambiance of the hall, and we loved it. The pool hall was a great place to meet your high school buddies, for smoking cigarettes, telling lies, and boasting of time spent with the opposite sex. However, the biggest attraction was shooting a game of nine ball on the pool tables for fifteen cents per game. For those who had no ability on the pool tables, there was the gallery section to sit and pontificate, or at least be seen. It was in the gallery section of the antiquated, wooden folding stadium seats, that I first spotted the old man, "Pops."

It was rumored that the old man was homeless, a wino, a derelict—the stories were countless. It was not until I met a "friend of a friend" that I got the background on this man. This old craggy face, with deeply embellished facial lines, was not that of a lush; this was the face of a man who sailed several times around the world on old three-masted schooners. His eyes had seen the treachery of rounding the Cape in a howling gale, to see crewmen lost overboard and never recovered, while he himself survived to enjoy the sublime tranquility of a sunset in the Caribbean Islands with his schooner safely moored in a harbor.

After graduation from Pensacola High School, with an insatiable interest in photography, I drove down to the Union Pool Room to see if Pops might still haunt this old building. Luckily for me, he was still a fixture in the old place. I explained that I wanted to make an attempt at portrait photography, and asked if he would mind being my subject. The old man walked out of the pool room with a very unsteady gait, and sat on a wooden box in front of a railroad car.

I made only one exposure with a hand-held camera, no tripod. It was my first attempt at portraiture, and in my opinion, still my best, even after thirty years of photography. It's as if all his rough edges have ben polished by a tough life. His eyes have seen what we have never seen, the eyes of a very quiet humble simplicity, no airs. Simple truth—his face tells all.

It has been my experience with portraiture that a great many people when approached from out of the blue will consent with very little prompting to allowing you to take their photograph. Perhaps it appeals to a place inside of everyone that is flattered to think that someone else finds them suitable as a subject for "art." Maybe it's just that deep down, everyone wants to be a fashion model. Don't be afraid to ask someone who strikes your photographic fancy if he will let you take a few frames of him. Suggest that you send him copies of the photos when they are printed. Who doesn't like to get a token print "on the house?"

EQUIPMENT

Camera: Mamiya C3 Twin Lens Reflex
Lens: 80mm
Lighting: Direct sunlight
Film: Kodak Plus-X
Development: D-76
Print: Kodak Ektalure-X (no longer manufactured)

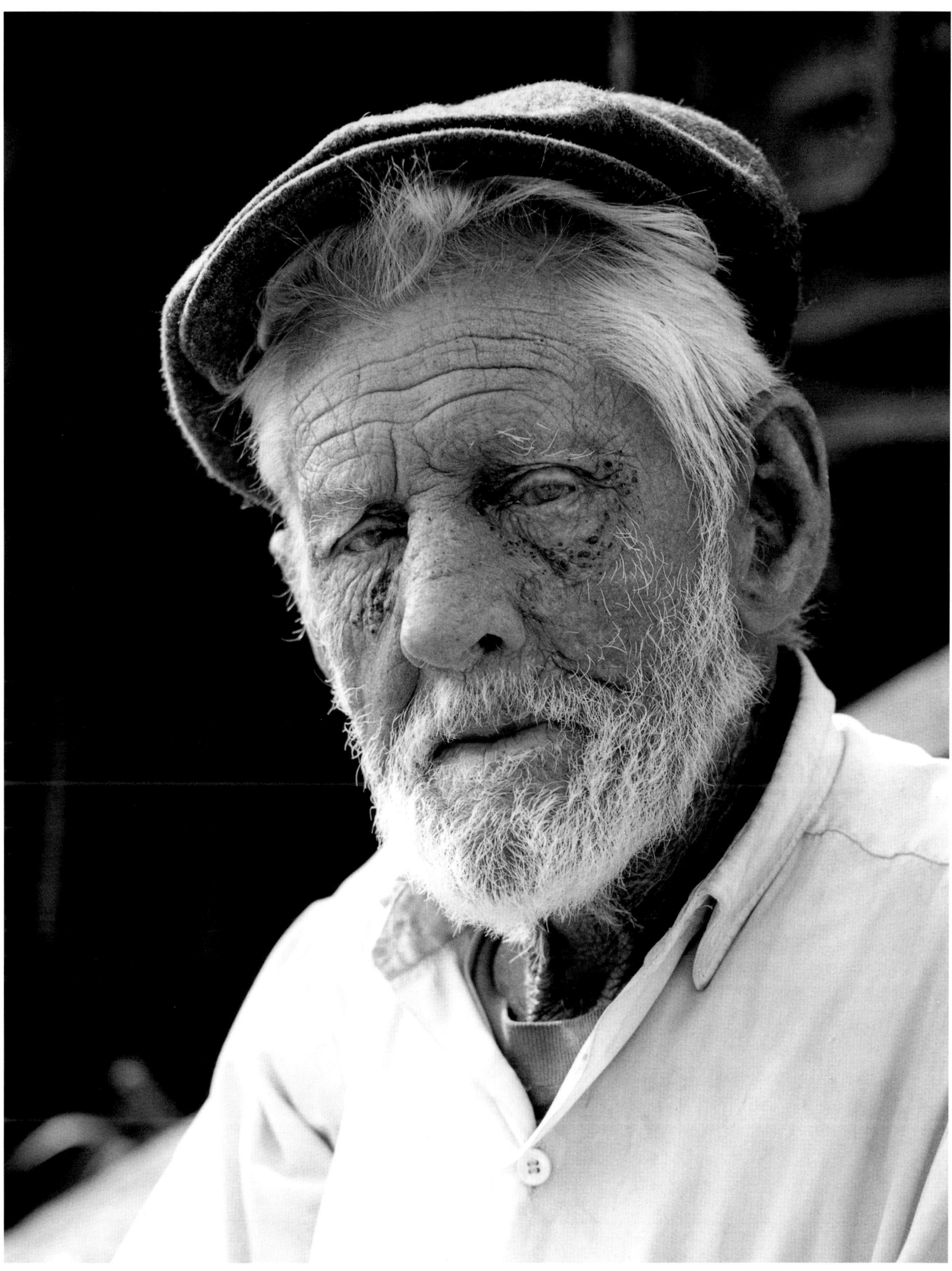

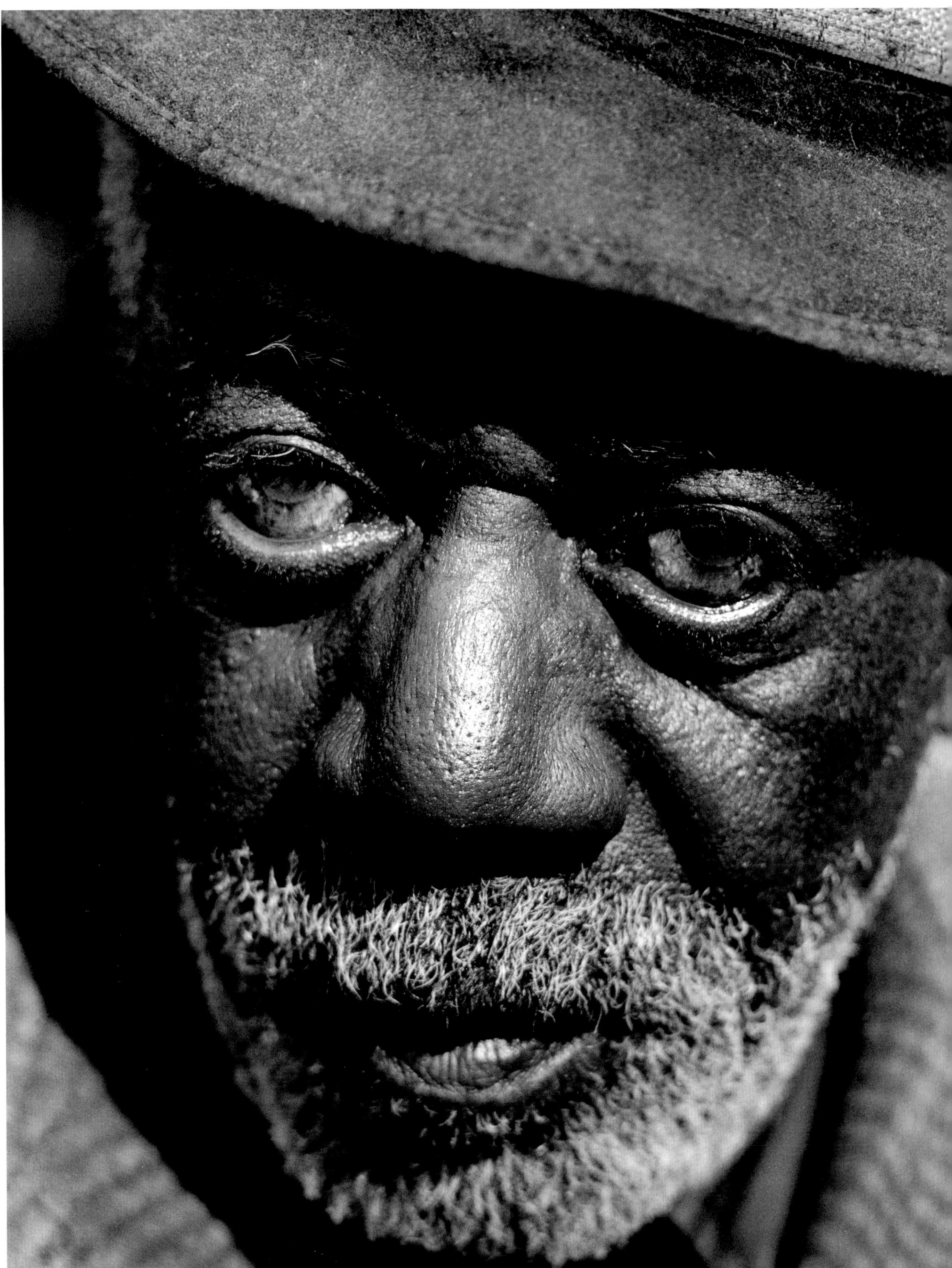

It was 1969, and I had observed Roosevelt on numerous occasions, sitting on the stone parapet wall surrounding Jackson Square, adjacent to my first studio. On a sunny spring morning, I walked to the Square under the guise of photographing the children playing around the fountain. My intended target, however, was not the kids, but Roosevelt. I realized immediately upon arrival that what I was doing was ridiculous: I am hardly a paparazzo, much less a surveillance photographer.

I approached my subject, introduced myself as a professional photographer, and asked might I take his picture. In a low gravely voice he said, "No way." I explained that there might be a possibility of his face being in a magazine, or at least the local newspaper. He still expressed no interest. In desperation, I asked what would it take to get his photograph. "It's easy," he replied. "Just walk two blocks to the Royal Package Store and get me a bottle of Mattingly & Moore Bourbon. It'll only cost you three eighty-nine plus tax." I acquired this fine bourbon for Roosevelt, and we went to work. He sipped between shots, and I clicked away.

The effort was well worth it. The image shows a face and eyes that tell a story—a life consumed by exploring the genie in the bottle. The white beard offsets his charcoal face and hat, with the light coming across the forehead to frame the eyes. You would think that he would be full of despair, but his strength and sense of self show through with great power.

When setting up your portrait, do not compose it so that there is a great deal of extraneous or misleading information visible in the frame. This is a good idea for all of your photographs, but it is especially important to a good portrait. Remember to previsualize your image, and with practice you will be able to see the details quite strongly in a short amount of time.

For example, you can see how the brim of Roosevelt's hat creates a heavy, dark shadow that helps to give definition and create a visual line between the tonalities of his skin and the fabric of the hat. If I had asked him to lower his face, his eyes would have been lost in the shadow, and the impact of the photo would have changed. The same is true if his head were tilted higher, leaving less of a hard shadow, and taking away from the impact of the image.

Also, you can use the Zone System for portraiture as well as for landscapes or still lifes. The concepts are the same, only you are dealing with a person instead of a skyline. You might want to practice this in a studio situation or at least somewhere with constant and steady lighting at first, until you become adept at using the System. You will be quite pleased with the outcome, I am certain. Your portraits will take on a whole new life as you increase your control over the final print.

EQUIPMENT

Camera: Mamiya C3 Twin Lens Reflex
Lens: 180mm
Lighting: Direct sunlight
Film: Kodak Plus-X
Development: D-76
Print: Kodak Ektalure-X (no longer manufactured)

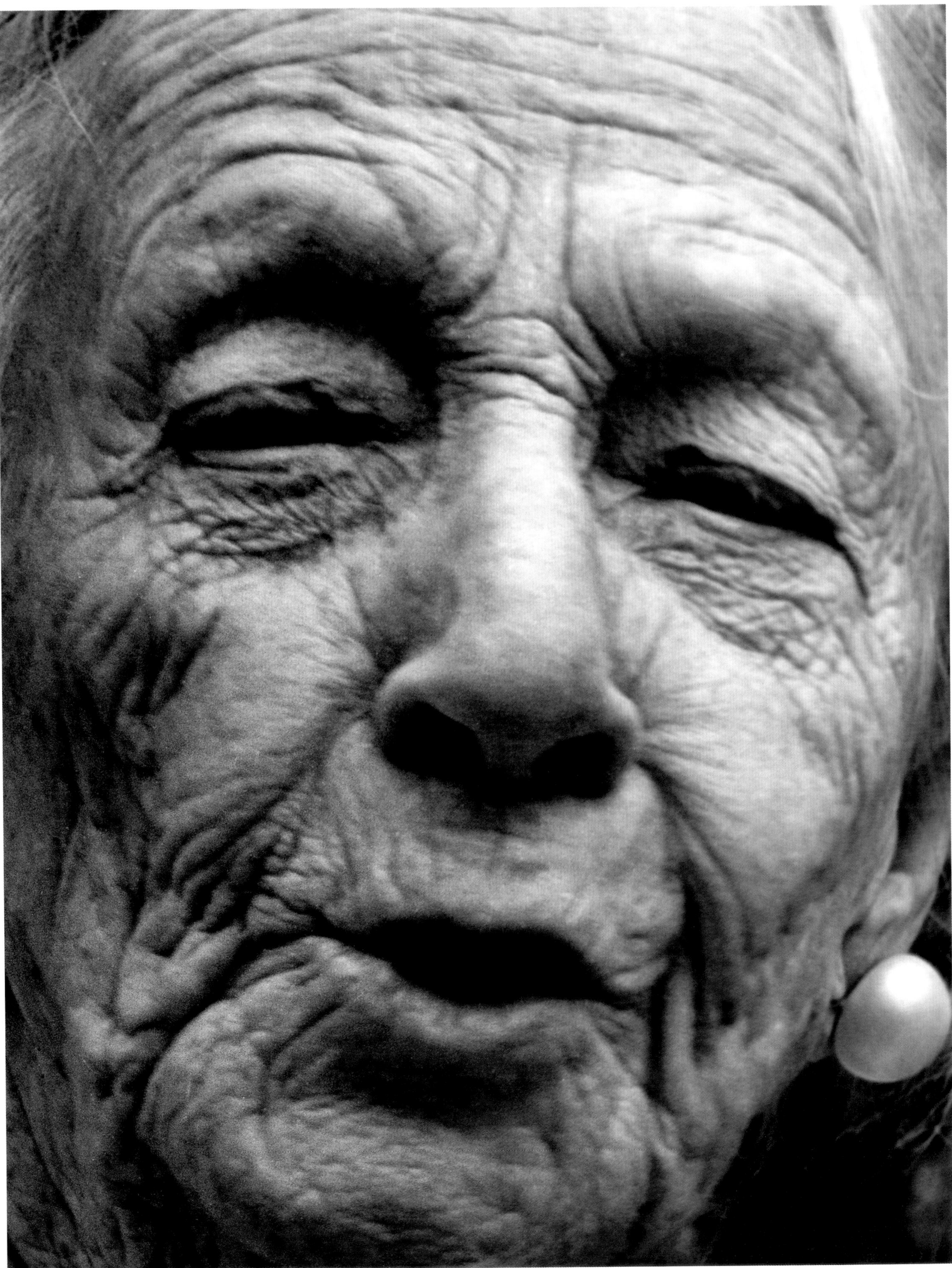

If you have the opportunity to be the photographer for a one hundredth birthday party, by all means accept the assignment. There are some people who simply grow old, and become very feeble and mentally fuzzy. This was not the scenario with this high-spirited lady, however.

It was 1969 when I showed up with camera in hand and knocked on the door at West LaRua Street. I was surprised to be greeted not by a nurse from hospice or a caretaker, but by the birthday girl herself. "How are you doing, young man?" she asked. "Are you here to take my picture?" I replied, "Yes, Ma'am." She eyeballed me closely and then asked how old I was. "I'm twenty years old." She laughed and told me that I was just a pup. At that point, I was feeling like one. This lady, who had a good eighty years on me, had already taken control over the shoot!

I asked her where she would like to have her photograph taken, and she said the front yard. My camera was loaded with ASA 100 film, and at the time I didn't have enough sense to bring supplementary lighting such as a portable electronic flash. I was at the mercy of the available light filtering through the oak trees, and without a tripod, which meant the camera had to be hand-held. I was completely nervous, a fact I'm sure she picked up on, since she said she would make my job a little easier for me."I'll sing a little verse from the opera *Porgy and Bess,* a song called 'Summertime,' and you take whatever picture you want." With that, she started singing, and I clicked away.

EQUIPMENT

Camera: Mamiya C3 Twin Lens Reflex
Lens: 80mm
Lighting: Overcast daylight
Film: Kodak Tri-X ASA 100
Print: Kodak Polymax Fine Art Fiberbase

The Mask

If you have never been to New Orleans, you are denying yourself a wonderful photography excursion. If you've never been to Mardi Gras in New Orleans on Fat Tuesday, the day before Lent, you are missing an even greater photojournalistic experience. Demented people, and those not so demented, plan all year for this day of feasting, drinking, and dancing in the streets to the wee hours of the morning. When they come out of the woodwork, have plenty of film, as the photo opportunities are everywhere. To make your assignment even easier, everyone in costume wants his or her picture taken. They have no idea whether you are a budding amateur or a seasoned photojournalist on assignment for a national magazine.

I shot this image in 1989 at Mardi Gras. I had been fortunate enough to have been invited to stay at a friend's apartment in the French Quarter, right at the heart of the action, which was excellent for photographic opportunities. Also importantly, if I needed a break from mingling with the revelers, I had a safe haven where I could retreat, either to change cameras and film or simply to sit on the second floor balcony and watch the parade of drunks passing by below.

I met my hostess at a neighborhood bar at about five o'clock, and found her to be quite excited over something. "Did you see the man in the African mask that just walked out of the bar?" she asked. I had not, and asked her what was so unusual about an African mask at Mardi Gras, where masks were extremely plentiful. "It's his eyes," she exclaimed. "His eyes are fantastic. We've got to find him so you can take his picture."

The last thing that I wanted to do was be in search of an African mask in the middle of two hundred thousand people who also happen to be in costume. Better sense prevailed, and I suggested to Meme that instead of walking the streets in pursuit of this mystery man, he might return to the bar if he was in need of another drink. It was good thinking on my part, for somewhere around eight o'clock our man in the mask strolled back into the bar for a refill. Meme wasted no time in cajoling this man into walking one block north, to the courtyard of her apartment to have his portrait taken. He agreed without hesitation, but only with the stipulation that I had to mail him an 8x10 of the photo, and that I would never reveal his name. I have honored both of these requests.

As for the photo, at first it seems like a quaint Mardi Gras mask at a costume party. Then you realize there is a very primitive guy in there. Perhaps this isn't a Mardi Gras reveler at all, but rather a bushman, or a voodoo high priest.

Props can help to bring out a great deal in a portrait, or can even make or break the photo in and of themselves. Keep your eyes open for interesting objects that you might be able to incorporate into a photo, even if you haven't got a particular image in mind yet. If you have storage space for props, it's not a bad idea to just stock up on them, knowing that you'll have a future use for most of them. The actual props themselves might turn out to be the subject of your photo, either a portrait where the model is secondary to the image, or a fascinating still-life. Experiment with different items you find, and visualize in what way you can best use them to make your print as artistically pleasing as possible.

EQUIPMENT

Camera: Hasselblad 500C
Lens: 150mm
Lighting: Vivitar 283 Portable Strobe (hand-held at a 45-degree angle), blue blanket for background

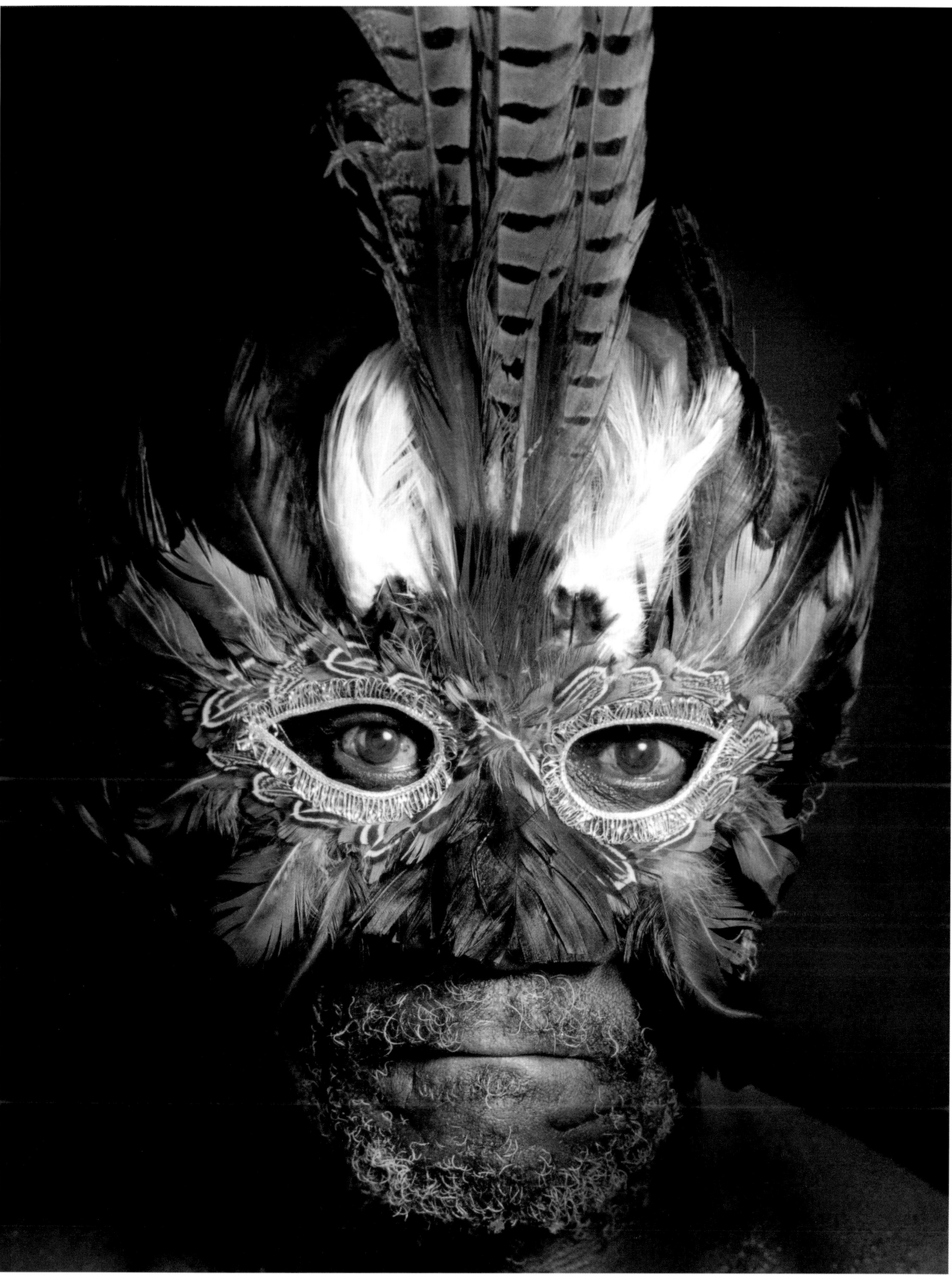

The Gate of Heaven

On a commercial assignment to photograph the historic Christ Episcopal Church in my hometown of Pensacola, Florida, one of the last negatives to be exposed was the adjoining chapel off of the main sanctuary. At the time this exposure was made, looking into this beautiful old chapel, my mind was thinking in terms of architectural photography, not multiple image prints. Architectural photography has to be precise in terms of correct camera perspective control so there is no distortion, and the artificial lighting used by the photographer can be balanced with the ambient light streaming through the windows. This is more of a mathematical calculation to document the architect's and designer's work than a creative experiment on the part of the photographer, although the three persons should share equal credit for the finished image to be published.

After reviewing my contact prints from this assignment, I saw the possibility of a multiple image art print. What does the entrance to heaven look like? I have no idea, and I'm sure that no one at any level of authority can give a definitive description either. Nevertheless, I am sure that the majority of people on this beautiful planet have given thought, whether they admit it or not, to eternal life. This negative gave me the opportunity to mirror my dreams of what the "pearly gates of heaven" might resemble.

The basic image of the doors served as a starting point, but I needed an "S-curve" image at the bottom doors of the chapel. The classic "S-curve" has been incorporated in the works of artists for thousands of years to draw the viewer into the image. I found this "S-curve" in a negative in my file of water, sand and bird images, and this element was blended into the bottom of the print. The cloud negative was the final element added to the top and sides of the wrought iron doors. I had several ideas of how to title the finished print, but Ken Karadin, director of music at the church, exclaimed upon viewing the print, "That is 'The Gate of Heaven,'" which to me seemed the perfect title.

I strongly suggest that you keep a well-organized file of some sort in which to keep your negatives. It will make the creative aspects of your work that much easier and speedier for you to accomplish if you have easy access to the negatives that you might wish to blend. Consider file types such as I've mentioned in the previous paragraph, or "doors," "automobiles" or whatever system suits you. Trust me, it will only help you in the long run.

EQUIPMENT

Camera: Hasselblad 500C
Lens: 50mm
Accessories: Bogan tripod
Lighting: Two 300 watt incandescent bulbs in silver reflectors
Film: Kodak Tri-X ASA 400 (rated at 250)
Development: Kodak HC 110
Print: 11x14 Ilford Variable Contrast Fiberbase paper, #3 Filter

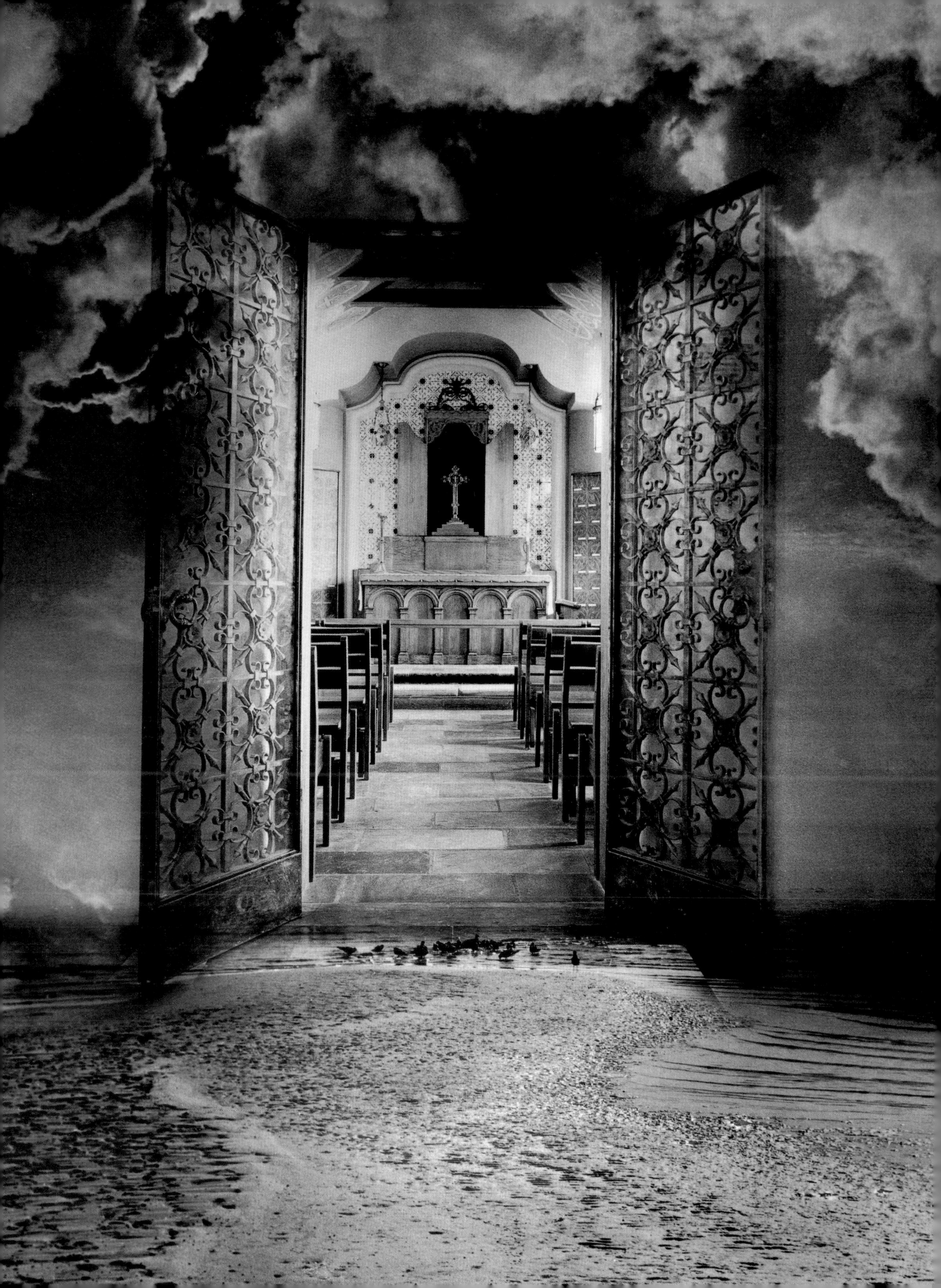

Antique Car and Vines

Luck has a great deal to do with finding interesting subject matter for your photography pursuits—provided you are not mowed down by a tractor, or fired at with a double barrel shotgun for trespassing. Luck was the case in this print. On a trip to a friend's farm in Alabama, I spotted this rusting old Buick behind an old frame structure which I mistakenly perceived to be either public or state (Alabama) property. After receiving permission to enter the property with camera and tripod, I exposed several frames. Always be sure that you have permission from the property or landowner before wandering about on what might be private property; the time spent sorting out legal difficulties is always better-spent in doing actual photography.

After viewing my contact prints, I realized that I had not given much thought to the background. At every camera angle I had chosen, there was a great deal of distracting clutter and debris behind the car (if you keep a fine old rusting car like this, who says the yard has to be manicured?). For the final print I constructed a "paper mask" for the car negative to eliminate the background. After making this exposure on the paper, I moved the same sheet of paper to the next enlarger and overprinted the vines.

Don't be afraid when you are starting out with techniques such as this to go through a lot of photographic paper as you hone your skills. It will take a bit of practice before you achieve the level of work that you are setting for yourself, and you'll probably find yourself going through quite a bit of paper in the process. When starting out, purchasing a box of paper with a large quantity of sheets inside (fifty or a hundred) is the most cost-efficient way to go. I would further suggest that you set yourself projects at first that do not require you to use an entire 8x10 or 11x14 sheet of paper, but rather try something of a smaller scale. Buy the larger paper and trim the sheets in the darkroom to a smaller size, a half or even a quarter of their initial measurement (remember to not expose the photographic paper to anything other than a safelight before the developing process!). You'll find that you get more value at this point, and before very long you'll be proficient enough in your skills to keep your waste levels to a minimum.

EQUIPMENT

Camera: Mamiya C33 Twin Lens Reflex
Lens: 80mm
Lighting: Late afternoon sun
Film: Kodak Tri-X ASA 400 (rated at 250)
Print: Ilford Fiberbase in Dektol

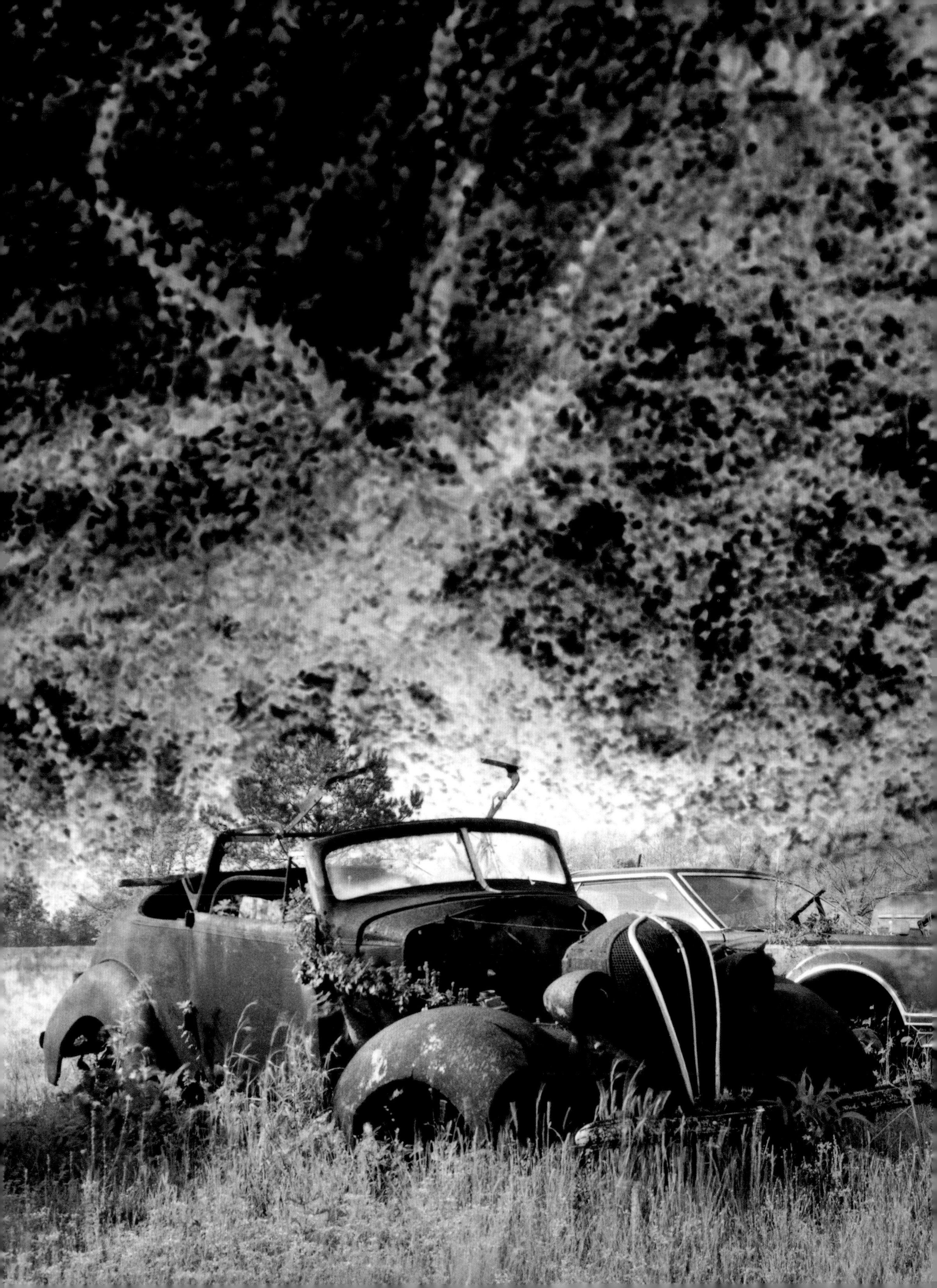

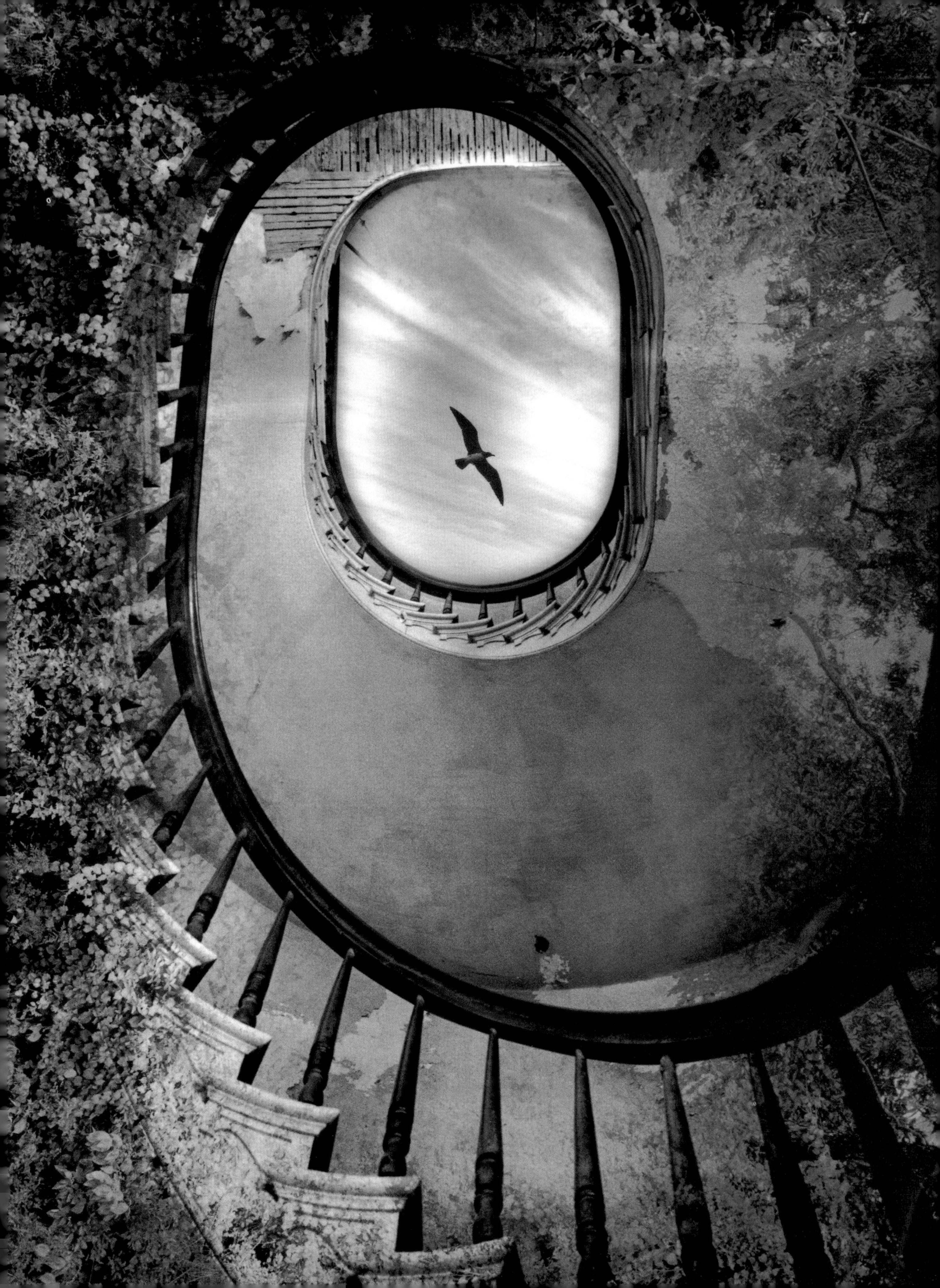

The building of three-story spiral staircases has always been a true art form that is not seen in many homes today, partially due to the expense but also due to a lack of skilled artisans or craftsmen with this expertise. The beauty of this type of architecture has forever captured the imagination of artists. However, photographers seem to be the most fascinated with these architectural treasures.

At Ashland Plantation in Louisiana, I decided to look at the staircase from the lowest vantage point possible, the floor. The camera was prefocused to approximately thirty feet on the lens, and to ensure complete depth of field, the lens setting was set at f22. The lighting conditions were extremely low, with a "bracketed exposure" time that ranged from one to four seconds. A long cable release was used to ensure there would be no camera movement, since the camera was on its back, on the floor, without benefit of a tripod (you should always try to use a tripod on exposures of longer than 1/30th of a second to minimize blur). At the time of making this exposure, I had no preconception of a final print. This assignment was only the beginning of a three negative composite print.

The print was distracting primarily due to the view of a bare 100 watt light bulb suspended from the ceiling in the middle of the print. To eliminate this, I created a paper "mask" and sandwiched it to the original negative in a glass negative carrier. Sandwiching is a technique that is exactly what it sounds like—putting two or more items (such as negatives or masks) in the enlarger together and printing them all at one time, as one complete image. If you don't have a glass negative carrier, two pieces of clean, single strength glass will serve the same purpose. Having now successfully blocked out this part of the image, I could then overprint another negative into that area. The bird and clouds were incorporated in the new print, giving me the wispy openness needed at the top of the print. As a final element, vines were overprinted on the edges to bring the viewer's eye to the center of the composition.

Sandwiching negatives can give you some very interesting and creative images in the darkroom. Best of all, it's a very simple technique that can give a lot of bang for the buck. The face of a young woman superimposed over an image of a dry and cracked plain of mud, a portrait of a friend at one side of the paper staring at a mirror image of himself on the other side of the paper—you will have no trouble finding a myriad of uses for this technique in your darkroom works.

EQUIPMENT

Camera: Pentax 6x7
Lens: 50mm
Lighting: 100 watt bare bulb and ambient available room light
Film: Kodak Tri-X ASA 400 (rated at 250)
Print: Kodak Polymax Fine Art paper (fiberbase)

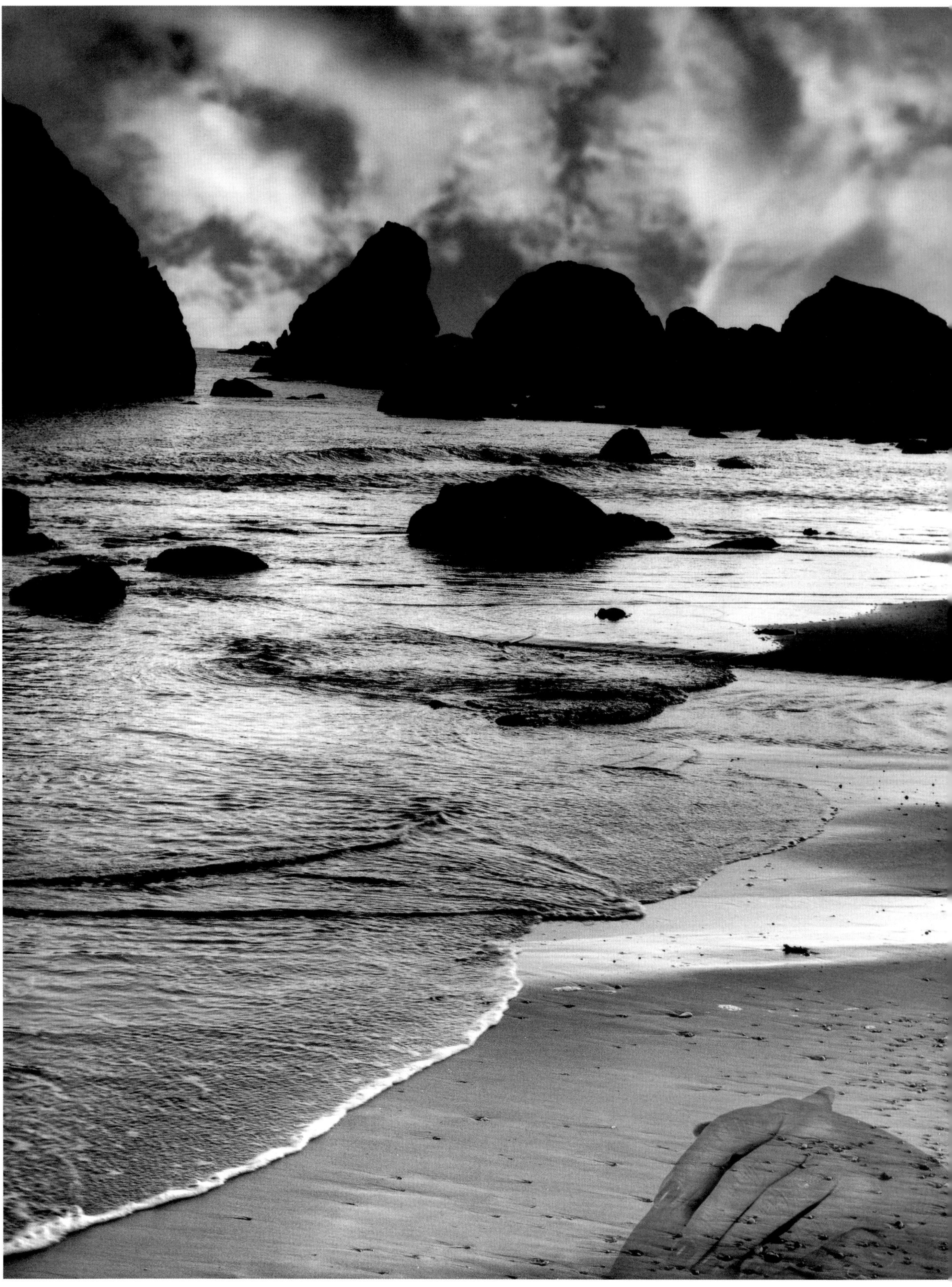

I have been asked more times than I can remember, especially at the opening night of Gallery Shows, "What are you trying to convey in this print?" In a number of cases, the most simplistic answer is, "Only to make you puzzled as to my thoughts, and lead you to supply your own interpretation."

The negative of this print was taken originally for a landscape series of the Oregon Coast in the early part of 1992. There was no thought of an added element being brought into the print. The sheer beauty of the late afternoon sun on the rocks and water made this a classic "West Coast" image favored by the pictorialists. Most landscape photographers lean towards the "craftsmanship" of superbly crisp, sharp images displaying the full tonal scale afforded by black and white film, and this print is no exception.

The negative was exposed through an older 4x5 wooden field camera, intentionally over-exposed, and consequently underdeveloped (commonly referred to as a N-1 development). There is an old rule for photographers that tells us to expose for the shadows and develop for the highlights. What this means in practice is that both exposure time and development time affect your negative in different ways. For example, changing the development time will not affect the shadow areas to a very great extent, but it will alter your highlights to a large degree. Basically, the longer your development time, the denser your highlights will become. The opposite is also true, that shorter times will lead to less-contrasty negatives. Again, if you are able to previsualize your image, to have a clear idea what you want the finished print to look like, you can utilize this technique to your advantage.

The concept of altering your exposure and development times to adjust contrast comes into its own when you start working with the Zone System (there is a brief discussion of the technique at the beginning of this book). N is considered the normal development time for your negative based on the manufacturer's suggestions. N+1 adds 25% to your development time and increases the contrast range on your negative. N+2 equates to the normal development time plus 50%. N-1 is 80% of the normal development time, N-2 is 60% of the normal time, and these both will flatten the contrast range of your negative.

The straight version of this print sold well for several years, but after some time I thought an alteration might bring more interest to the image. An assignment for the University of West Florida for a calender featuring hands gave me the overlay image (additional negative) that blended in perfectly in the lower right corner of this landscape.

My subconscious mind sees the hands as being an intricate part of this image. However, I will leave the final interpretation to the viewer.

EQUIPMENT

Camera: Anba 4x5 Wooden Field Camera
Lens: 90mm
Lighting: Late afternoon sun
Exposure: f32 at 1/15th second
Film: Kodak Tri-X
Print: Ilford Variable Contrast, #3 filter

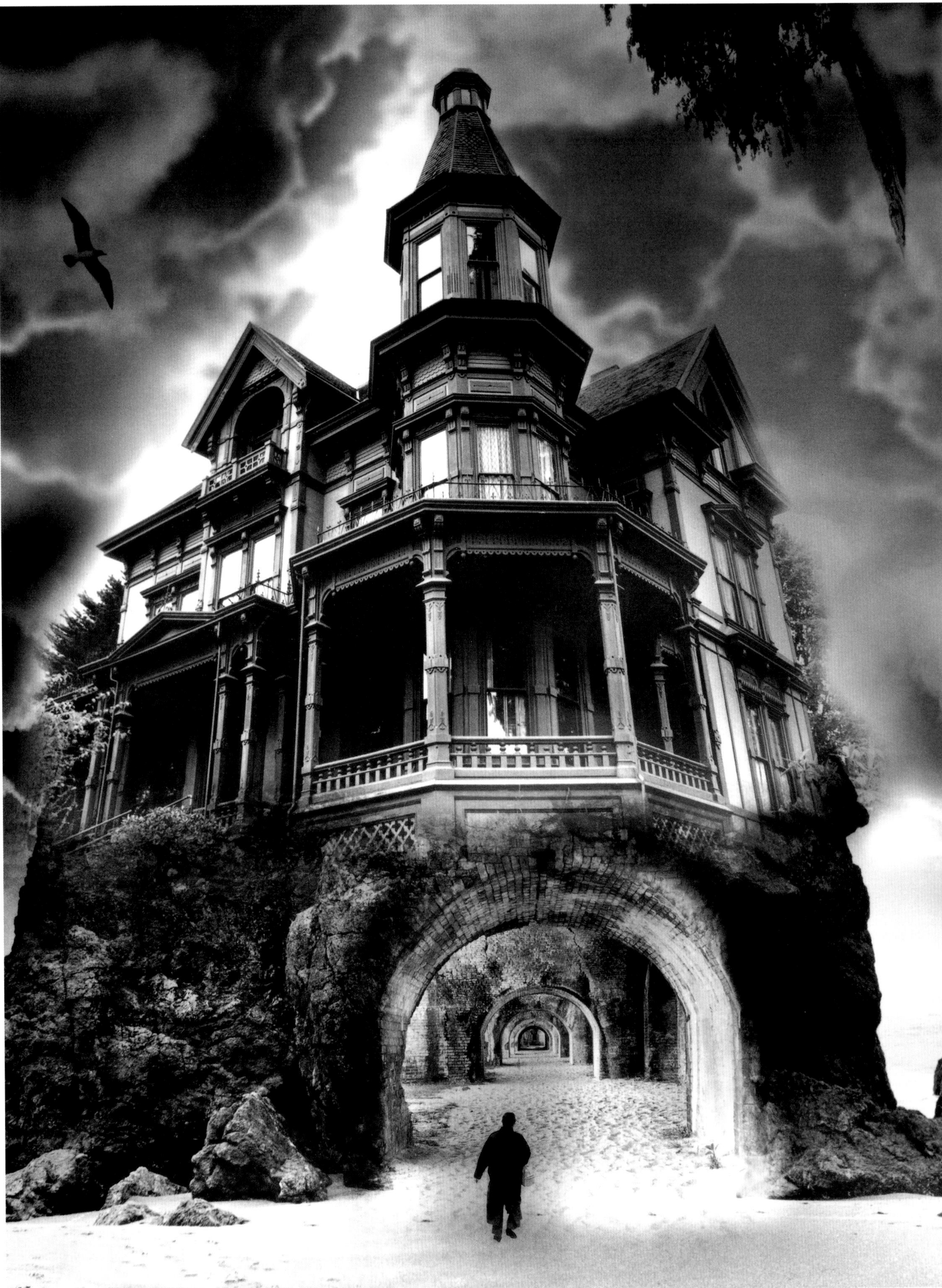

This particular image came about more by accident than design. A potential buyer of my art photography commented that she had a sizable number of prints of lighthouses from coast to coast, but she didn't remember seeing any of the old "lightkeepers" houses, or private residences. I responded that I didn't have anything in my negative file as a straight image, but could possibly "build" a fantasy version of what she was looking for by combining existing images into a dreamlike interpretation. After receiving a deposit from the buyer, I proceeded to assemble negatives that would create an image or illusion of the most immense and solid home for any coastal dweller, especially the lightkeeper.

The original version of this print, which served as a starting point, is the image known as "The Tunnel" as seen on page 75 of this book. The initial thought process of the print started with the rock formation photographed on the Oregon Coast in 1992. This negative was made in the traditional style of the early West Coast photographers by using the 4x5 Field camera, Schneider 90mm wide angle lens, and employing the Zone System (discussed earlier in this book) throughout exposure and development. The opening to the rock, obviously, was non-existent. The brick arches forming the tunnel came from a negative made at Fort Pickens, a Civil War fortress on Santa Rosa Island, which is located at the western end of Pensacola Beach, Florida. I now had the foundation for the print, without the house for the lightkeeper.

On the same trip to Oregon for the coastal series, I spent one day in the attractive city of Astoria, mostly as a "sightseer" in their downtown shops and art galleries. I made a wrong turn and ended up driving down a one way street in the wrong direction, but fortunately dead-ended at a beautiful but neglected and abandoned mansion. The negative of this home, made at this dead-end street, served as the perfect match with "The Tunnel," because the top of the rock blended well with the stone foundation of the mansion. The only missing element was the lightkeeper himself—a person to identify with, as well as to give the image a sense of scale. Looking through my contact sheets taken in Paris in 1987, I remembered a 35mm negative that I had taken of a "little man" walking in the rain, down a side street in the Left Bank in the City of Lights. The "little man" proved to be the missing link that laced this new print together. The buyer of this commissioned print was most pleased, and pleaded with me not to let anyone know that this was a composite photograph. So, as readers of this confession, don't tell anyone.

EQUIPMENT

Camera: Rock formation—Anba 4x5 Wooden Field Camera; Pt. Pickens Arches—Mamiya C33; Oregon Mansion—Pentax 6x7
Lighting: Available light on all negatives
Film: Kodak Tri-X on all negatives
Print: Kodak Polymax Fiberbase, Dektol Developer

Ocean View

Living on the Gulf Coast is as close to having a small piece of the Riviera as possible. The Gulf Coast, by my definition, extends from the shores of the Mississippi Sound, to as far east as Apalachicola, Florida. In all due respect to my fellow Floridians, we have the most beautiful beaches in the world, and I would not trade any Gulf Coast property for the finest Miami Beach condominium. Tucked away, in the Panhandle of Florida, this is a great lifestyle; however, the rest of the world is discovering Northwest Florida, much to the dismay of the natives.

Readers of this book will notice while flipping through the photographs that I have a certain penchant for the Gothic style of architecture. I try to incorporate this theme as often as possible, simply because it's a style that I favor. In regards to this print, "Ocean View," this house is not on the water, nor is it even close, in reality. However, if I could have a beach house, this would be it!

The negative of this old home, in all of its fading glory, was made and exposed in a very neglected area of downtown Pensacola. This house had great lines and character, and I felt it would therefore blend well with supplemental negatives, specifically a heron and some cloud images from my negative file. How do you create this whimsical fantasy, an illusion that is precise in architectural details, giving you a near perfect rendering of your proposed waterfront dream house? The answer is simple, and as old as photography itself: traditional darkroom manipulation, no computers required.

In the darkroom, I placed the negative of the house in my primary enlarger. Using three enlargers side by side, I referred to the primary enlarger as the Bessler 4x5 chassis, coupled with the Ilford Multigrade Head, as opposed to the standard condenser head. Having made subsequent tests on the two additional negatives (the heron in water, and the cloud formation), the exposure times were recorded. The rest was routine work. The 11x14 paper was placed under the Ilford enlarger, and exposed for the house. Slight dodging was needed below the steps of the house, to allow the overprint of the second negative. The paper was moved to the second enlarger and the exposure of the heron and water was made. Lastly, the same sheet of 11x14 paper was placed in the easel under the third enlarger for the final element, the addition of the dark, ominous cloud formation.

Have we achieved anything in this overlay of negatives? I believe so—we have an enigma in the fact that this is a fantasy house and not a true waterfront. The blue heron adds to the mystery of this image, as does the menacing sky. It's as if time itself is wearing down this house—the waves polishing its soul.

EQUIPMENT

Camera: Pentax 6x7
Lens: 55mm
Accessories: Yellow filter
Lighting: Direct sunlight
Film: Ilford HP-4
Print: Ilford Fiberbase VC, #3 filter

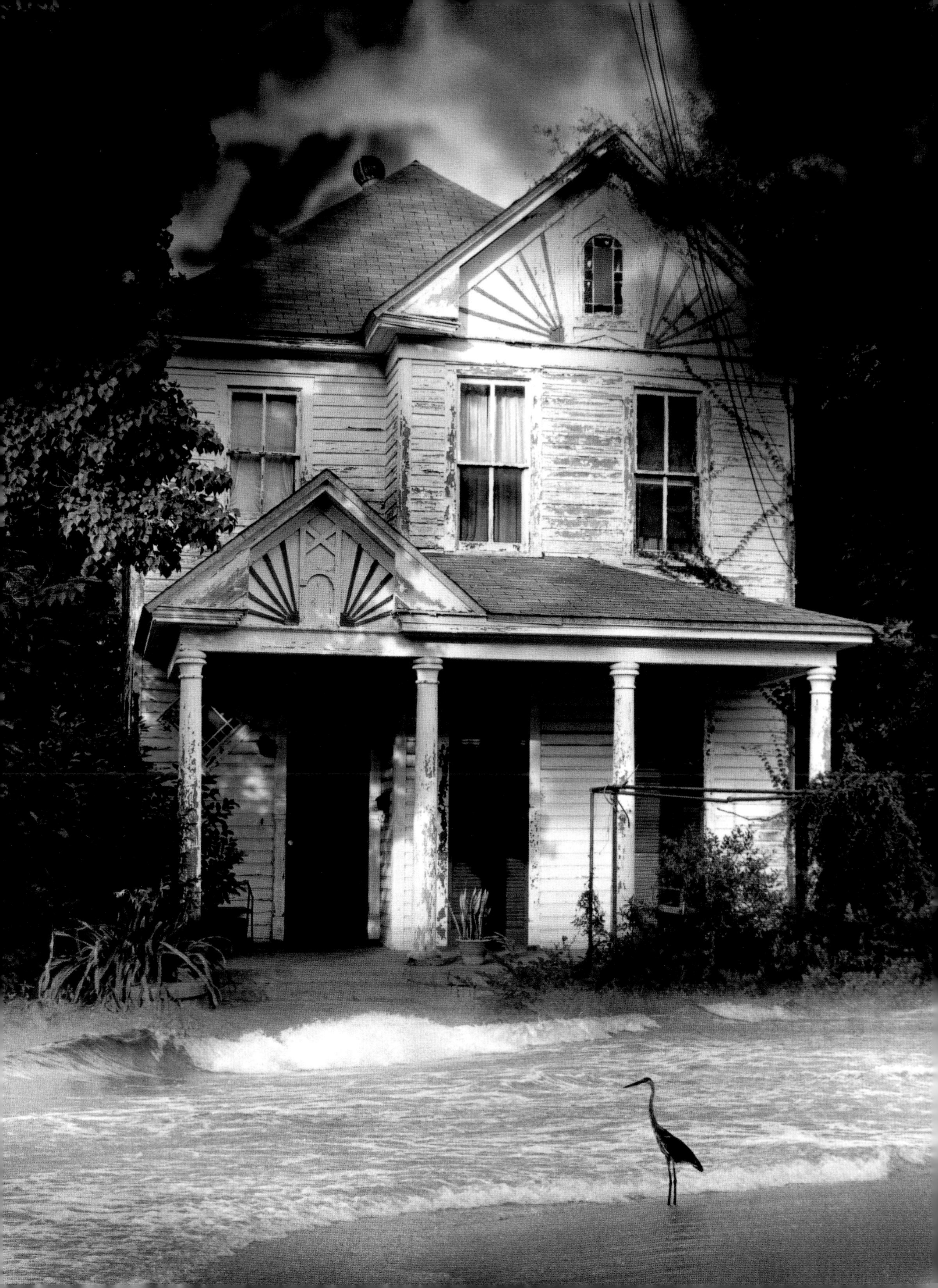

The Card Room

This is pure fantasy, a forest wonderland that just so happens to reside in the clouds. As a child, did you ever want to create your own secret hideaway? We all have these memories. I remember mine well, and it is this image here, an illusion of the perfect room.

In this print, I hope that the theme is obvious. I have always enjoyed a good card game and this room, designed by a friend who is a noted decorator, caught my eye. I was commissioned, not to play cards, but to do architectural photography for the "Decorator's Showcase House" in Pensacola. Seeing this room, while photographing this fine antebellum home, reminded me of a room that you see only in your dreams. Nancy Woodcock, a fine and talented decorator, was responsible for transforming a mundane room into one that you would pay to walk in.

Using a 6x7 Corfield architectural camera (a fine piece of equipment made in England), I made the exposure of the room under strictly available light, with no supplemental lighting. After viewing my first 8x10 test print in the darkroom, it took no magician to see the potential. All I had to do was add the clouds and vines, and it became a surrealistic print made in heaven. This is now a room where one can sip 100 year-old Scotch, and touch the timeless and deathless realm that only comes through heart-warming conversation with an old friend.

You will notice a great many of my prints, this one included, have a filter used on the photographic paper when I am in the darkroom. This filter is used to alter the contrast of the image, but not always for purely technical reasons. If you expose your negative correctly in the beginning, then your print should be fine without any other contrast manipulation at all.

However, there are times when artistically you might want to change the contrast, and this is where the darkroom work comes in. If, for example, you decide that your print should have a higher degree of contrast, you can use either a variable contrast paper (with which you can alter the contrast by use of filtration in the enlarger when printing), or you can use a graded paper. This paper is available in grades 0 through 5, with the contrast values shifting from soft to hard as the grade increases. Not all papers are made in all grades, and not every manufacturer uses the same scale, so you might need to experiment with different paper grades to see which you prefer. Of course, variable contrast paper is less expensive in the long run, since you don't need to purchase each grade separately. Instead, you only need a filter pack in order to have a wide range of contrasts available to you.

EQUIPMENT

Camera: Corfield 6x7
Lens: 47mm Schneider
Lighting: Available ambient room light
Film: Kodak Tri-X
Print: Kodak Fiberbase VC, #2-1/2 filter

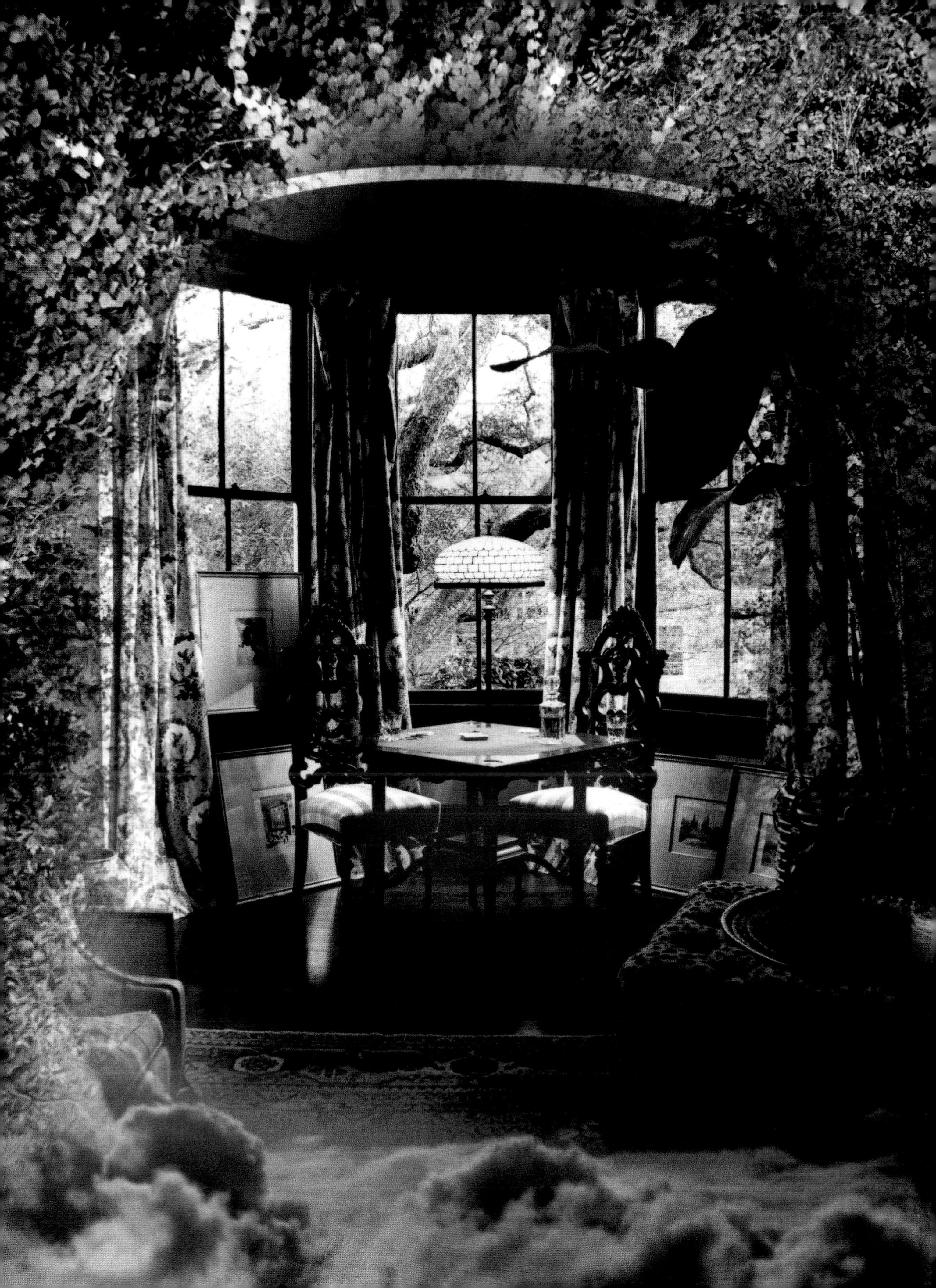

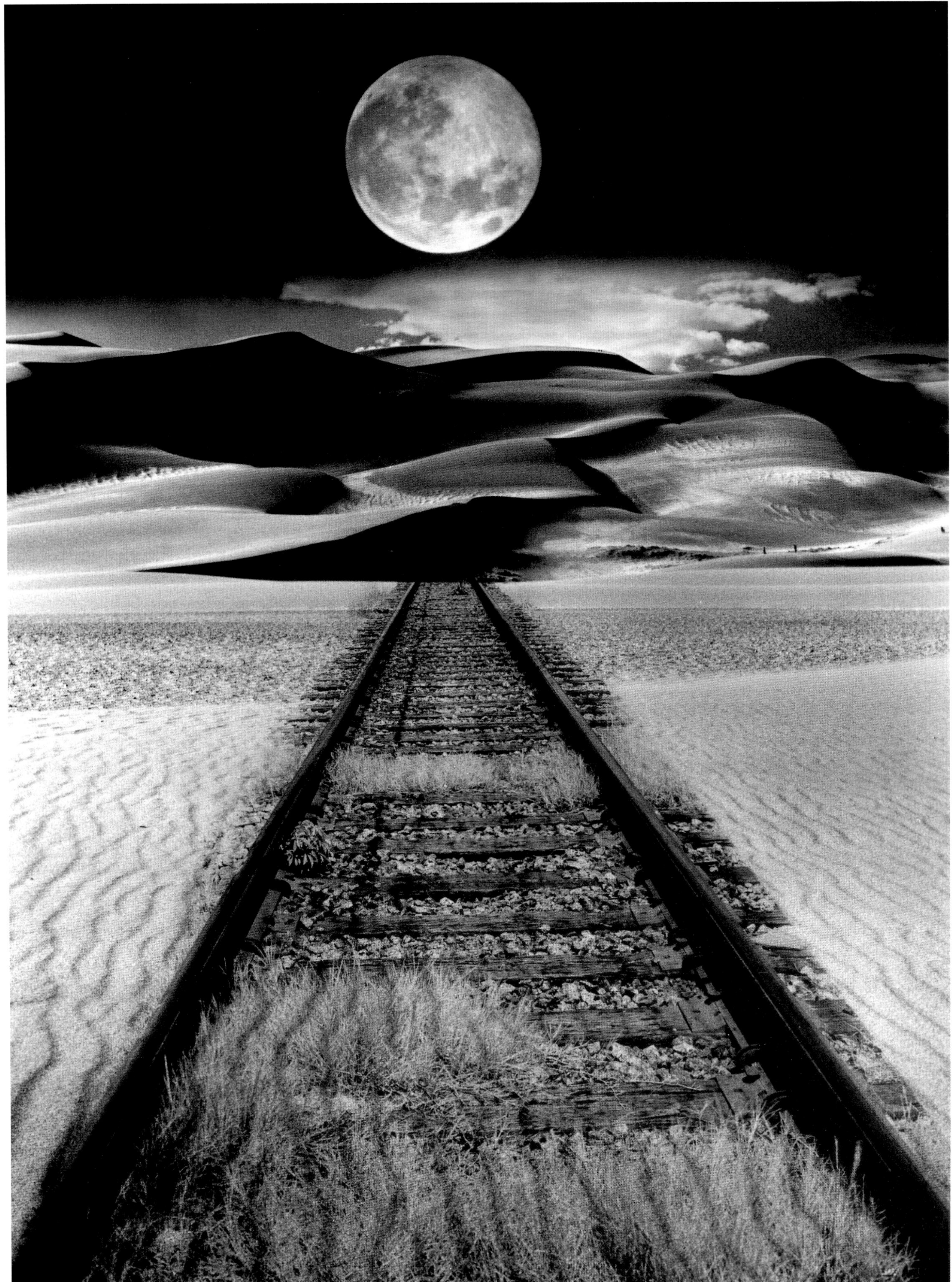

Most people are entranced by a full moon, but an autumn moon in a foreign setting makes it all the more intriguing. This fantasy image with the tracks takes you into a bizarre land: a desert which seems to mirror the lunar landscape so far away.

While visiting a friend in Taos, New Mexico, I planned a day trip to the Great Sand Dune National Park in Colorado, several hours to the north. For this photo trip, all my equipment was large format, all 4x5 cameras and lenses. The mistake I made for this intentional trip was not checking the position of the sun for the deep shadows needed to photograph the dunes. I assumed, incorrectly, that it would be a morning shoot. Once I arrived, I realized that I would have to kill about six hours and wait for the late afternoon light. About an hour before the light would be perfect, I began my trek through the sand to set up the 4x5 camera and tripod. Being accustomed to the sand on Pensacola Beach, I was quite taken back and surprised by the fine and soft texture of the sand making up these dunes. It was as if I needed snow shoes to keep from sinking to my ankles. Nevertheless, my mile hike was well worth it in spite of the wind blowing a small gale. A very good negative resulted from these endeavors.

I printed this negative as a straight image for several years, and without sounding modest, it was a popular print, and sold well. The concept of "Moon Tracks" came about three years ago. By a fluke, I stumbled across a negative of railroad tracks that I knew immediately would easily overprint on the dunes print. With the first test print of railroad tracks and dunes completed, I needed an additional element to balance the top of the print. Why not integrate the moon into this image? With the moon now added, we have a curious print that always makes viewers ask, "Where is this?"

The composition of this new print is an invitation to a journey, a concept that I find repeating itself in my work. I want the photograph to take you into worlds that are completely new, or that have only been visited in our dreams.

EQUIPMENT

Camera: Dunes—Anba 4x5 Wooden Field Camera; Moon—Nikon F-3; Railroad Tracks—Hasselblad 500C
Lens: Dunes—90mm Caltar; Moon—300mm; Railroad Tracks—90mm
Lighting: Available light on all negatives
Film: Kodak Tri-X on all negatives
Print: Kodak Polymax Fiberbase

The Tunnel

The entrance to this old Civil War fort is purely a world within worlds. I had imagined landing on some distant land and finding these ruins of another age, of another culture.

The principal negative in this composite print is not the rock, but rather the arches and tunnel, which I photographed for the first time in 1988. It is somewhat ironic that you can revisit a scene that is totally motionless, and with your tripod in the exact position as for the previous assignment, come up with a totally different mood. Of my three excursions to Fort Pickens, this negative of the tunnel had the best lighting. The only other mechanical exercise was total sharpness, from the point closest to the camera to infinity. We can assume that with the camera on a sturdy tripod and the lens stopped down to f22 our depth of field will be precise.

The tunnel and arches proved to be a great starting point for my ideas. I remembered a very sedate negative that I made of a rock formation on the Oregon coast; it had the perfect tonal qualities and texture to blend with the Fort Pickens negative.

In the darkroom, I placed the negative of the Oregon rock formation in the first enlarger. Projecting this negative on the easel, I drew in pencil where the area would be dodged so that I could point the tunnel in this same position. With the tunnel negative in the second enlarger, I overprinted this negative in combination with the negative that had already been exposed in the Oregon rock negative in the first enlarger. With this accomplished, my last step was to darken the top of the print with a further element. Hence, a cloud formation from my negative file was put into play.

This might be referred to as a hedge bet, but I like giving the interpretation of the print after seeing if I have successfully combined the negatives to my satisfaction. This print worked well with all three above mentioned negatives. The photograph suggests the sky, rock and sand of a forgotten, archaic landscape—to be visited not by us, but perhaps someone else.

EQUIPMENT

Camera: Tunnel—Mamiya C33; Rock—Anba 4x5 Wooden Field Camera; Cloud—Unrecorded 6x7 format camera
Lens: Tunnel—55mm
Lighting: Available light on all negatives
Film: Tri-X for tunnel and rock, Ilford HP-4 for clouds
Print: Ilford Fiberbase VC

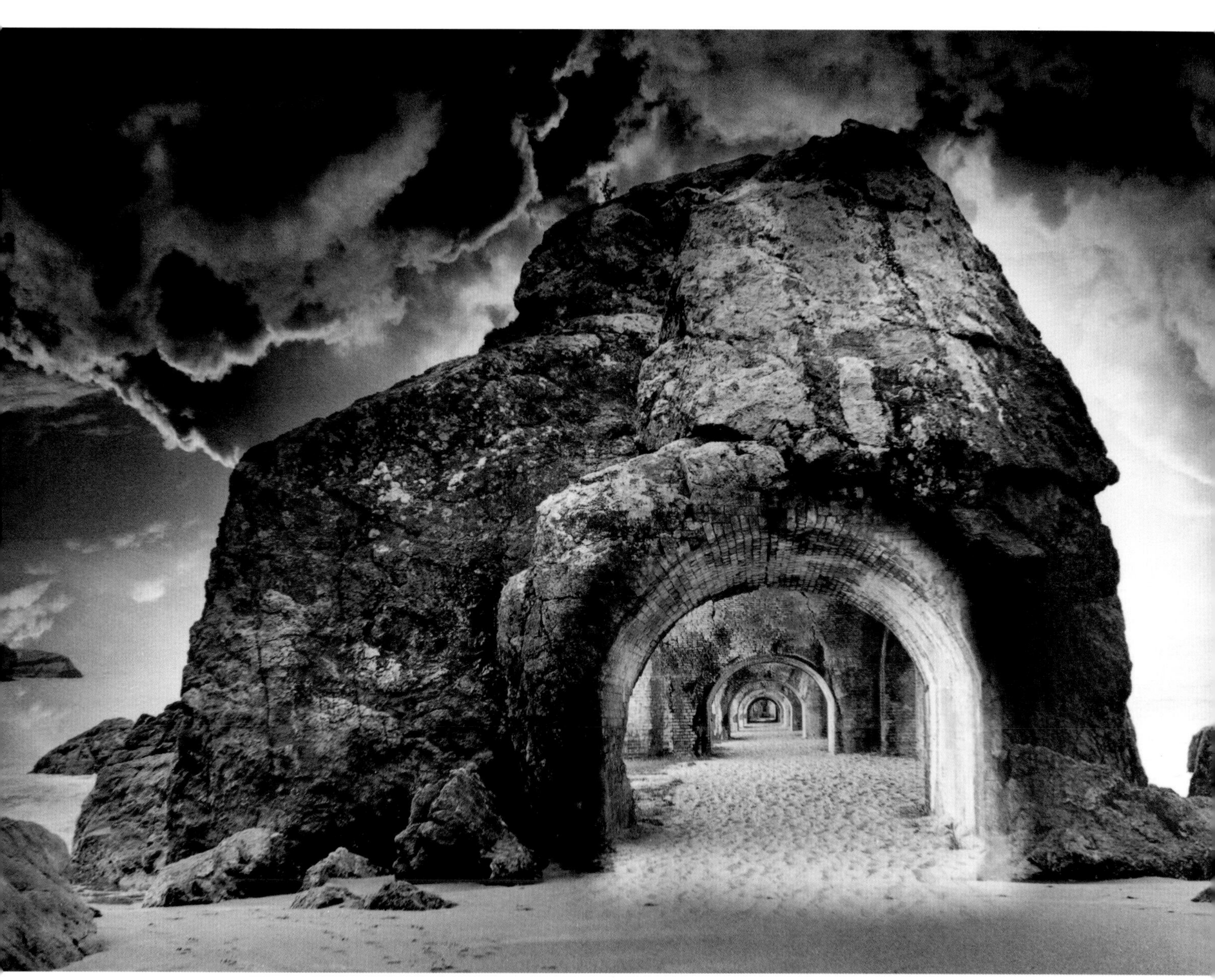

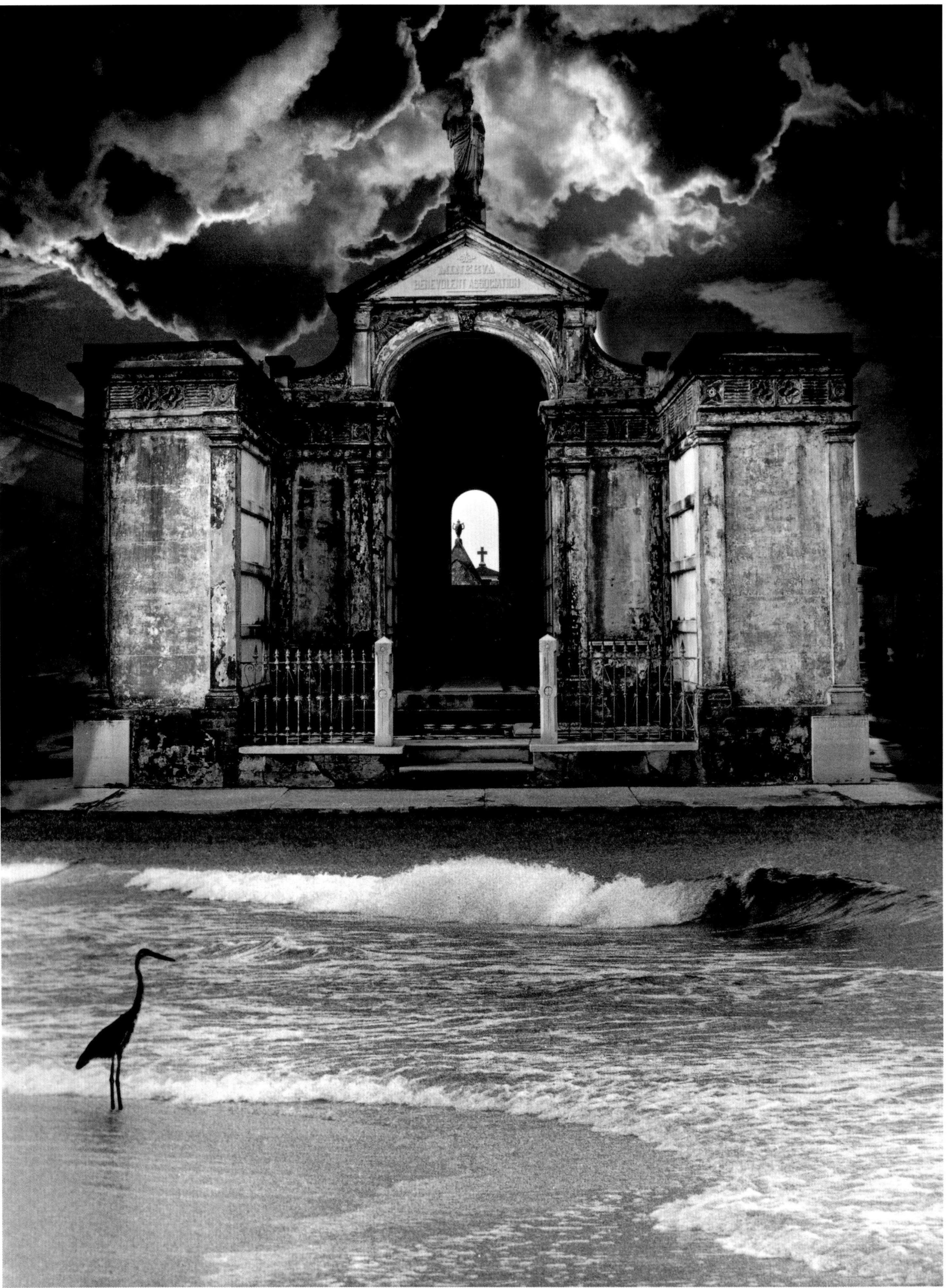
BENEVOLENT ASSOCIATION

Metairie Tomb

I was taken by the old weathered stone textures of this ancient crypt. Looking at the narrow window with the steeple and cross in the background gave me a glimpse into another world.

As as "old haunt" who combs the ancient graveyards in search of another image, I believe that Metairie Cemetery in New Orleans has the finest mortuary architecture in the world, and some of the finest photographic opportunities. For those who have departed this life, there is not a finer resting place, or one that is more visited. These fine marble and granite tombs were the successful endeavor of architect and sketch artist John H.B. Latrobe, and tomb maker and contractor Albert Weiblen, who accumulated a great deal of wealth in their development of funerary architecture. To duplicate these tombs today would surpass the cost of a fine home in an upscale urban development. The wealthy had the means to afford these monuments to themselves, and with no income tax at that time... well, what's the cost of immorality?

This old society tomb (multiple vaults), which was in a dismal state of disrepair, caught my eye as an ideal image to incorporate additional negatives. As a person who loves sailing and the ocean, I had a vision of all the departed "tucked away" folk in this tomb as being "seafarers." Accordingly, I made a negative of the tomb with the implicit idea of adding the negative of the water and heron below the base of the tomb. With this accomplished, my last component was the addition of a negative with a very swarthy appearance to suggest adverse weather.

I stumbled across a quotation that I had been saving, which proved to be a greater interpretation of this composite print than I could write. It was made in 1513 A.D. by Fra Giovanni. The contemporary verse would read something like this: "The gloom of the world is but a shadow. Behind it, yet within our reach, is joy. There is radiance and glory in the darkness... we only have to look."

EQUIPMENT

Camera: Pentax 6x7
Lens: 55mm
Accessories: Yellow filter
Lighting: Available light, indirect sun
Film: Ilford HP-4
Print: Ilford Fiberbase VC, #2-1/2 filter

The Guardian Angel

Photographers and artists sometimes extract ideas from dreams or, even more consequential, a real-life experience. These concepts and ideas can sometimes produce images that are seen at first only by the subconscious mind, but are later reproduced on canvas. This was the case in the construction and formation of this very simple image.

At this point in the book, it's no secret that I'm a "haunt" of the old cemeteries and graveyards. I'm always looking for the ultimate Gothic image with which to blend another negative. On an excursion to New Orleans with my sister, we stopped in Bay St. Louis, Mississippi, which happens to be the half-way mark between New Orleans and Pensacola. There was a beautiful sunset over the Mississippi Sound with a 1920s pier and gazebo in the foreground. It was an ideal photo, although it might have been better for a color calendar than a black and white art print. I asked my sister to stop the car by the side of the road so that I could record the scene. After exposing several negatives, I picked up the camera and tripod and turned to cross the road. Immediately, there was a piercing horn blast from a sixteen-wheeler that missed mowing me down by only a few inches. I had forgotten that I was on a four-lane divided highway. Although shaken, I was still alive; I had been spared. Do I believe in angels? Yes, I do. It wasn't my time to go.

A quote from John Calvin goes something like this: "The angels are the dispensers and administrators of the Divine beneficence toward us. They regard our safety, undertake our defense and exercise a constant solicitude that no evil befalls us." With Calvin's words and my near-death experience in mind, I made a mental note to recreate an image of this guardian who had protected me. I found this angel in Metairie Cemetery, New Orleans.

The technical notes on this image are quite simple. The angel is a granite figure atop a very modest tomb. The sky was overcast, giving me a dark and bleak rendition of this beautifully sculpted angel. A normal meter reading from the camera, or hand-held meter, would have rendered the granite angel a very dark gray. To create the tonality I desired, I simply turned to the principles of the Zone System, mentioned in the front of the book, and "moved" the granite from Zone V to Zone VII. This translates to overexposing by two stops, making the torso of the angel light gray instead of dark gray.

The last element was to add a negative from my file of a sunburst and cloud formation, which easily overprinted the bland lack of sky in the original negative. As a last element, I added a bird from my negative file. In no time, with three negatives in one enlarger, my vision of the Guardian Angel came to life.

EQUIPMENT

Camera: Pentax 6x7
Lens: 90mm
Lighting: Overcast daylight
Film: Kodak Tri-X ASA 400 (rated at 250)
Print: Kodak Polymax Fine Art

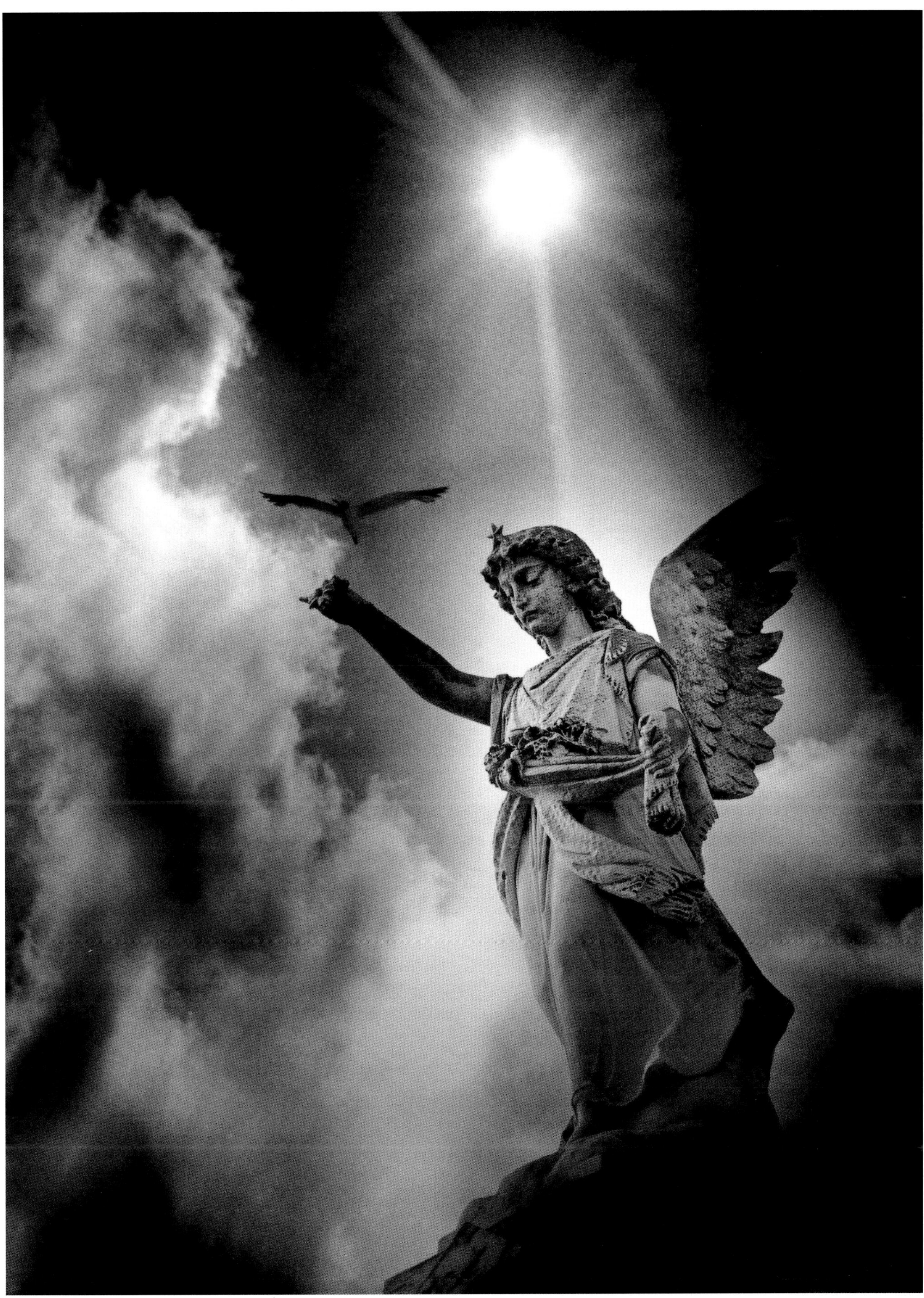

Bates Motel

This is a house on the top of a haunted hill—not a movie set, but an abandoned home in Astoria, Oregon, that I found on a side trip to photograph the Oregon coast. It was almost as if it were meant for me to find it, there at the end of a dead end street. Seeing this Victorian architectural gem made me wish that I had packed the 4x5 camera to correct for the distortion created when shooting at an inclined angle with a fixed back camera. Nevertheless, I resorted to my original idea of the haunted house image, and realized that the distortion of the house would not take away from but enhance the final print.

Upon my return to Pensacola, the first 8x10 proof of this house did not reflect my initial feeling of a "spook house," even though the lines and character of the architecture suggest this. The sky was totally washed out and devoid of any clouds. Secondly, the street and parapet brick wall below the home suggested Victorian suburban living, circa the 1890s. Flipping through my contact prints of seashore scenes, I found a negative made near Portland, Maine that was the perfect match. It was a walkway to the beach, and the foliage on both sides of the boardwalk conformed with the grass surrounding the mansion. A perfect arrangement, I thought. After carefully dodging (removing) the original street scene below the house, I overprinted the Maine negative with the boardwalk under the foundation of the house. The sky and bird were added as the final elements, and my version of "Bates Motel" was complete.

EQUIPMENT

Camera: Pentax 6x7
Lens: 55mm
Lighting: Overcast daylight
Film: Kodak Tri-X ASA 400 (rated at 250)
Print: Kodak Polymax Fiberbase

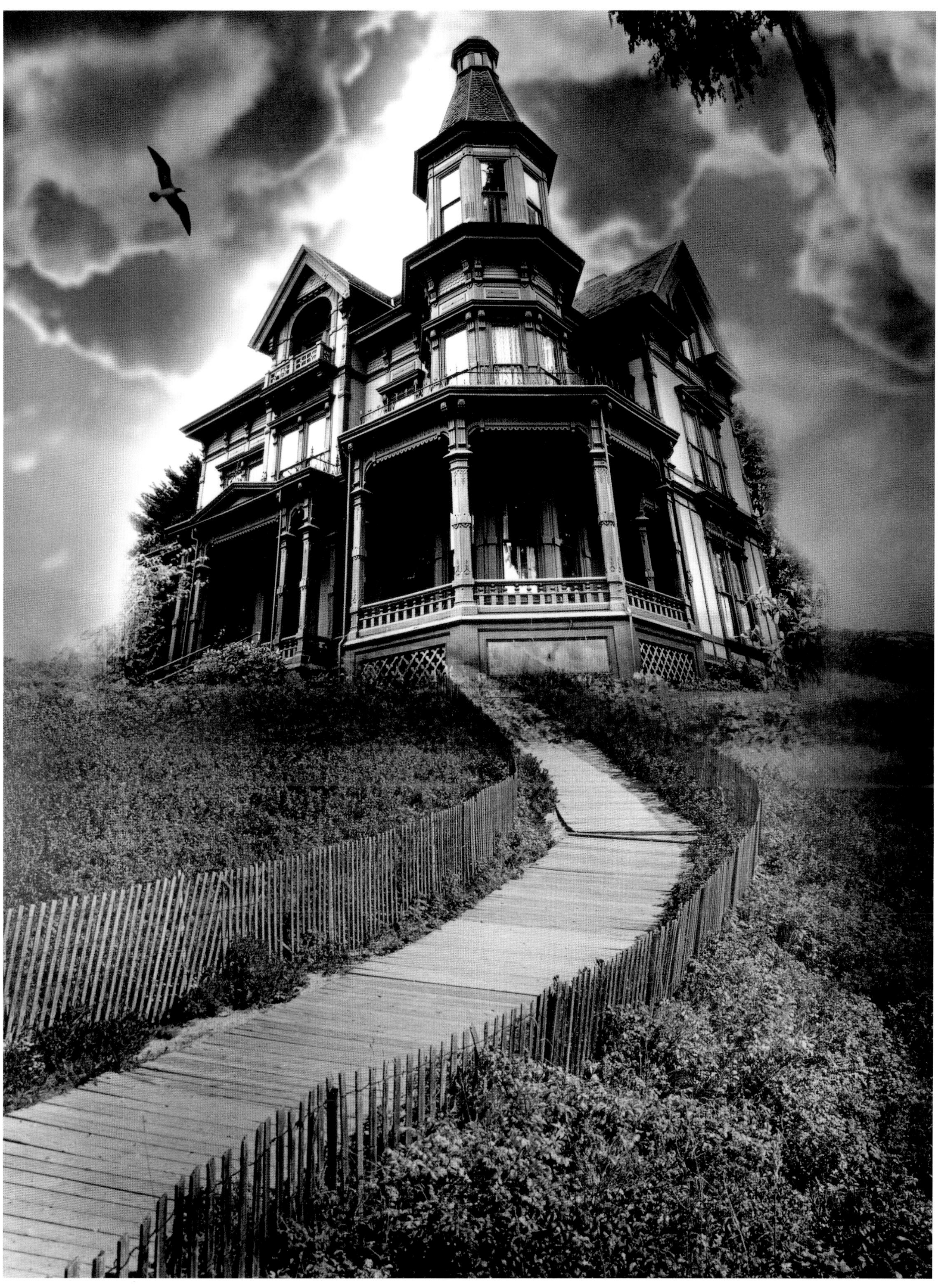

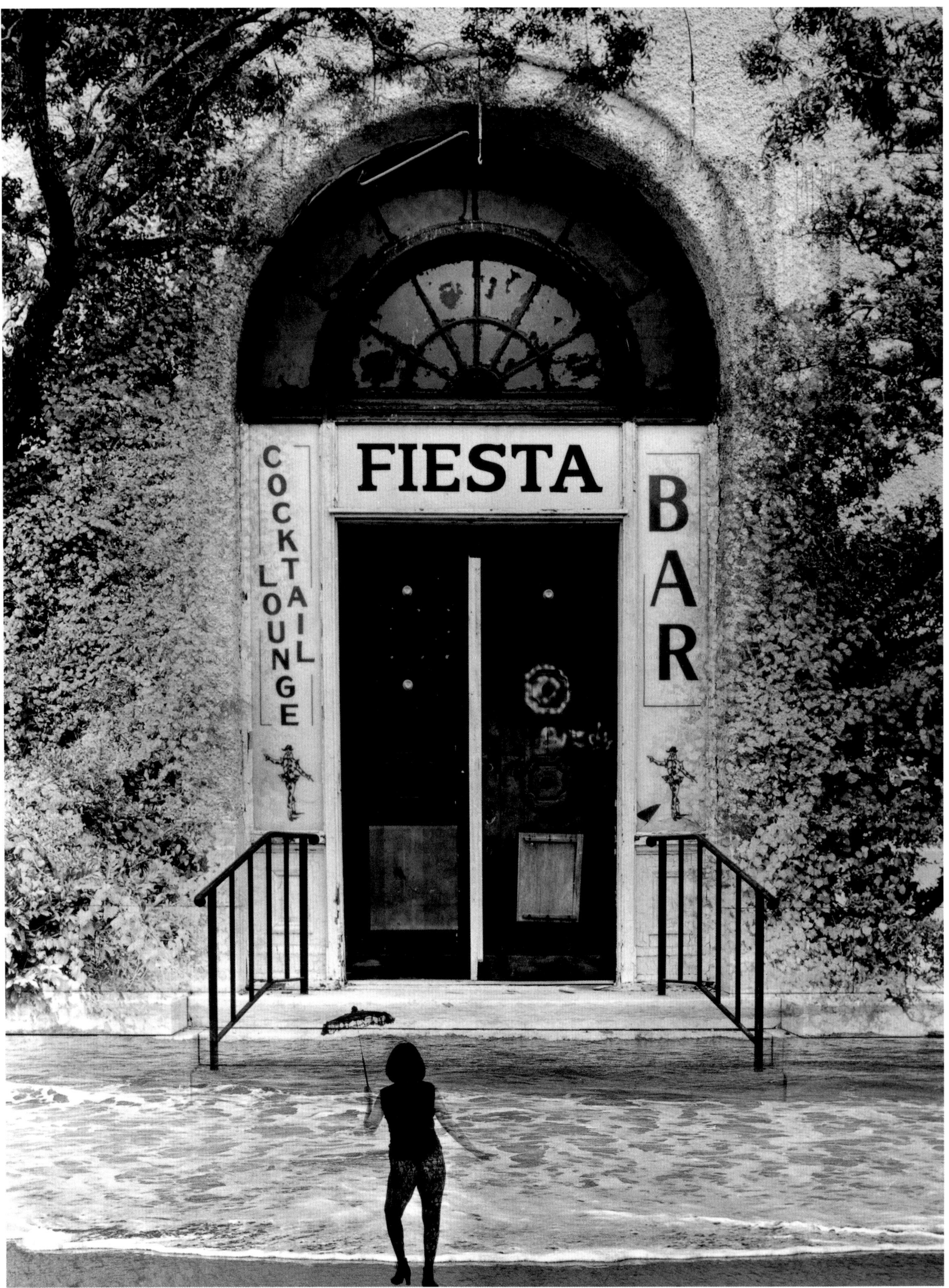
FIESTA
COCKTAIL
LOUNGE
BAR

This old side bar of the former San Carlos Hotel was the beloved watering hole of many of Pensacola's finest citizens—politicians, bankers, stockbrokers, lawyers, hoodlums, pimps and prostitutes. This fine, timeworn hotel finally met its doom with the wrecking ball several years ago, to make room for a new United States Federal Courthouse. Several days prior to the demolition of this section of the hotel, I had several sheets of 4x5 film still loaded from an architectural assignment that I had just completed. I had no interest in making a negative of the full exterior, which had been done for the last seventy-five years by more than a dozen photographers. However, I had no recollection of anyone zeroing in exclusively on an image of the entrance to the Fiesta Bar. I decided that it was my job to document this infamous bar for prosperity.

I made a negative with a pleasing composition and exposure, but with no one shouting for an immediate copy of this print, I filed it away and almost forgot about it. Several years later, I received a letter from a casual acquaintance who had purchased prints from me in the past. He asked if I had anything in my files that would portray prostitutes and sleazy bars. Knowing that I had nothing on file as a single image, I offered to combine several negatives in the darkroom. If he wasn't pleased with my interpretation of his fantasy, I could always market the print to someone else.

The composite print of "Fiesta Bar" required four dissimilar negatives. This was absolute for my operation, as I have only four enlargers in the darkroom. The first exposure was of the facade of the bar. The second enlarger held the negative of the "prostitute" (a studio model shot against white seamless paper and lit with an electronic flash). This was overprinted in the bottom of the print. The third element was the overprinting of the water between the lady and the base of the door. Lastly, I incorporated a negative of vines to frame the top and sides of the final image.

The buyer of this commissioned print was amused as well as pleased. He asked me what I had been thinking when putting it all together, and I replied, "Don't shut the bar yet! I'm coming in for the last call like the ghost from New Year's past."

EQUIPMENT

Camera: Hotel Exterior—4x5 Anba Wooden Field Camera; Studio Model—Hasselblad 500CM; Water—Pentax 6x7; Vines—6x7 format (camera not recorded)

Lighting: All exterior available light except for studio model

Film: Combination of Tri-X and Ilford Delta

Print: Kodak Polymax Fiberbase

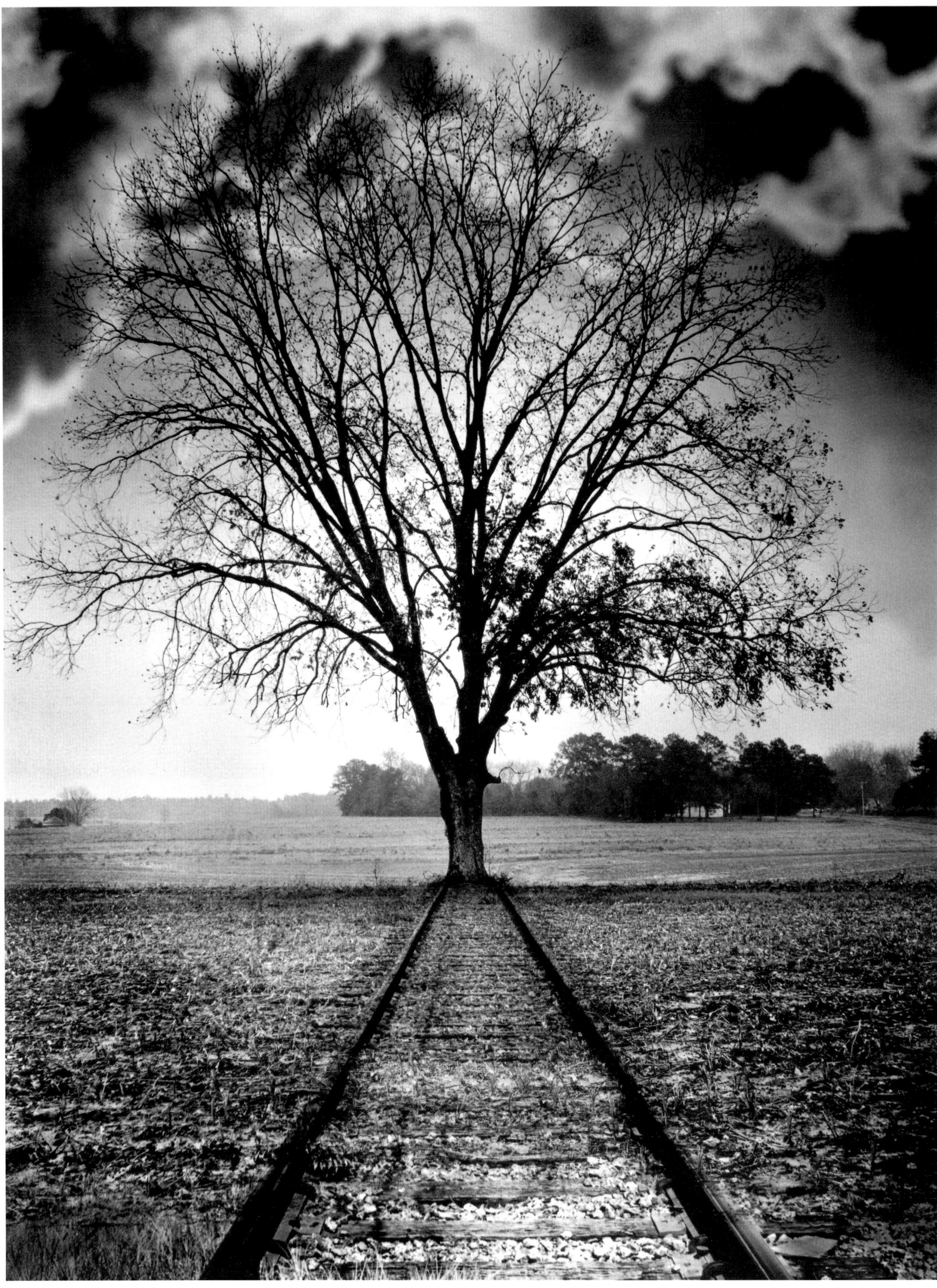

I've never seen anything—and I mean nothing in the manmade world—that approaches the beauty, elegance and uniqueness of a single tree framed against a sky.

I would rather be lucky than smart regarding my photography, and that applies to this image. I received an invitation to join an old friend for a weekend retreat at his family's farm in Alabama. I arrived too early—5:30 in the morning. I walked through the door of this old farm house (which has never been locked in the last century) and found that everyone was still asleep. There was a note in the kitchen, left by my host who had anticipated my early arrival. It gave instructions for me not to wake anyone. "Go take some pictures," the note read. "Wake us up when you get back."

I heeded the advice of my host and left the house on a photo expedition. I drove down a road that had not seen asphalt in a long time, not knowing where I was going on this cold, gray morning. Without expecting it, I suddenly found myself near an imposing, old, bare pecan tree in the middle of a vacant field.

I was armed with an arsenal of different cameras for this trip, and it looked as if I had loaded most of my studio gear in the car. However, I gave this tree my best effort by using the biggest machine I had in the bag, the 4x5 view camera. I can't think of what nut other than me would be out at six in the morning, freezing to death, to photograph a near-dead pecan tree. This was an exercise that only Matthew Brady, the Civil War photographer, would have enjoyed.

The straight version of this scene was exactly as I had interpreted: the simple elegance and lines of the tree. The print sold well as is for several years. In spite of successful print sales, there is always the tendency to alter, or modify what is already a productive image. The railroad track negative was part of my disjointed "to do" file, and at this point it had never been blended with another print. Observing the two negatives on the light box, you could see that they were obviously made for each other. The new version of this print was made by a simple overprint of the tracks, and the addition of clouds.

This image should not lead you into another world, but rather give you the solace of a long journey's end. You're home, and this is the end of the line.

EQUIPMENT

Camera: Anba 4x5 Wooden Field Camera
Lens: 90mm Caltar
Lighting: Tree—overcast sky; Tracks—direct sun
Film: Kodak Tri-X
Print: Ilford Multigrade Fiberbase, #3 filter

Mass at High Tide

This beautiful church is only sixteen feet tall. It's another fine example of the beautifully crafted tombs to be found in Metairie Cemetery in New Orleans. Mortuary architecture of this style is uniquely characteristic of New Orleans and Paris, France (most notably the Cimetiere du Pere-Lachaise, at the fashionable address of "16 rue du Repos"). From a layman's view, I favor the tombs of the New Orleans' architects.

Before driving home from a portrait assignment in New Orleans in 1998, I made a hasty stop at Metairie Cemetery to pay my respects, and give a quick knock on the door of my grandparents' and great-grandparents' respective tombs. There was no response to my knock, which made me somewhat relieved, since it was getting dark.

Leaving this gigantic cemetery of countless tombs, I remembered seeing this miniature cathedral-like tomb from a previous visit. It had tremendous potential for a multi-image print. However, I envisioned it as being architecturally correct with no distortion, so a portrait camera was not the right tool for this shot. I used a Corfield Architectural Camera (which can be manipulated to keep the lines of a building straight, instead of converging). With the light slowly fading, I positioned a tripod with the English-made Corfield camera. This is a unique architectural camera in that it uses a Mamiya 6x7 back, coupled with a Schneider 47mm wide angle lens, on a camera body not much larger than your standard 35mm camera. The quality of the finished print resembles the 4x5 format, with a third less equipment.

As mentioned above, I made the exposure with the intent of incorporating a secondary negative into this image. The lushly manicured lawn below the tomb was blocked out in the initial exposure on paper. Moving the same sheet of 11x14 paper to the next enlarger, I printed a negative of rushing water taken at the Rio Honde in New Mexico directly below the base of this mausoleum.

With the print now finished, we can somehow see how the strong, sharp and angular lines of this tomb contrast so well with the rushing water. Sometimes it is the completely unexpected that comes together the best. The subtle glow lends an almost eerie and holy air to this image.

EQUIPMENT

Camera: Corfield Architectural Camera
Lens: 47mm Schneider
Lighting: Dusk and fading daylight
Film: Kodak Tri-X ASA 400 (rated at 250)
Print: Kodak Polymax VC Fiberbase

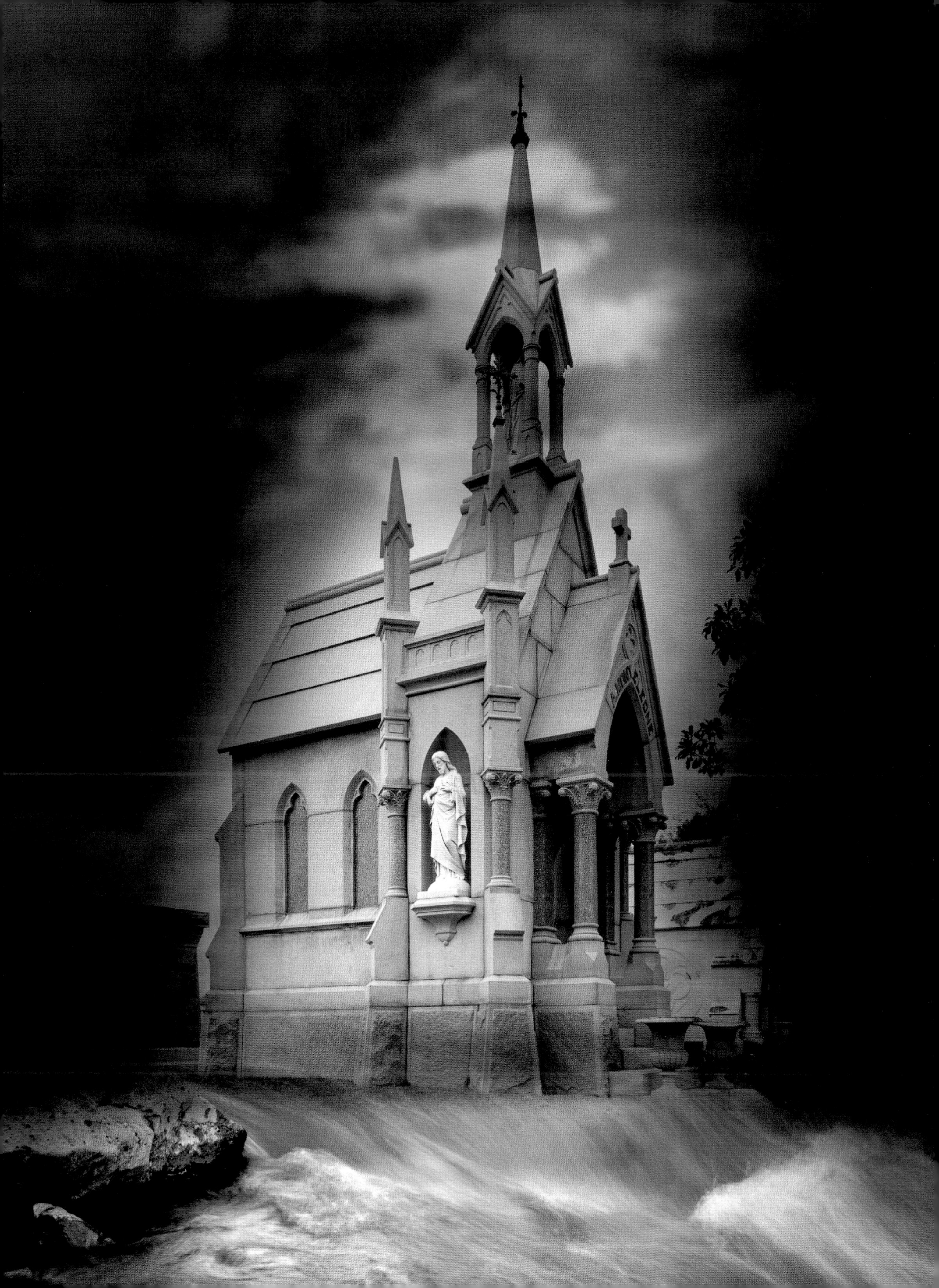

The Lost City

My schedule is such that travel to Egypt is out of the question. Granted, it would be a great expedition to photograph the pyramids and the illustrious Sphinx. As a photographer who enjoys the art form of combining multiple images, negatives such as these would be quite an asset to my file. The noted photographer Bert Stern took note of a similar idea in the early 1950s. Stern, while enjoying a martini in the staid, old Oak Room Bar in the Plaza Hotel in New York, had a similar vision. Looking through his martini glass, he envisioned the pyramid behind a martini in the sand, with the reflection of the pyramid inverted, as on a ground glass of a large format camera. This concept by Stern resulted in one of the most successful ad campaigns ever launched by Smirnoff. Forty years later, the historians of Madison Avenue have mixed opinions on whether to give the credit for this vision to Bert Stern or to the "proof" of the vodka being poured that afternoon.

Bert Stern made the journey to Giza, Egypt in 1955, and came home with incredible images on color transparency film. Wanting a similar image, and not having the time to travel to Egypt, I remembered a negative in my file from Metairie Cemetery in New Orleans. It was of the Brunswick Tomb, one of the most recognized shrines to any family in Metairie Cemetery. It is a pyramid, with steps leading up to the door of the crypt, flanked on the left with a statue of a patrician queen, facing a miniature Sphinx. I wedged the camera, tripod and myself between the statue of the queen, and made a classic "portrait" of the Sphinx, as observed in this print. The sand came from a negative of sea oats on Pensacola Beach, and was printed below the base of the tomb. The sky was darkened by simple burning of the upper edges of the print.

EQUIPMENT

Camera: Corfield 6x7 Architectural Camera (Mamiya RB Back)
Lighting: Overcast midday sunlight
Film: Kodak Tri-X
Print: Kodak Polymax Fiberbase

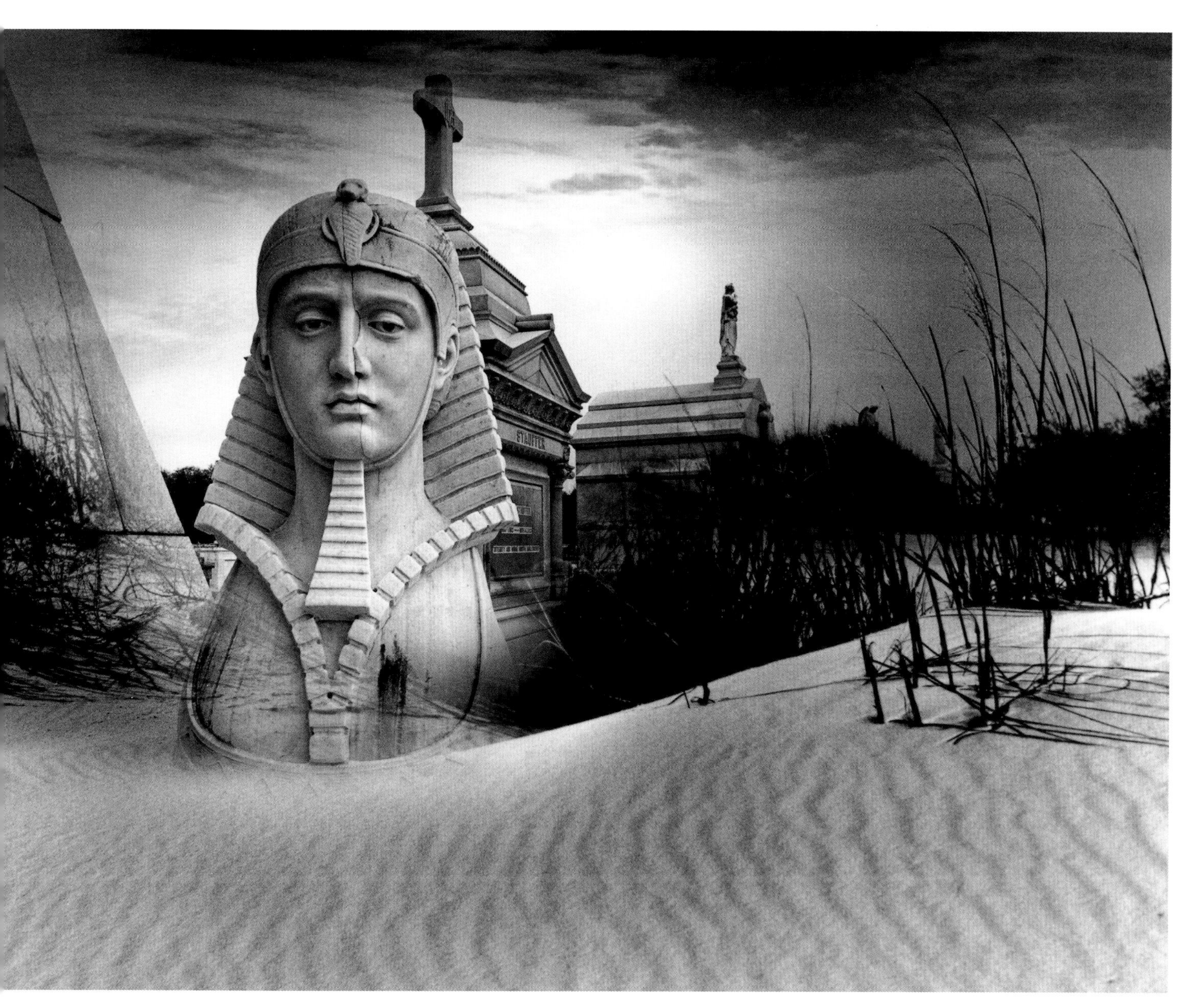

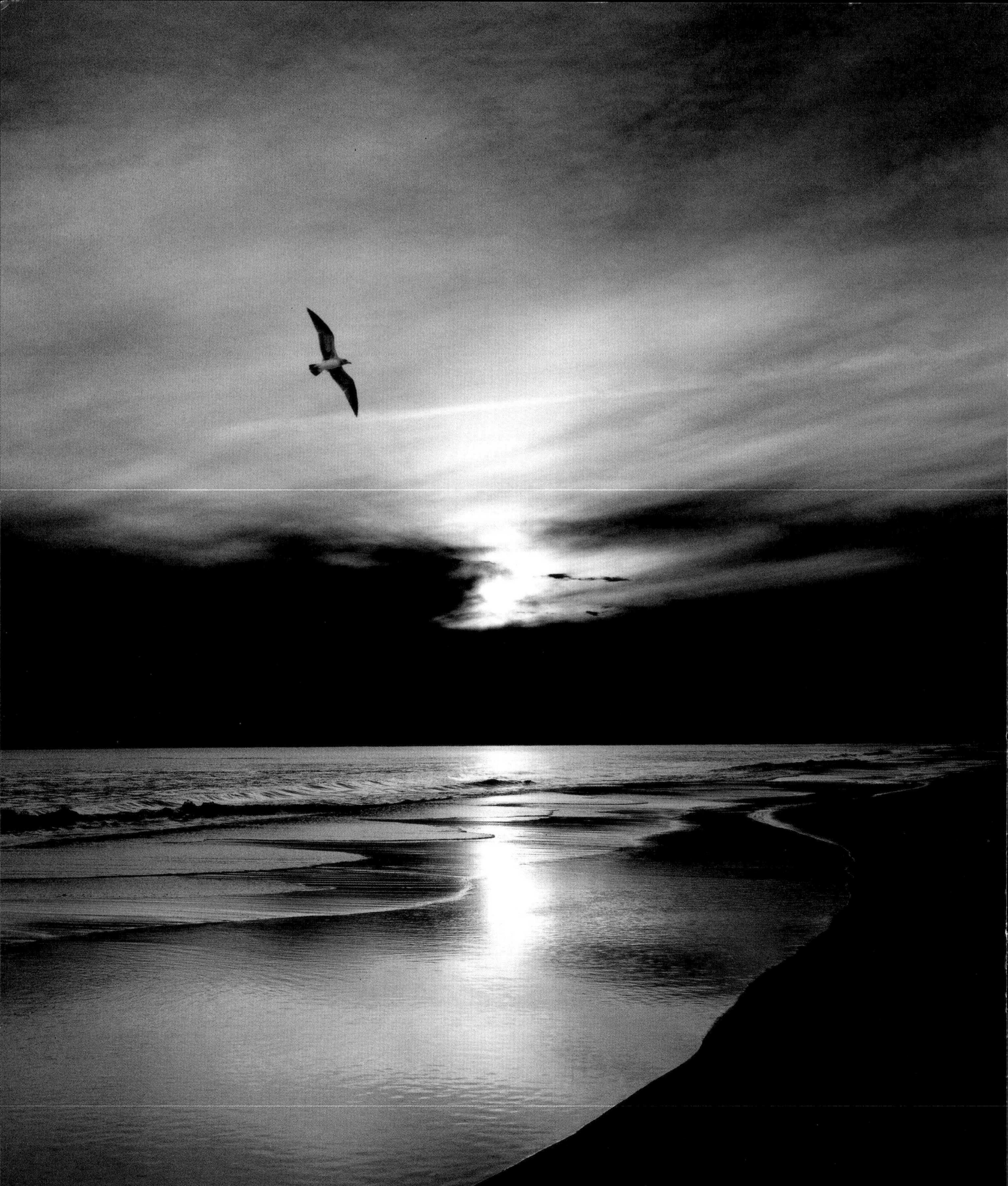

Winter Sky Gulf of Mexico

Professional photographers in most cases leave a commercial shoot with the satisfaction of an assignment well-executed, and with the expectation that the client or art director will be equally pleased. The "lagniappe" that is truly a bonus is to fall upon an image that can be incorporated into your personal work while you are still on the client's payroll. This was the case in the making of this print.

I had been commissioned for architectural photographs of a newly constructed Catholic Church on Santa Rosa Island, in my hometown of Pensacola. The architect was one who preferred black and white prints for the tonal scale, as opposed to the slick, glossy look of 16x20 color prints.

I was given total freedom to select the angles and views of the exterior of this sanctuary for images that would best exemplify the architect's design. I exposed approximately eight sheets of 4x5 film from various perspectives, and then started to pack my gear. Before loading the car, I thought it might be worthwhile to walk about 50 yards to the water to observe the sunset. Without hesitation, and afraid of losing the light, the 4x5 camera was remounted on the tripod to record this scene.

To intensify what was already a beautiful scene, I decided that an underexposure of the negative would give me the dark sky and sand. To intensify the highlight of the waves, an overdevelopment of the negative would be required. The negative delivered all of the tonal scale that I have mentioned in the forward on the Zone System. The final print was burned in at the top to darken the sky and make a more dramatic print.

As an afterthought, the negative of the lone seagull was added for the final element. Somehow this solitary bird in flight is caught in suspended animation. Like most of us, it is trapped between heaven and earth, light and dark.

EQUIPMENT

Camera: Graflex 4x5 View Camera
Lens: 150mm
Accessories: Red filter
Lighting: Sunset
Film: Kodak Tri-X
Print: Kodak Polymax Fiberbase

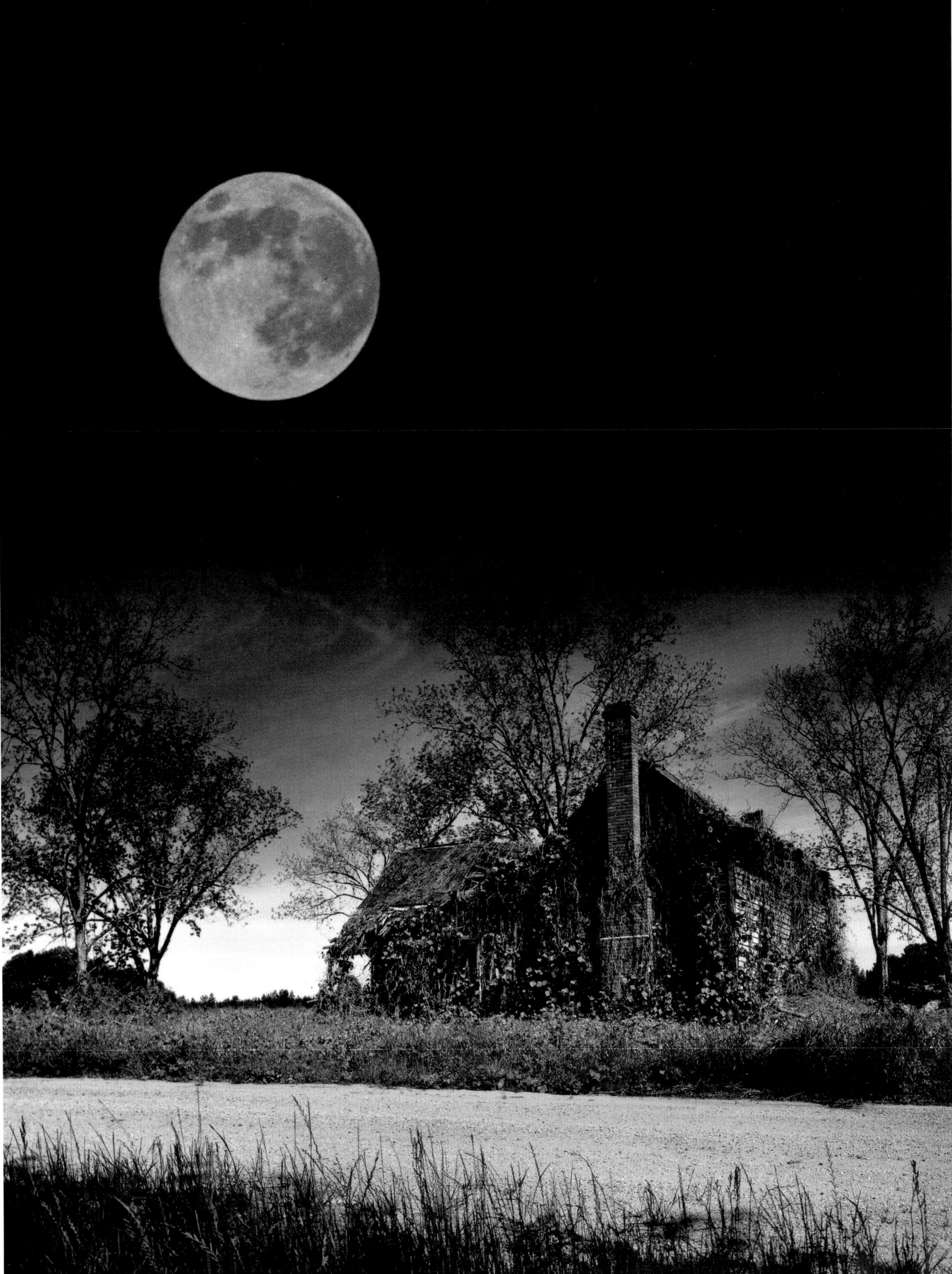

It's been alleged that a mustard seed can move a mountain. I'm not sure whether I subscribe to that hypothesis, but on the other hand, in the South we have kudzu vines that can eat and swallow a small house in one summer.

On a visit to see friends at their farm in Alabama, I made a wrong turn and ended up on a clay road, with no apparent end in sight. In all deference to my Alabama friends, some of these trails that are referred to as "roads" will never be on a map anytime in the next century. Driving down roads such as these can bait the mind of photographers—if I go just another mile or two, will I come across some fantastic photo opportunity? I kept driving, much to my discomfort, as my old BMW seemed unable to miss any of the mud or potholes. At the top of a small hill I found the setting that would make for an ideal weekend photo workshop: an abandoned shack, possibly a slave cabin, being consumed by kudzu vines.

The late afternoon light on this October afternoon was perfect for the old cabin. It proved to be a very elementary set-up: camera on the tripod and a dark yellow filter on the lens. This served a dual purpose, darkening the sky and lightening the surrounding grass which was now dormant. I made four or five exposures with the view camera. As it was now getting dark, I moved on, eventually landing at my friend's weekend retreat.

My first view of the negatives convinced me that I had a satisfactory image. It wasn't until I viewed the test print, though, that the emotion and sentiment for this little house registered in my mind. This was the home of someone unknown to me. How plebeian he might have been is inconsequential; I'm sure the patriarch of this tiny cabin was a king in his children's eyes. This backward little home, in all probability, had Christmas celebrations that we all would love to have witnessed, and a full moon would have likewise enhanced this celebration.

The original negative was printed "as is" for several years. However, the image of the moon at Christmas was still in the back of my mind. Finally succumbing to my original concept, I overprinted a negative of a full moon above the old house. Slight dodging and burning was required, but after the initial effort, the two negatives blended quite well.

EQUIPMENT

Camera: Calumet 4x5 View Camera
Lens: 90mm Caltar
Accessories: Yellow filter
Lighting: Late afternoon sun
Film: Kodak Tri-X
Print: Kodak Polymax Fiberbase, #3 filter

St. Louis Cemetery No. 1

Most people have heard that when New Orleans floods, the water pushes the caskets out of the ground, and there are bodies floating down Bourbon Street. This depicts the ghost boat ferrying these departed souls to Bourbon Street Heaven. Of course you will note the boat is empty.

The city of New Orleans, embraced by the gigantic Mississippi River, is a town that is actually below sea level. The site that Bienville had selected for New Orleans in 1718 created problems almost from the beginning. A year after the little town was laid out, the Mississippi overflowed and a low levee had to be constructed to keep out the water. From that day to this, drainage has been a continual, expensive problem, which had only really begun to be resolved in the early 1900s. This small narrative explains why no one is buried underground in this city; your final resting place is in a tomb, above ground, and hopefully an elegant one.

In this old cemetery, the remains of Marie Laveau, the best know of the voodoo queens, are at rest... maybe. This onetime hairdresser of the 19th century was a dominant soul among the superstitious members of New Orleans, and many respectable citizens consulted her for wisdom and advice as well. However, her main source of income was the sale of gris-gris (pronounced gree-gree), a luck charm for good or for evil, take your pick. Gris-gris was a concoction of salt, gunpowder, saffron and dried dog dung.

This image was made approximately twenty feet from Marie Laveau's tomb, with the negative being exposed in direct sunlight. The test print of the composite view of the tombs had possibilities in its own right, but as mentioned above, a modest amount of humor can spice up a New Orleans scene. A negative of a dory from Maine was incorporated in the final print by cutting a paper mask to block out the area now seen as water, and overprinting the boat.

Here's a neat tip for you regarding contrast control. If an image, such as the tombs here, comes out too contrasty in your original negative, you can take steps to create a more pleasing image. First, reshoot the same image so you have an undeveloped negative once more (if you can purchase a low-contrast film, this will help as well). We are going to use a water bath on this new negative, which will reduce contrast. First, develop the film for one minute in developer with normal agitation. Then place the film into water (or empty your developer tank and add water) for three minutes, using no agitation. Finally, return your negative to the developer (or empty the water and put fresh developer into the tank), and then another three minutes in the water. This should reduce the contrast in your negative once your developing process is complete. You may need to experiment with developing times for your film type in order to get the best results from this technique.

EQUIPMENT

Camera: Pentax 6x7
Lens: 55mm
Accessories: Yellow filter
Lighting: Direct sun
Film: Ilford HP-4
Print: Ilford VC Fiberbase, #3 filter

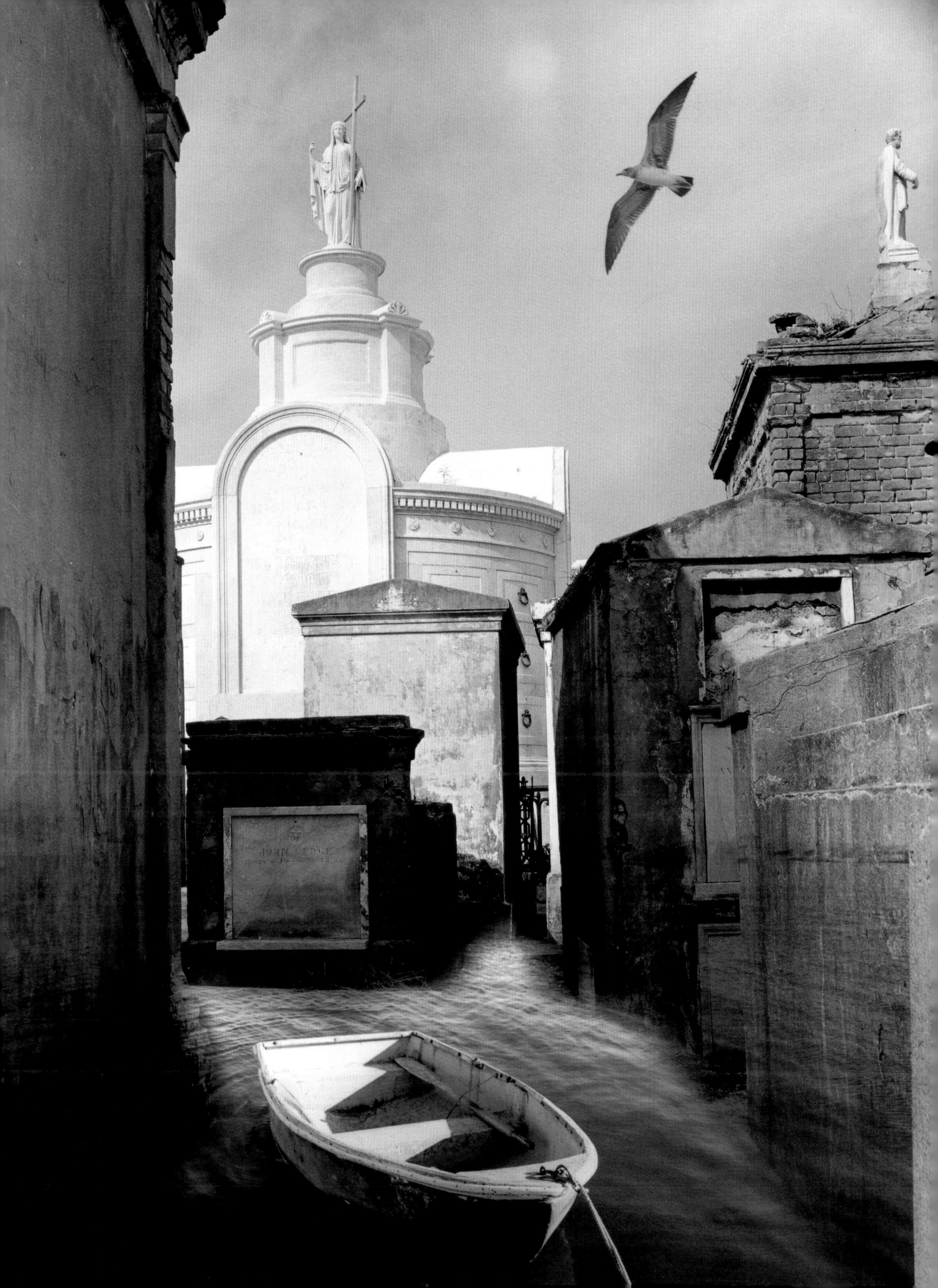
JOHN

Staircase in Forest

A theme that I'm always drawn to is the architectural lines of great staircases. This is a house that I would like to have, one that you could get lost in, one decorated with a nouveau forest.

This is not intended to dishearten students or beginning professional photographers, but the combination of these two images is best achieved with a minimum of a medium format camera, ideally one with a 4x5 negative. When prints with the intricate detail of leaves and vines are made larger than 8x10 with the 35mm camera, you tend to lose the tonal scale and sharpness seen in the larger format.

The first negative of this combination print was made on a trip to photograph the Oregon coast. For those who have never been there, Oregon's magnificently rugged coastline with its sandy beaches interspersed with rock formations that resemble "stacks" is a photographer's paradise. If you become jaded with all this splendor of water and rock, a thirty minute drive inland at most any point will deliver you to timberlands and wilderness as seen in this image. To the best of my recollection, this negative was made approximately half-way between Portland and the northern coastal town of Astoria. At the time, there was no specific intent for a final image; it was merely one for the negative file of forested terrain.

Flipping through this book, you will note my appreciation of the classic "S-curve" of spiral staircases. Not one wanting to show favoritism to a specific period of architecture, I decided to incorporate this negative from a home that I had photographed with a traditional staircase with a "federal" window at the landing. Blending these two prints gave me more problems than anticipated. I normally dodge the area of the first print by hand to overprint the subsequent image. Due to the asymmetric zig-zag of this staircase, a paper mask was cut to block out the area of the forest where the staircase was finally printed. It was simply trial and error in the beginning. However, good prints are often very time-consuming. Finally, this one fell into place.

As mentioned above, we now have an image of a house that is overgrown from the inside—overgrown with nature and wilderness.

EQUIPMENT

Camera: Calumet 4x5 View Camera
Lens: 90mm
Lighting: Available light
Film: Kodak Tri-X
Print: Kodak Polymax Fiberbase

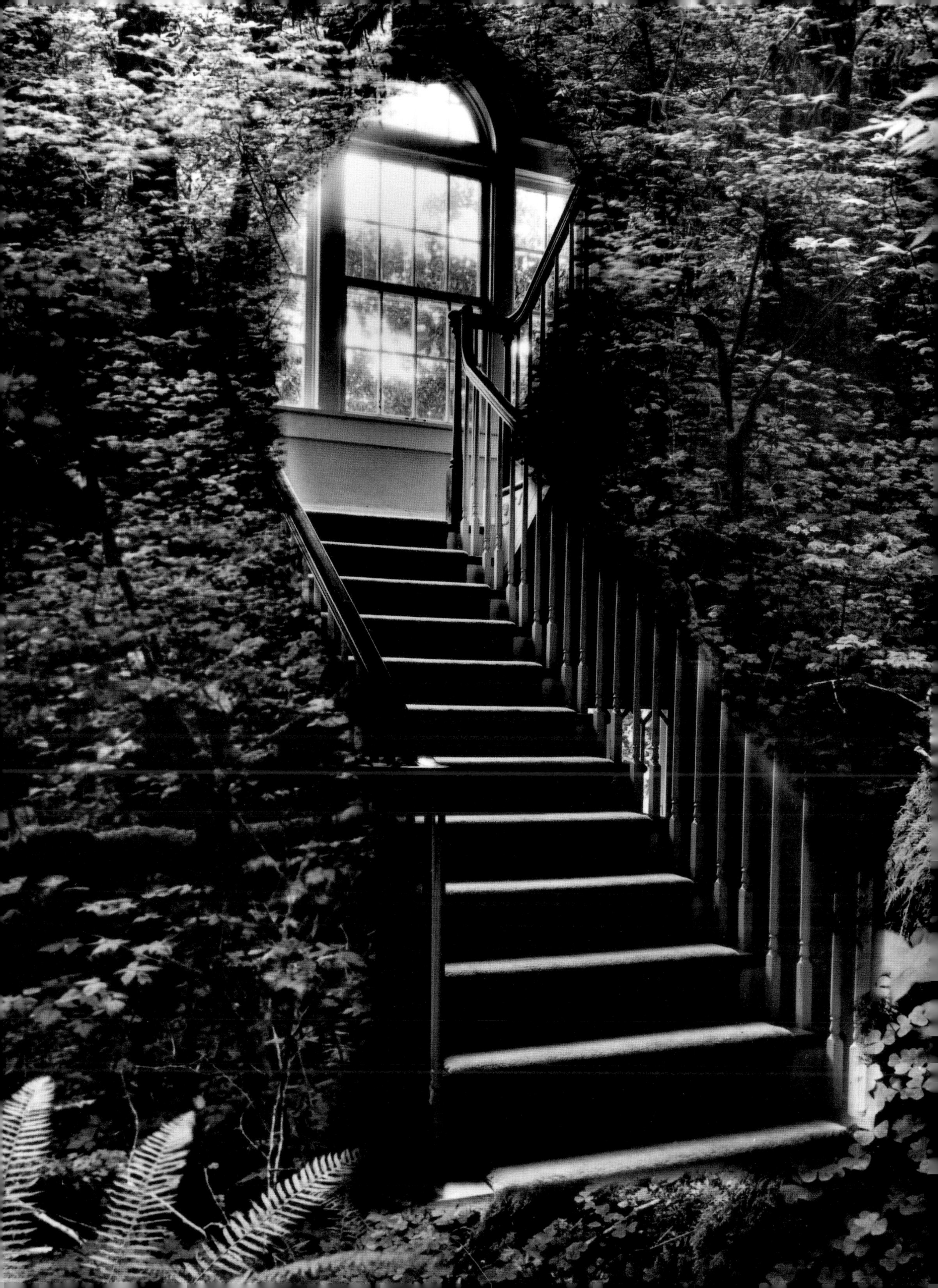

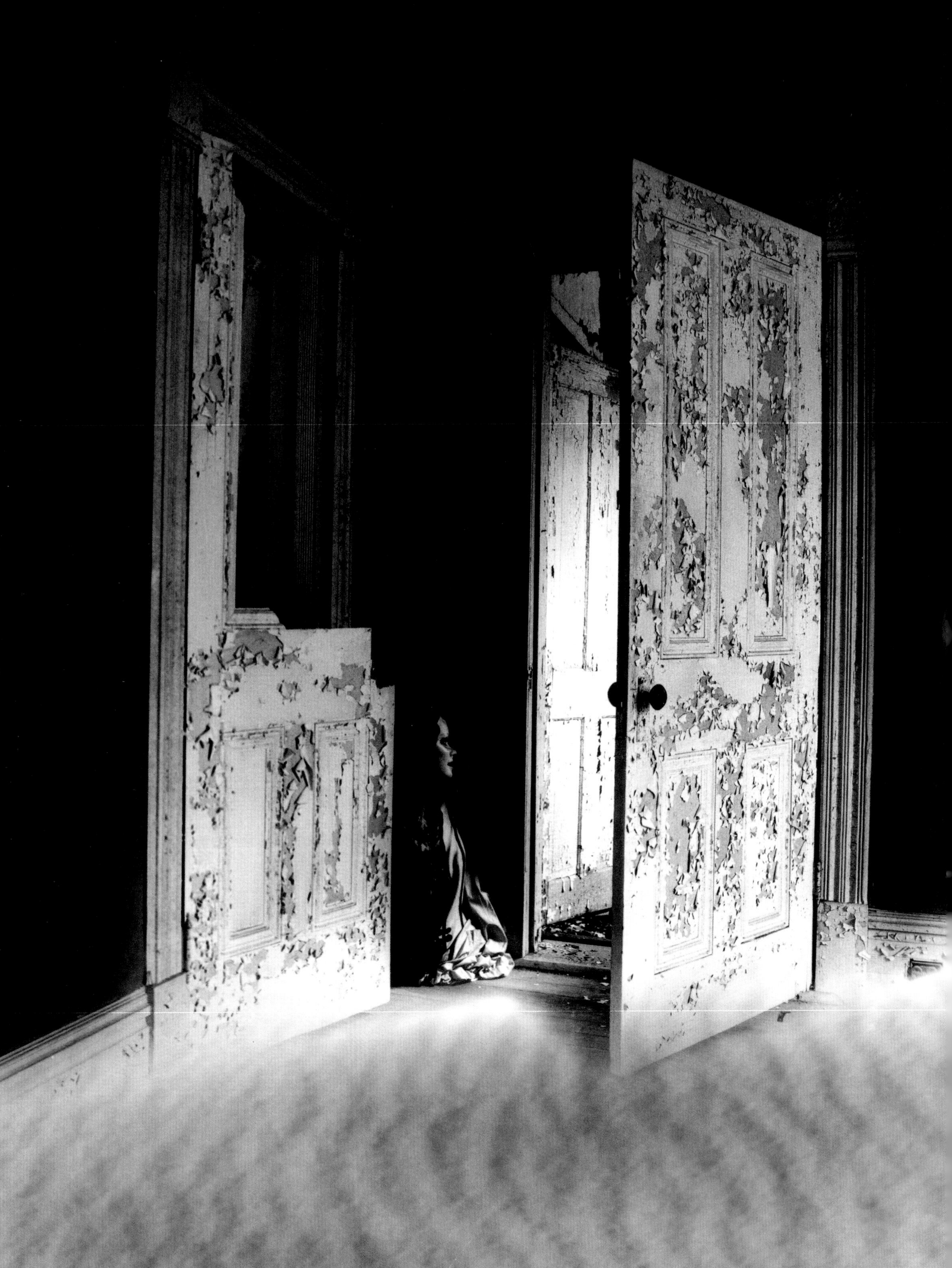

The legendary rock band founded by Jim Morrison would have been the proud of this outlandish photo. Morrison is long-since dead and in repose in the Cimetiere du Pere-Lachaise in Paris, though he could possibly have selected this image for their next album cover—if it was considered bizarre enough.

At openings of art shows and exhibits, I am always privately amused at some of the questions asked of me regarding the surreal photography. At an exhibit in Birmingham several years ago, a gallery patron spent virtually all of an hour looking at this print, totally mesmerized. John McClusky, owner of the gallery, found me in the crowd and said that there was an "aging hippie" that wanted to meet me. Thinking that I'd made the first sale on this opening night, I introduced myself. He looked at me, looked back at the print, looked at me again, and then asked, "What kinda dope ya smoking?" Not expecting a question such as this, I confessed to enjoying a good cocktail now and again, but I didn't partake of the "weed." Looking back at me through somewhat bleary eyes, he replied, "Too bad, you could have been a great photographer." I appreciate critics such as this. They keep things somewhat in perspective.

This idea was not inspired by any "mind altering" substances, although it doesn't hurt to have a partially demented sense of humor. Lance Mortensen, a friend who was an airline pilot and weekend preservationist, rescued this old house from the wrecking ball. With the house saved by court order, Lance prevailed upon me to photograph the interior prior to the contractors starting their restoration.

As a prank to Lance, I placed a mannequin in the upstairs bedroom under the guise that it was there when I arrived. While taking these photos, a homeless man (who had obviously camped out in this dwelling) walked in. Seeing me kneeling on the floor with my camera on a tripod, and the mannequin in the background, he took one last sip of his Thunderbird wine and tossed it out the open window. With an unsteady gait, he retreated and said, "Good luck buddy—and you better be nice to that lady."

As an added element, sand from Pensacola Beach was incorporated into the bottom of the original print.

Yes, this would have been the style of Jim Morrison and The Doors.

EQUIPMENT

Camera: Hasselblad 500CM
Lens: 80mm
Lighting: Lumedyne Portable Strobe with silver umbrella
Film: Ilford HP-5
Print: Ilford Variable Contrast RC

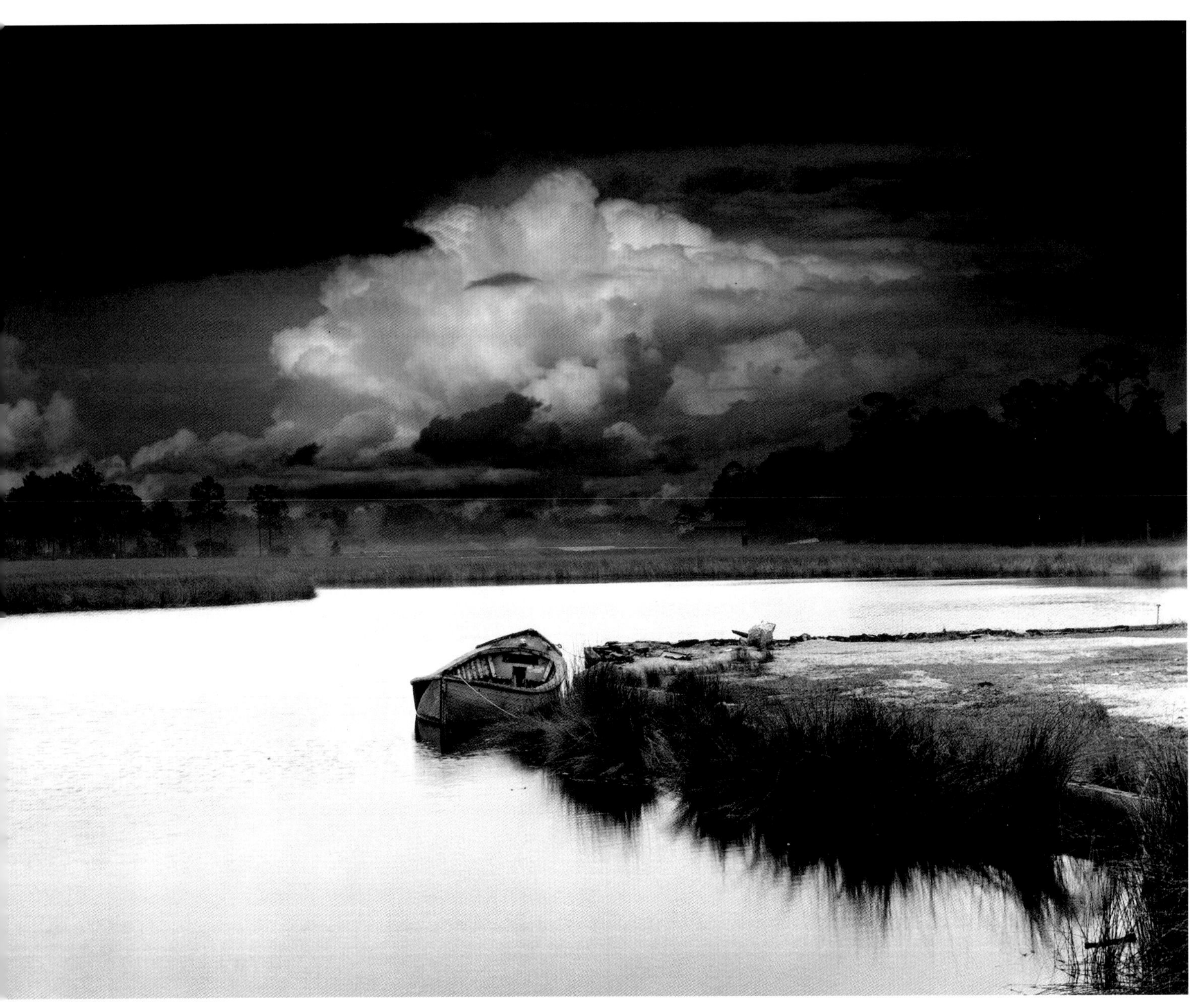

Dory Grand Lagoon

The dory is a small boat with classic lines that is synonymous with New England. It's not often seen on the Gulf Coast, where our small launches are primarily referred to as dinghies and rowboats. The Cajuns in Louisiana refer to them in their native French as "pirogues" (pronounced pee-rows), a small boat used to navigate the inland waters.

In 1972, I had been on a commercial assignment to photograph one of the first condominium developments on the beaches of Perdido Key, which is the division of the Florida and Alabama line on the coast. This scene caught my eye on the early, foggy morning as I was zooming across the ancient Gulf Beach Highway bridge in my dilapidated Volkswagen. This dory was completely out of place in Northwest Florida, which prompted my making a 180 degree turn for another glance at this placid scene. With plenty of 4x5 film left over from the architectural assignment, I set up my large camera and tripod in the middle of the bridge and made the exposure.

The simpleness and tranquility of the dory, bayou and saw grass made a print that easily stood on its own merit, with no alterations needed or expected. However, it bothered me that there was a lack of a dominating skyline with an ominous cloud formation. The print needed to be capped off somehow—it lacked a finishing touch. Therefore, I pulled the splendid cloud formation seen in this print from my negative file. I exposed the expanse of water and the dory on the sheet of paper in the darkroom (the sky was so light in the original print that it needed no dodging). The new sky and clouds were overprinted in the upper half of the print.

EQUIPMENT

Camera: Calumet 4x5 View Camera
Lens: 90mm Caltar
Accessories: Yellow filter
Lighting: Early morning fog
Film: Kodak Plus-X
Development: D-76
Print: Kodak Ektalure-X (no longer manufactured)

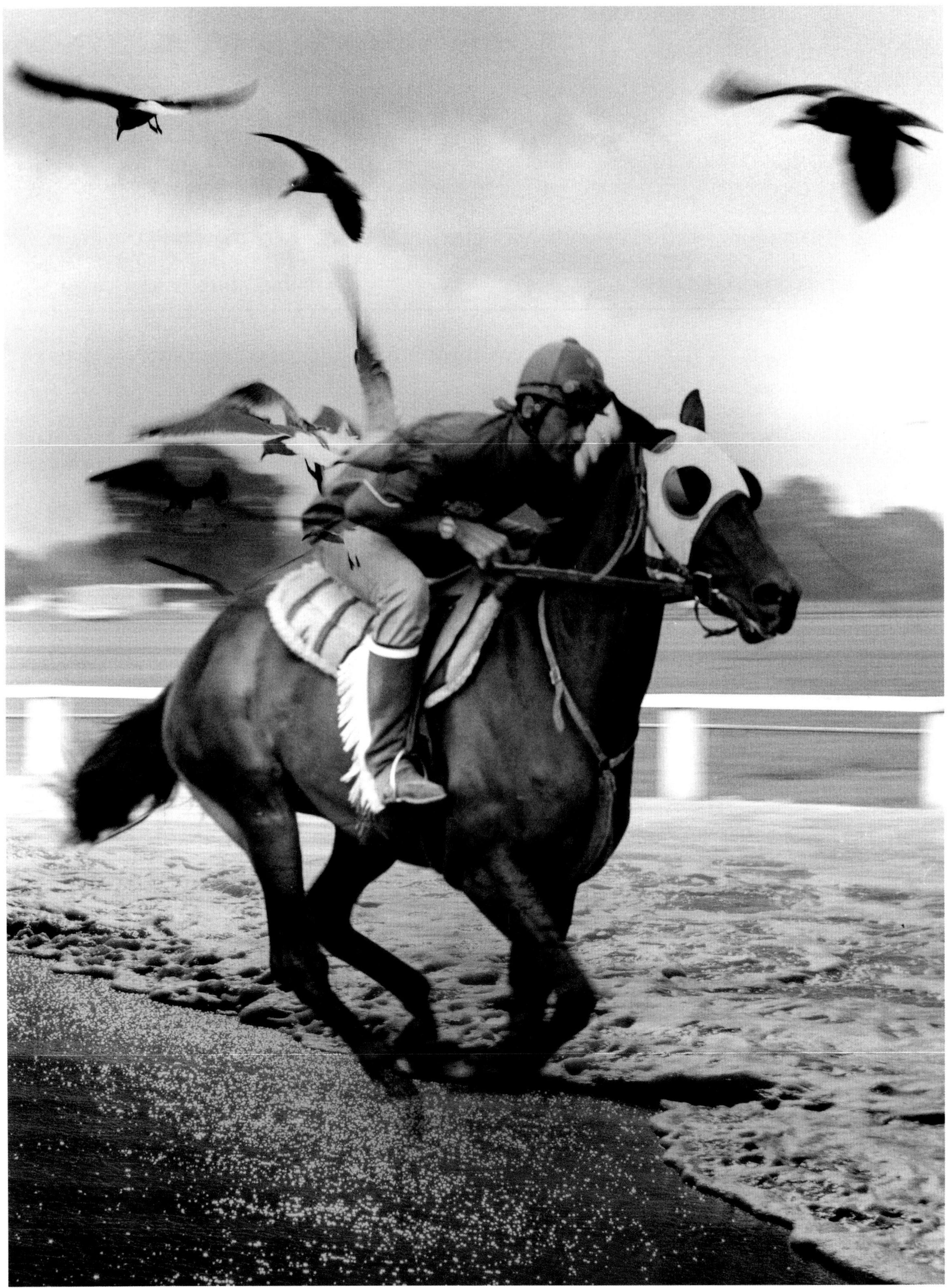

This is the Kentucky Derby meets Alfred Hitchcock's *The Birds*. Flight is the main theme here: the flight of the birds and the flight of the horse.

On a photo excursion through the Louisiana Cajun country several years ago, I found more photo opportunities than could possibly be absorbed in the allotted three days. These small towns and parishes in the delta country seem as though they are suspended in a time that has long since passed. If there is a Louisiana town that can truly be called "Cajun," it is Lafayette, located about one hundred and twenty miles west, as the crow flies, from New Orleans. One of the greater pastimes in this town of fun-loving people is the sport of kings, horse racing, down at Evangeline Downs, the local track.

The track is not open to the public during the day. However, with a small bribe and my sister's good looks, we received permission to photograph the preliminary trial runs. There was not an abundance of activity on this day. However, one jockey was running his horse through a demanding workout. I positioned myself at the finish line with my Pentax 6x7, which looks like a very large 35mm camera but uses 120 film. To accomplish a shot such as this, where the subject is moving rapidly in front of you, you must pan your camera to follow you subject as it passes by. The panning action will give the intended blur to the background, but at the same time will ensure that the horse and jockey are crisp and frozen in the print. Also, you must pre-focus on the area where your subject is going to be as it passes you. There is rarely time to be able to focus on the fly in such a situation.

The early exhibitions of this print attracted only marginal interest. Even this was mostly from the equestrian crowd, which is a small fraternity—not like the masses you find in a Saturday night bowling league. Not wanting a good negative to go to waste, I decided to add a bit of offbeat humor to this print. I overprinted two negatives onto the original print, first the birds, and then the water lapping at the horses hooves.

EQUIPMENT

Camera: Pentax 6x7
Lens: 90mm
Lighting: Direct sun
Film: Ilford HP-4
Print: Kodak Polymax FIberbase

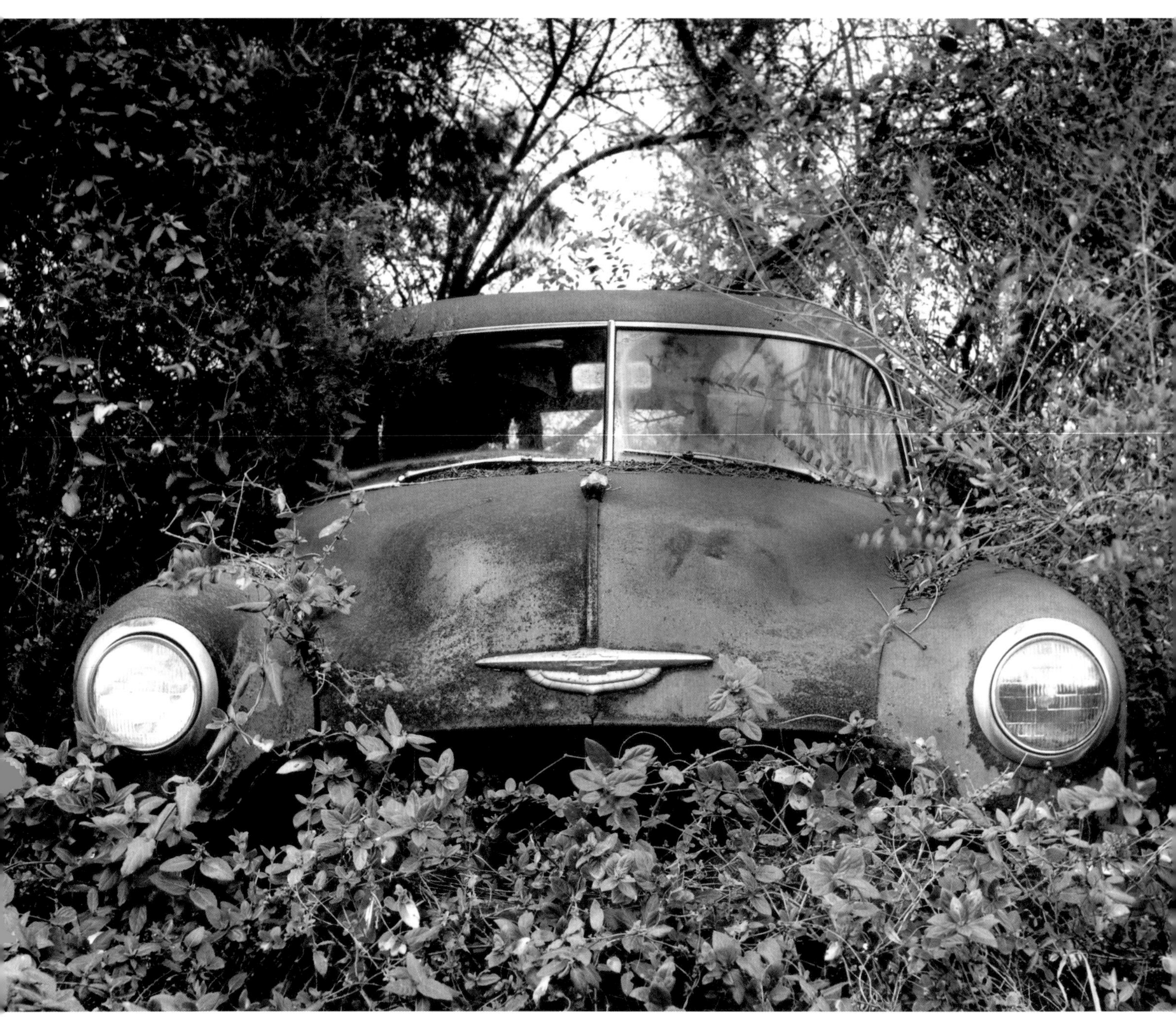

I have mentioned before that luck has a great deal to do with finding unique settings to photograph. This was the case with this old car nestled in the woods. I had completed a photography assignment in Brewton, Alabama, and was heading home along Highway 29 when I spotted this rusting hulk of a car, not too far removed from the road. This vast expanse of pine timberlands and undergrowth was no doubt part of the state of Alabama's wildlife preserve, which I assumed meant that there should have been no problem with me entering the land (I was wrong about this, as I was soon to find out).

I parked my car on the roadside and hiked a short way through the undergrowth to set up my camera and tripod. After taking initial light readings with a Pentax Spotmeter, I was preparing to make my first exposure when I heard footsteps behind me, and then the unmistakable and chilling sound of a shotgun being pumped. I turned around slowly to see a deranged-looking man in a tattered flannel shirt, missing several teeth, and holding a shotgun at an angle that was very unsettling.

There were a few moments of silence which seemed to go on for years, and then the man said forcefully, "Hey buddy! Da last guy stole da grill out of my car. What is you lookin' fer, that is, before I shoot ya?" After a considerable amount of stuttering on my part, I convinced the owner of this property that I was a photographer, and not a thief specializing in used car parts. He agreed to let me take my photograph (fortunately, I had a tripod to stabilize the camera, since my nerves were now pretty well shot). He then escorted me from his property.

The original print of the car proved to be extremely popular, with the only disparaging remarks coming from car collectors, who don't seem to be serious buyers of art photography. Some contended that this was not the body style of a '53 Chevy. Some suggested it was an earlier model, while some advised me that it was a later version. In any event, the restlessness I find in repeated printing of the same negative is a good reason for change; I decided the car needed someone in it.

The ghostly image of the lady behind the steering wheel is a copy negative of an oil painting of my great-great grandmother. With a tiny paper mask attached to a sturdy wire, I dodged the windshield of the car, and then moved the paper to the next enlarger to transplant grandmother, circa 1850, behind the steering wheel.

EQUIPMENT

Camera: Mamiya C33 Twin Lens Reflex
Lens: 35mm
Lighting: Overcast daylight
Film: Kodak Tri-X
Print: Kodak Polymax Fiberbase

The Pyramid

This is another example of how I use the fine funerary architecture found in the New Orleans cemeteries to create a composite print of something not seen anywhere else before (with the possible exception of your subconscious mind). This one uses many of my favorite elements, like clouds and water, to create a dreamlike atmosphere.

Metairie Cemetery in New Orleans covers one hundred and fifty acres and contains more than seven thousand graves. Established in 1872, this old graveyard was formerly the site of the Metairie Racetrack for horse racing. Likewise, its streets and avenues follow the oval shape of the original racetrack. Unlike some of the deterioration seen in the other burial grounds in this city, this one is notable not only for the spectacular tombs and mausoleums but also for the pristine landscaping and graceful trees. There are a number of extremely flamboyant and ostentatious mausoleums to be found here, most notably the pyramid-shaped Brunswig Tomb, which gave me the start for building this multiple image print.

This flashy tomb features a large marble sphinx that was perfect for a surreal image. The initial negative was made as a direct frontal view, which is normal in the majority of my work. In the darkroom, the projected image of the tomb was outlined in pencil on the 11x14 easel. I then went to work, subsequently blending three additional negatives into this scene.

The pyramid was coupled with the view of the underside of a bridge in Pass Christian, Mississippi, on the Gulf Coast. The required masking of the negative took more time than I care to admit to (this sort of work can be time-consuming for professionals, too, so don't get discouraged if it takes you a bit of time to get your masks correct). The remaining negatives of the clouds and the water proved to be easy to overprint once the new image of the pyramid joined with the columns of the bridge was finished.

The new composite print reflects the sharp and angular objects I had seen, while adding a different kind of drama. Here, the Egyptian crypt sits atop the pilings of an abandoned highway overpass. There is an entrance above as well as below—chambers within chambers, worlds within worlds.

EQUIPMENT

Camera: Pentax 6x7
Lens: 55mm
Lighting: Available light on all negatives
Film: Kodak Tri-X
Print: Kodak Polymax Fiberbase

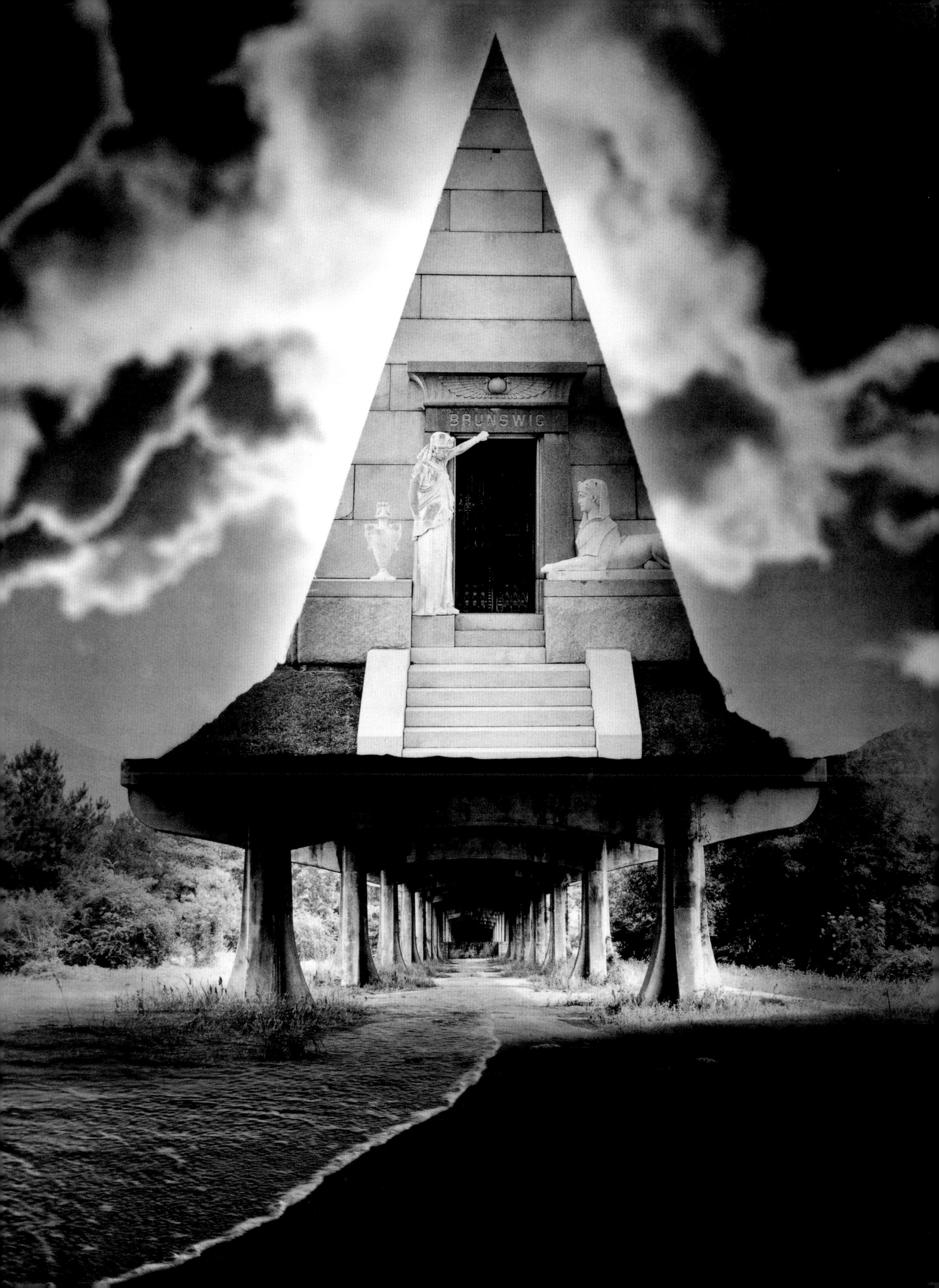
BRUNSWIG

Dory, Water and Tomb

This might appear to be a tourist snapshot from Venice, but I promise you it isn't the case. Like the image of "The Pyramid" seen on the previous page, this is another curious compilation of several negatives used to draw your mind into the tombs of the New Orleans cemeteries, and likewise the souls in repose within these chambers.

The making of a print like this is a unique combination of mechanical execution and creative activity. When I refer to the mechanical execution, I mean that the quality of your work will be determined by the proper exposure of the negative. The creative printing process is very much like the creativity of exposing the negative; in both cases, we try to appreciate and interpret them to our satisfaction. This explains why photographers and artists can work side-by-side with the same subject matter and each arrive at a different interpretation. Knowing this, it makes it easy for us to make varying prints from the same negative. If you look closely through this book, you will see certain negatives that have appeared more than once, but are mirrored in the later print in a totally different theme and perception.

My original thoughts in designing this print were to have something macabre, maybe a translucent ghost figure walking out of the tomb, with skeletons floating in the water. I scratched this idea, afraid that it would spook small children. I opted for a more subtle approach by using the negative from Maine of the dory, which I felt made the print believable. The edges of the tomb were blocked in the negative so that I could overprint the soft texture of the clouds around this crypt.

The empty dory is a wonderful symbol of a kind of inner emptiness or maybe peace, and the granite stone, clouds and water provide a wonderful contrast.

EQUIPMENT

Camera: Pentax 6x7
Lens: 55mm
Lighting: Available light for all negatives
Film: Kodak Tri-X
Print: Kodak Polymax Fiberbase

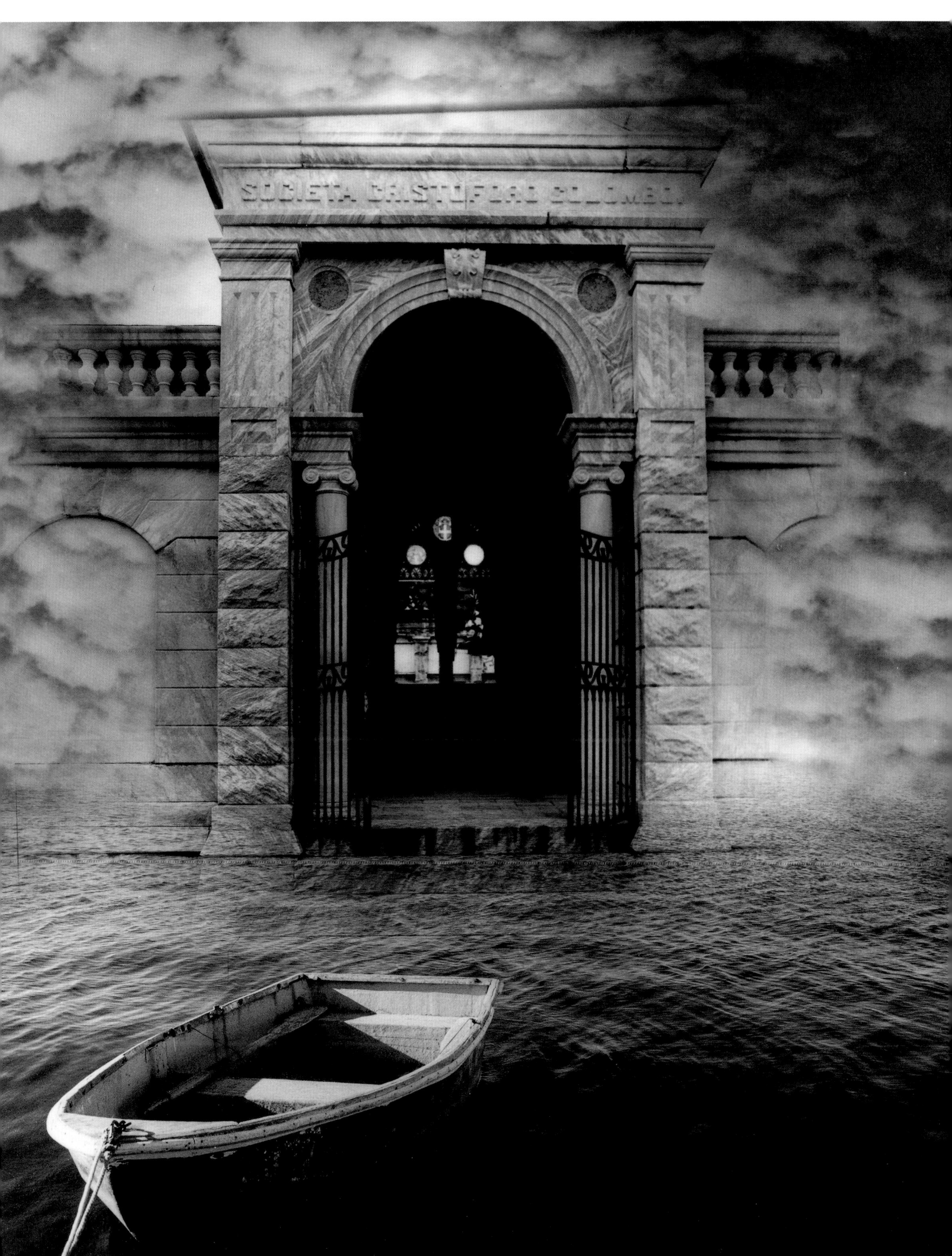
SOCIETA CRISTOFORO COLOMBO

Ghost Dancing

There are no two ways about it: this is my grade school piano teacher. She's the one who would rap my knuckles with the ruler when I didn't have perfect posture, and had garlic breath that would make a child wither on the piano bench.

Idiosyncratic and sometimes humorous ideas are obviously tucked away in the subconscious mind for a long time (at least in mine). The image of this room with the grand piano was taken at the request of my niece, Ashley Wiltshire Spotswood, for design and architectural purposes. Ashley is a very talented artist in her own right. She is a gifted painter and currently is a managing partner in a large-scale company specializing in the fabrication and distribution of fine iron furniture, as well as being their primary designer.

Searching for another client's print, I happened on to this print of Ashley's living room that I had totally forgotten. The piano brought back visions of playing scales in my teacher's old home, which as a child frightened me to death. It was a Victorian two-story home built sometime in the early 1900s, and smelled of dust and old plaster.

Although I didn't have the talent to become a noted pianist, or even to learn to read music, I had memorized a few tunes that I could play easily enough to give the impression that I knew what I was doing. As soon as the teacher left the room to powder her nose, I struck up a "boogey woogey" tune that would have made Little Richard proud of me. Invariably, my teacher would come running back into the room, with her white hair looking as if she had been electrocuted, shouting, "James! James, stop playing that nasty music on my piano!"

To immortalize my former piano teacher in this print, I needed three negatives in addition to the one of the room. First, the skeleton. It was darker than the back-lighted window, which made this only a matter of overprinting the negative on the window. The negative of the flowing water required a dodging of the floor, which was a considerably darker tone than the water. The last bizarre element was the addition of hands coming out of the water.

So, for my dear old piano teacher, this is my visual/artistic revenge: a flood in her own piano room.

EQUIPMENT

Camera: Hasselblad 500CM
Lighting: Available room light
Film: Kodak Tri-X
Print: Kodak Polymax Fiberbase

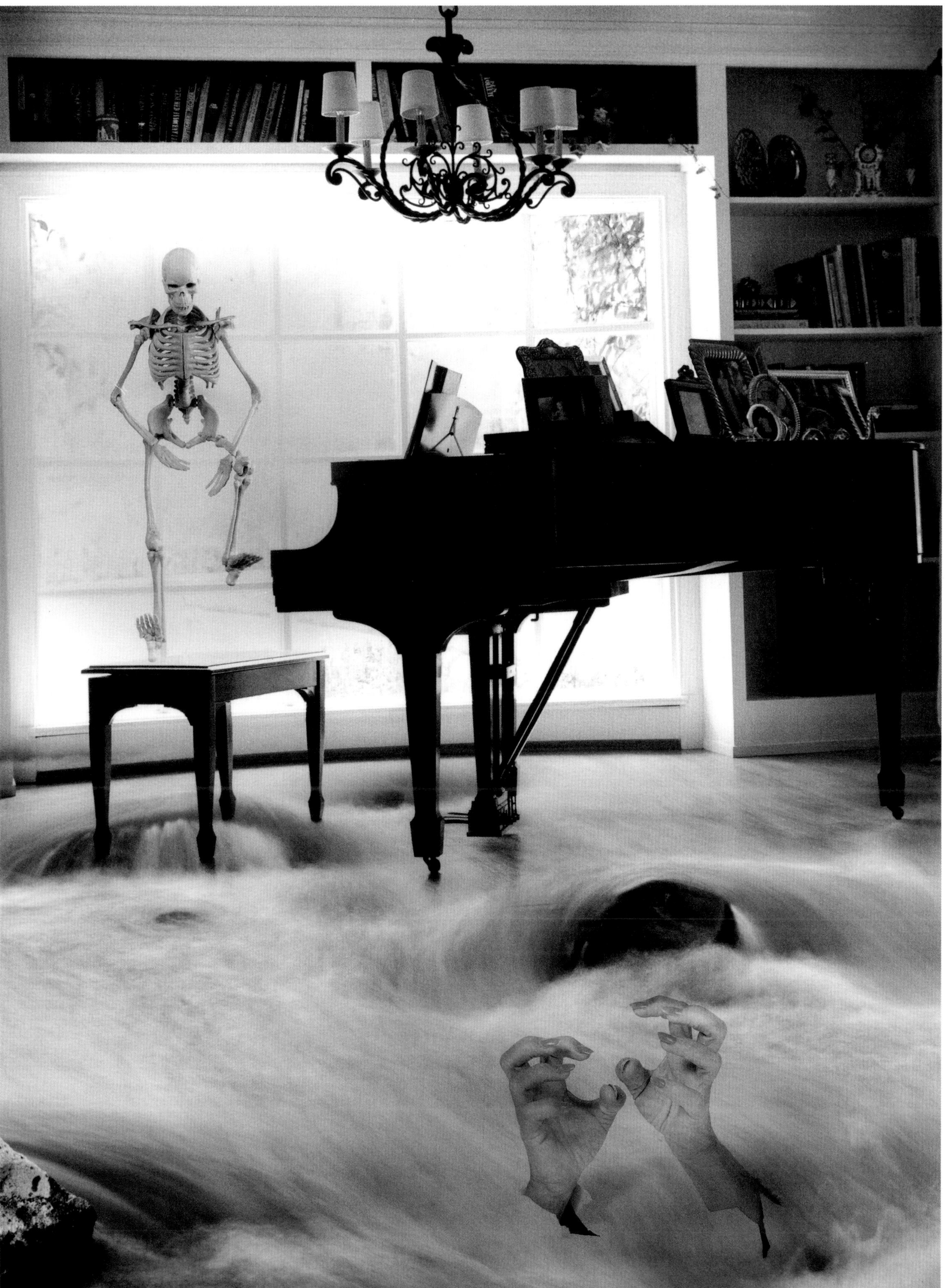

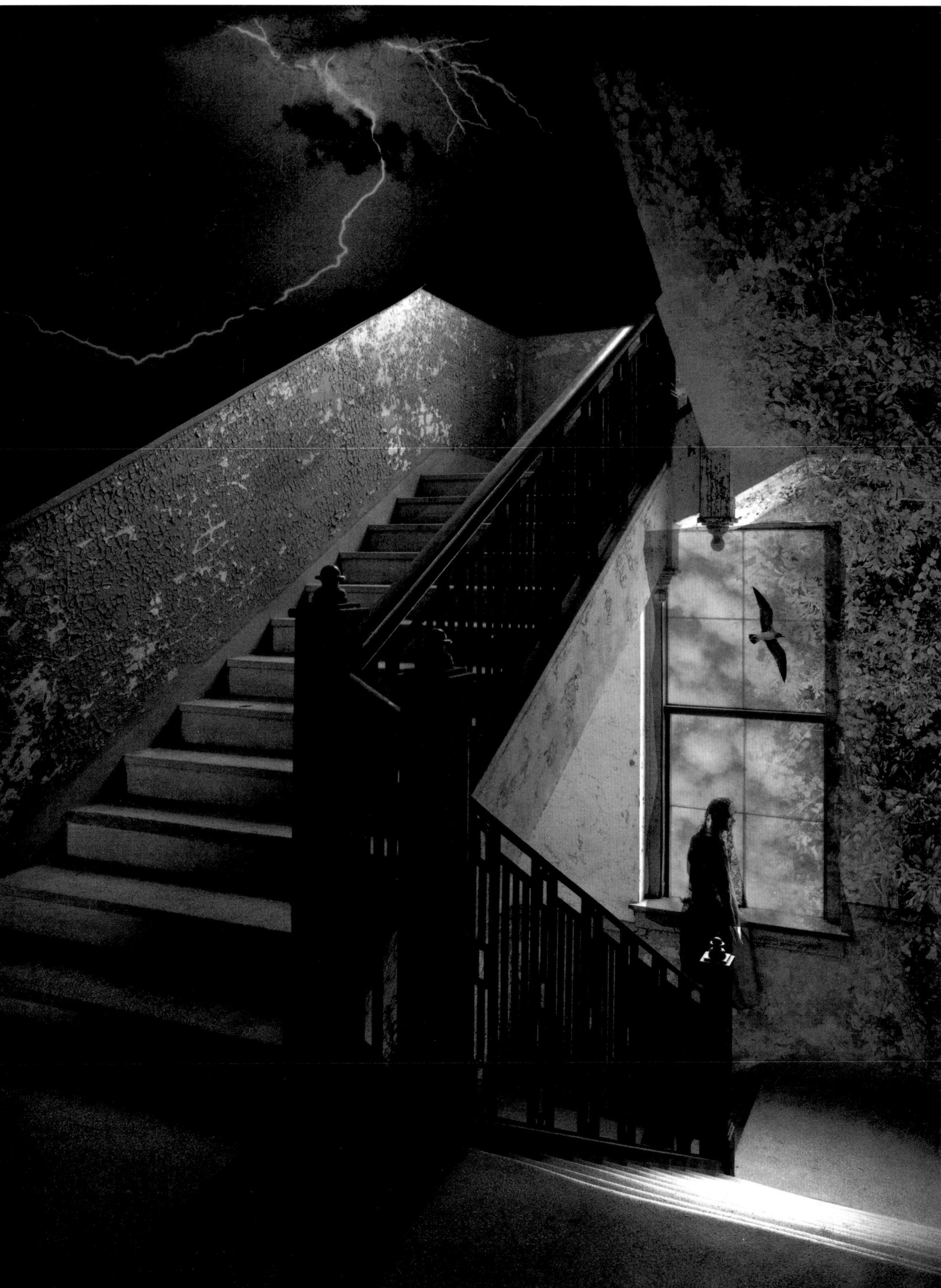

One can imagine the asylums of the last hundred years as places where souls died, shut away from the world, society and humanity. Very dark, and very lonely.

The inspiration for this bizarre photograph came from a vintage black and white movie I saw on cable. I picked up on the film mid-way through the first hour, and so did not note the title. In the film, there was a scene depicting a very distraught and disturbed woman locked in her room, peering out a barred window onto a dark and ominous sky. I concluded that there was a possibility of creating a still image that would convey this perception of lonely people, locked away and forgotten.

Several months later I was visiting a friend's art studio, which is housed in a four-story stone building that was the original Sacred Heart Hospital in Pensacola. This old gothic hospital has been subdivided by developers into a multi-use facility and is now home to offices, art studios and a restaurant. The wing of the building where my friend was renting was still under renovation, and that's where I discovered this staircase. It was made of handsome wrought iron, and I felt it contrasted well with the peeling paint. I now had a location for my vision.

This was definitely an image for the 4x5 view camera, primarily to prevent distortion due to the height of the ceilings, but also for the detail afforded by the larger negative. Due to the low light level which would require an exposure time of approximately four seconds, I decided I would use a mannequin from my studio for my model. This meant I wouldn't have to worry about a live model moving even slightly during the exposure and disturbing the crispness of the negative.

I used four negatives to create this image. On the original negative (with the staircase and mannequin), I used black tape to mask off the negative in the area where lightning is now visible in the finished print, and exposed this on an 11x14 sheet of paper. Next I cut a black paper mask to block out the staircase and window while I printed the lightning. Third, I made another mask which covered everything but the window. This allowed me to print in the clouds. The last element was the lone seagull at the window, which only required a direct overprinting to get in.

In the finished print, this woman looks as if she's spent decades feeling like the solitary bird she spies out the window. She is empty, hungry, cold and trapped. She's dreaming of her life outside the asylum, and is a reminder of the insanity that lies around the corner in all our lives.

EQUIPMENT

Camera: Calumet 4x5 View Camera
Lighting: Ambient room light
Film: Kodak Tri-X
Print: Ilford VC Fiberbase

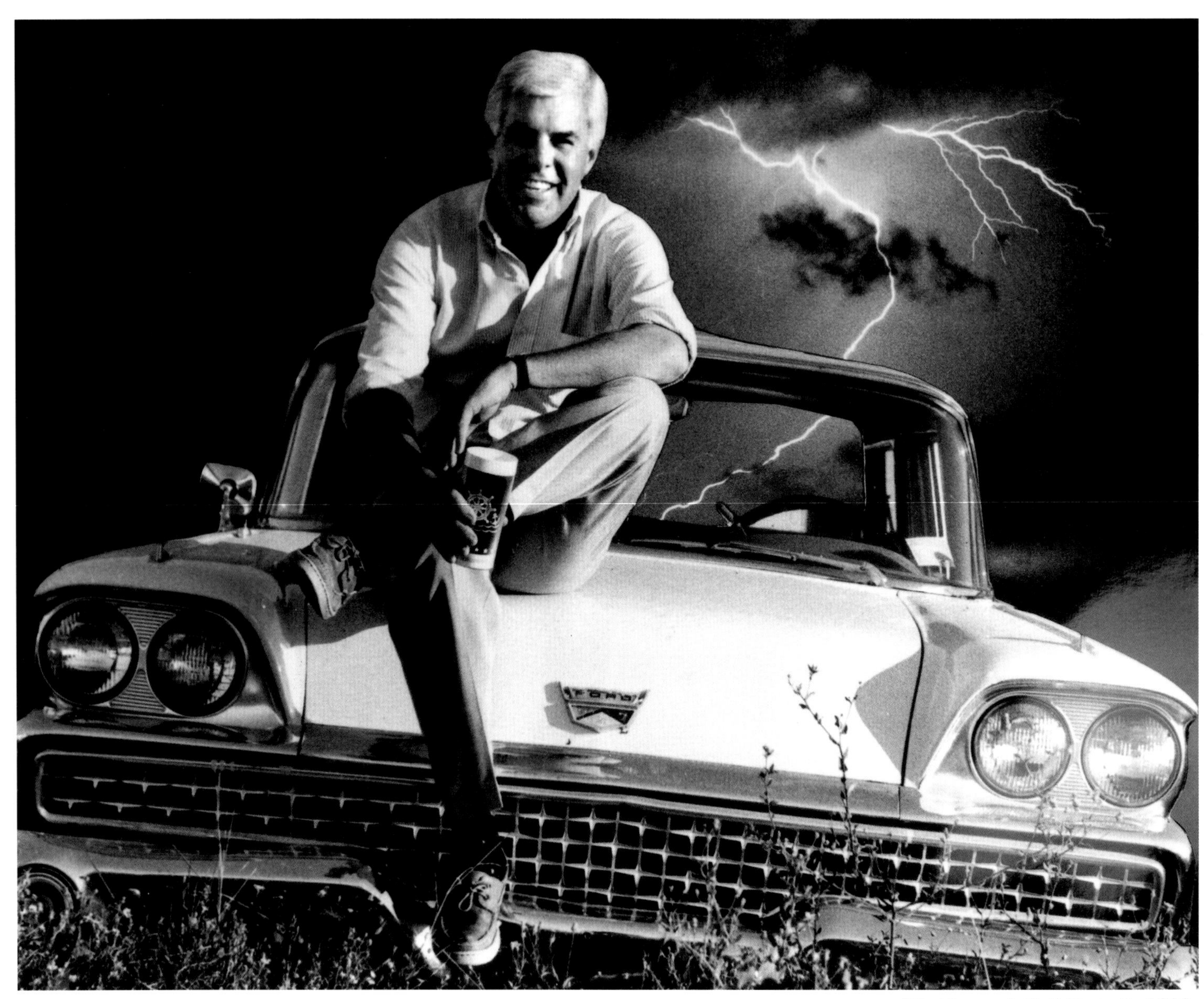

J.D. Hayward, *Self Portrait*, 1989.

About the Author

There are many artists and photographers who come strictly from the rigid workshops of the fine arts colleges and workshops; their eye has been fine-tuned and carefully coached by their instructors and mentors. J.D. Hayward did not fit into this mold. At age eighteen, without any formal training in photography, he quickly picked up a camera and created portrait and scenic images that immediately caught the attention of the professional photographers in Northwest Florida. One year later, the *Pensacola News-Journal*, becoming weary of their journeyman staff, hired Hayward as a freelancer for their new Sunday magazine, *Image*. For the next two years, Hayward's images were featured weekly on the front cover of the magazine.

Times got even better for Hayward when he opened a commercial studio in the old waterfront area of Pensacola. The contacts and assignments grew rapidly, and his creative talent was well-received. It was a great time to be a young and talented photographer: Vietnam was causing protests, skirts were getting shorter, free sex, drugs and rock and roll were abundant, and photography was being looked at with a new and unjaundiced eye. Through pure happenstance, Hayward was born at the right time, and found his place in the middle of all of this—photographing the late 1960s.

The early 1970s started to show a political and social change, and this sense of change washed over onto Hayward as well. He decided to make a career change, and began pursuing a degree in the Finance and Accounting Program at the University of West Florida. He completely dropped out of photography and joined the working ranks as a stockbroker with the firm of A.G. Edwards and Sons, where he remained employed for the next five years.

A trip to New Orleans in 1983 renewed and totally recharged Hayward's dormant photography genes. By blind luck, he walked into the photography studio of Johnny Donnell in the Old French Quarter. Hayward was taken with the superb quality of the black and white images of Southern scenes created by Donnell. He was more dumfounded to find that these fine prints had been created with a 35mm camera, and craftily printed on fiberbase paper by Donnell. Hayward's enthusiasm kept him (much to Donnell's dismay) picking the photographer's brain on every question he could think of regarding fine art black and white photography printing. After several hours of answering the unending barrage of questions, Johnny Donnell gave Hayward a box of Ilford black and white paper and suggested that he take a test run in the darkroom. Hayward put the knowledge he had gained to use, and was quite impressed with the results. Upon his return from this New Orleans trip, he built a darkroom far superior to any that he'd had before. By 1986, Hayward had been reborn as a photographer.

The following year, after much trial and error in the darkroom, a friend suggested that Hayward attend a workshop in Carmel, California, to fine tune his approach to the Zone System. By coincidence, one of the instructors was the noted photographer Allan Ross, who had been an assistant to and printed for Ansel Adams. Ross, upon reviewing Hayward's portfolio, immediately recognized the potential of the thirty-nine year old photographer—even with a ten-year break in his photographic career. Ross decided that, for Hayward's work to be truly recognized, he needed to gain skill in manipulating the tonal scale of the final print. In short, his print quality had to be equal to master black and white printers like Ansel Adams and Brett Weston.

Hayward was in the right place at the right time. Ross quickly corrected Hayward's approach to using a light meter, specifically the Pentax Spotmeter. Sitting on a rock overlooking Point Lobos State Reserve in California, Ross pulled a roll of white tape from his camera bag, numbered the zones from one to ten on it, and stuck it to Hayward's light meter. Ross then explained the Zone System, and how to find the correct exposure for a scene you previsualize based upon correct metering, exposure and development time. Hayward returned to Florida with a renewed sense of enthusiasm for his work and his future negatives. In a short time, the prints he began producing had the look of a master printer and photographer.

Art shows and exhibitions in the Southeast United States kept Hayward busy with his landscape images for the next three years. However, the demand for his portrait and advertising work diminished the time available for him to travel in search of the perfect image. Rene Margruete's surrealistic paintings had intrigued Hayward since high school, so without the time to be on the road in pursuit of new images, he started experimenting with combining several negatives in the darkroom into the same print, to explore the surreal on his own time. His early attempts were somewhat displaced, with no central theme or idea to hold them together. A photography professor from a community college observed Hayward's early attempt at surrealism and remarked to him, "It looks as if you have been influenced by Jerry Uelsmann's work." (Uelsmann has been the Graduate Research Professor of Art at the University of Florida since 1964.) Although he knew of Uelsmann, Hayward had never seen the master's work. Upon being shown original Uelsmann prints by the community college professor, Hayward exclaimed, "They are finer prints in quality (tonal scale) than Adams or Weston—and a lot more creative!"

Uelsmann's work made an impression on Hayward's mind more powerful than the professor would ever know. The images that had been on the drawing board in his mind would now be birthed. He was now a confirmed surrealist (which sounds like a religious conversion), and today, much to his esteem, buyers of photography are collecting the haunting works of J.D. Hayward.

Index

G

H

I

J

L

M

N

O

P

R

S

T

V

W

Z

Darkroom Manuals from Amherst Media

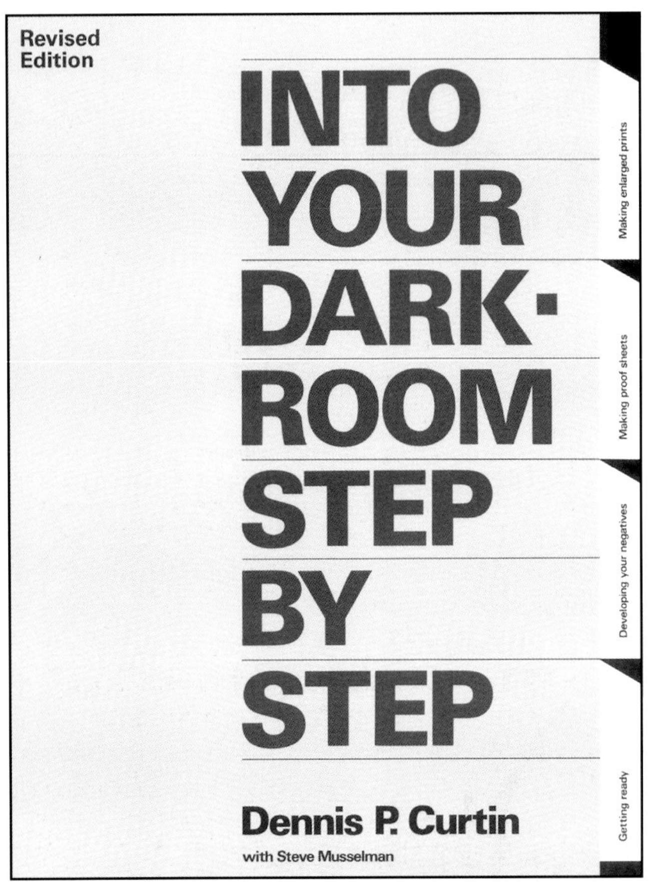

Into Your Darkroom Step By Step

The complete guide to doing all your own b&w darkroom work. For photographers who want to achieve results that are more expressive, less expensive, and printed better than a commercial alternative. Designed as a hands-on, step-by-step tool to use inside the darkroom. $17.95 list, 8½x11, 96p, hundreds of photos, Curtin, order no. 1093

FULL INFORMATION ON:

- Equipment
- Setting up your darkroom
- Developing negatives
- Making proof sheets
- Making enlarged prints

"...for photographers who wish to process their own work."
— *Publishers Weekly*

Build Your Own Home Darkroom

This timeless reference shows how to build a professional quality, yet inexpensive darkroom in your basement, spare room, closet, bathroom, or almost anywhere. Each project includes step-by-step building instructions. $17.95 list, 8½x11, 160p, many illustrations, index, reference tabs, Duren and McDonald, order no. 1092

FULL INFORMATION ON:

- Darkroom design
- Woodworking tools and techniques
- Light-proofing, ventilation, work tables
- Enlargers, light boxes and sinks
- Water supply panels and print drying racks

"...everything you need to know about constructing a darkroom..."
—*Popular Photography*

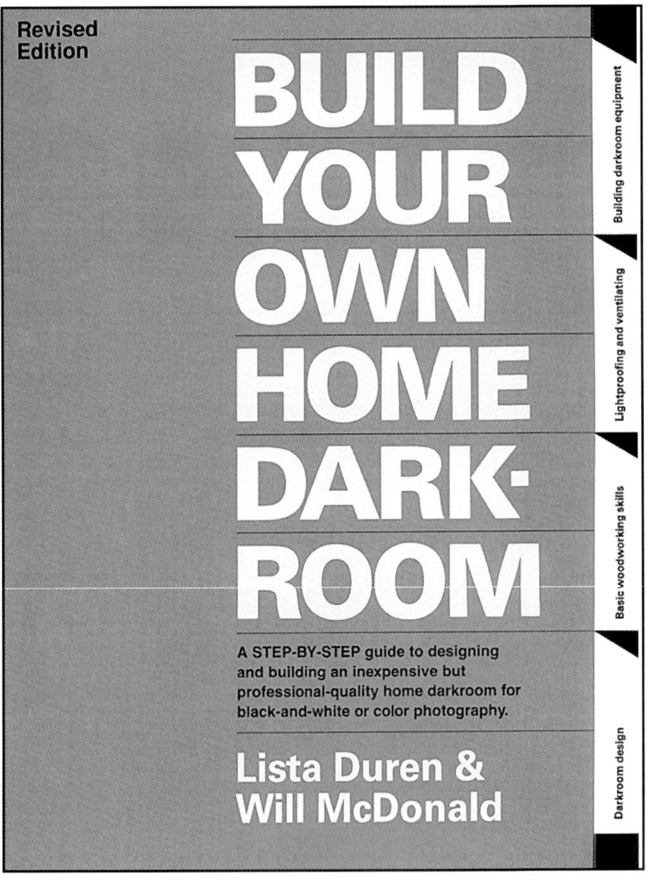

Other Books from

Amherst Media, Inc.

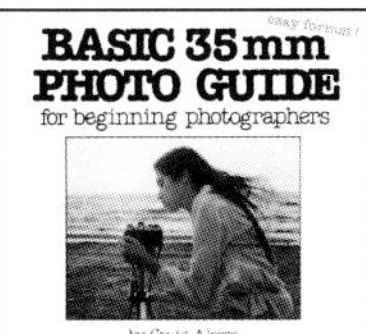

Basic 35mm Photo Guide

Craig Alesse

Great for beginning photographers! Designed to teach 35mm basics step-by-step — completely illustrated. Features the latest cameras. Includes: 35mm automatic, semi-automatic cameras, camera handling, *f*-stops, shutter speeds, and more! $12.95 list, 9x8, 112p, 178 photos, order no. 1051.

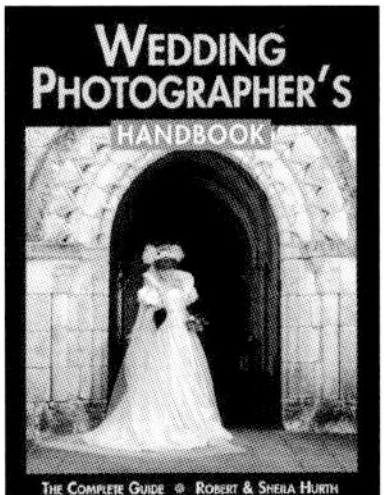

Wedding Photographer's Handbook

Robert and Sheila Hurth

A complete step-by-step guide to succeeding in the world of wedding photography. Packed with shooting tips, equipment lists, must-get photo lists, business strategies, and much more! $24.95 list, 8½x11, 176p, index, b&w and color photos, diagrams, order no. 1485.

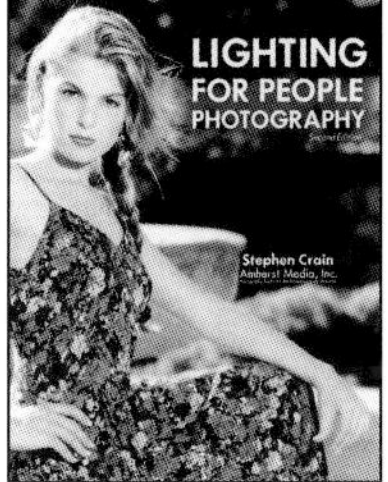

Lighting for People Photography, 2nd ed.

Stephen Crain

The up-to-date guide to lighting. Includes: set-ups, equipment information, strobe and natural lighting, and much more! Features diagrams, illustrations, and exercises for practicing the techniques discussed in each chapter. $29.95 list, 8½x11, 120p, b&w and color photos, glossary, index, order no. 1296.

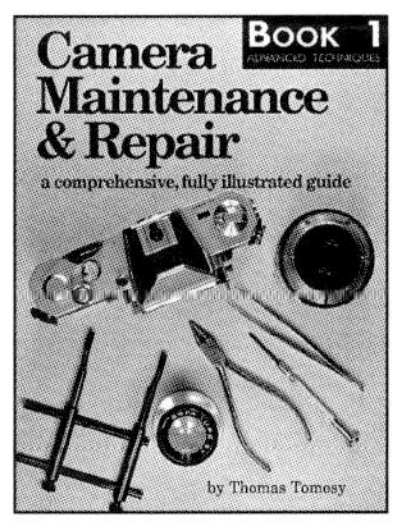

Camera Maintenance & Repair Book 1

Thomas Tomosy

A step-by-step, illustrated guide by a master camera repair technician. Includes: testing camera functions, general maintenance, basic tools needed and where to get them, basic repairs for accessories, camera electronics, plus "quick tips" for maintenance and more! $29.95 list, 8½x11, 176p, order no. 1158.

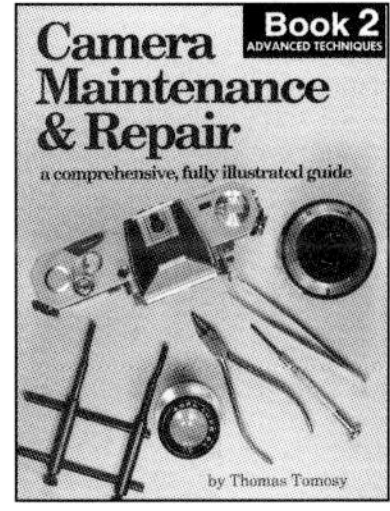

Camera Maintenance & Repair Book 2

Thomas Tomosy

Build on the basics covered Book 1, with advanced techniques. Includes: mechanical and electronic SLRs, zoom lenses, medium format cameras, and more. Features models not included in the Book 1. $29.95 list, 8½x11, 176p, 150+ photos, charts, tables, appendices, index, glossary, order no. 1558.

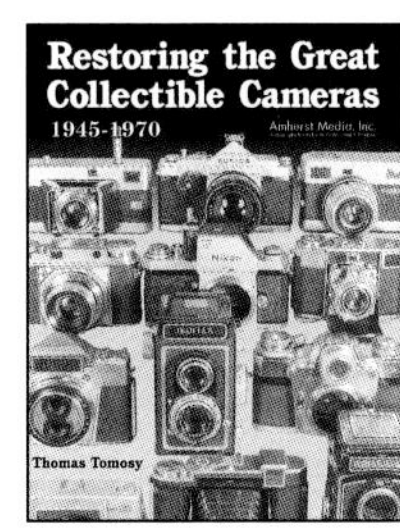

Restoring the Great Collectible Cameras (1945-70)

Thomas Tomosy

More step-by-step instruction on how to repair collectible cameras. Covers postwar models (1945-70). Hundreds of illustrations show disassembly and repair. $29.95 list, 8½x11, 128p, 200+ photos, index, order no. 1560.

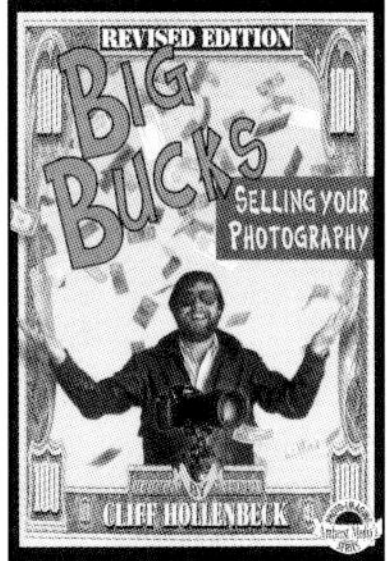

Big Bucks Selling Your Photography

Cliff Hollenbeck

A complete photo business package. Includes secrets for starting up, getting paid the right price, and creating successful portfolios! Features setting financial, marketing and creative goals. Organize your business planning, bookkeeping, and taxes. $15.95 list, 6x9, 336p, order no. 1177.

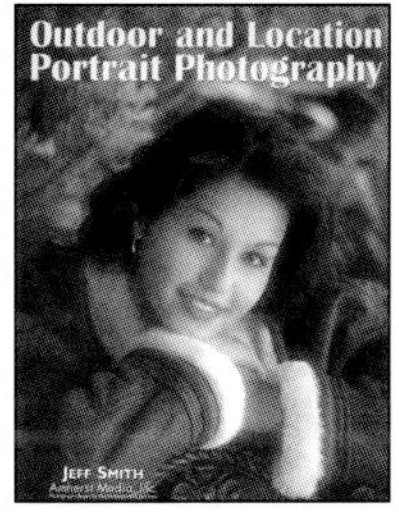

Outdoor and Location Portrait Photography

Jeff Smith

Learn how to work with natural light, select locations, and make clients look their best. Step-by-step discussions and helpful illustrations teach you the techniques you need to shoot outdoor portraits like a pro! $29.95 list, 8½x11, 128p, b&w and color photos, index, order no. 1632.

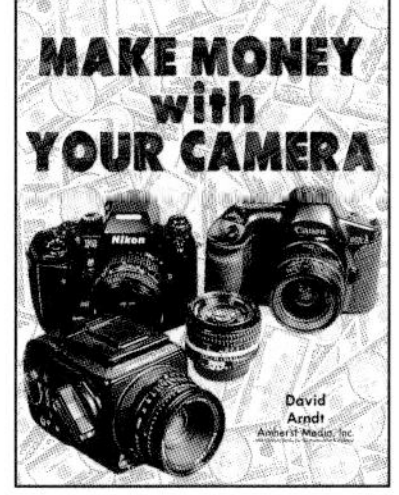

Make Money with Your Camera

David Neil Arndt

Learn everything you need to know in order to make money in photography! David Arndt shows how to take highly marketable pictures, then promote, price and sell them. Includes all major fields of photography. $29.95 list, 8½x11, 120p, 100 b&w photos, index, order no. 1639.

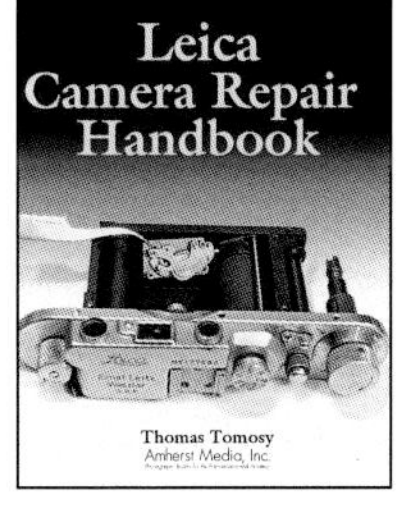

Leica Camera Repair Handbook

Thomas Tomosy

A detailed technical manual for repairing Leica cameras. Each model is discussed individually with step-by-step instructions. Exhaustive photographic illustration ensures that every step of the process is easy to follow. $39.95 list, 8½x11, 128p, 130 b&w photos, appendix, order no. 1641.

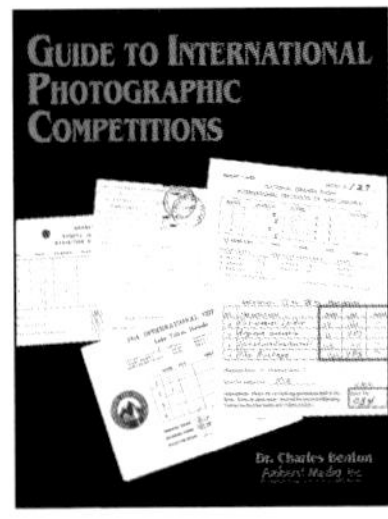

Guide to International Photographic Competitions

Dr. Charles Benton

Remove the mystery from international competitions with all the information you need to select competitions, enter your work, and use your results for continued improvement and further success! $29.95 list, 8½x11, 120p, b&w photos, index, appendices, order no. 1642.

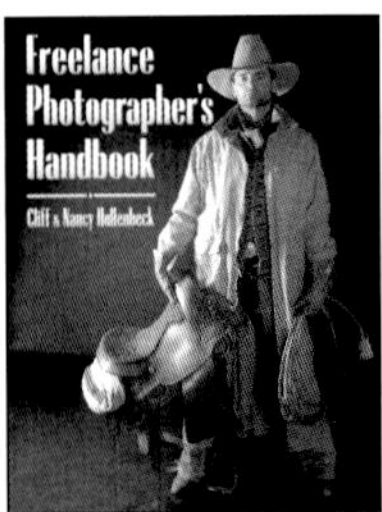

Freelance Photographer's Handbook

Cliff & Nancy Hollenbeck

Whether you want to be a freelance photographer or are looking for tips to improve your current freelance business, this volume is packed with ideas for creating and maintaining a successful freelance business. $29.95 list, 8½x11, 107p, 100 b&w and color photos, index, glossary, order no. 1633.

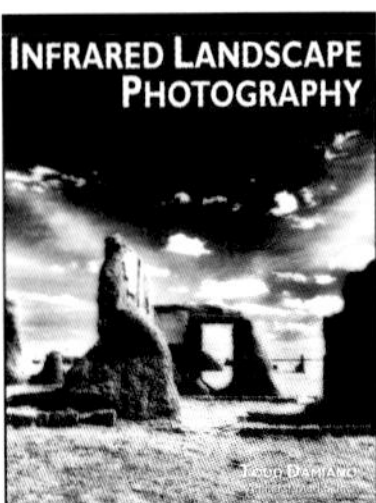

Infrared Landscape Photography

Todd Damiano

Landscapes shot with infrared can become breathtaking and ghostly images. The author analyzes over fifty of his most compelling photographs to teach you the techniques you need to capture landscapes with infrared. $29.95 list, 8½x11, 120p, b&w photos, index, order no. 1636.

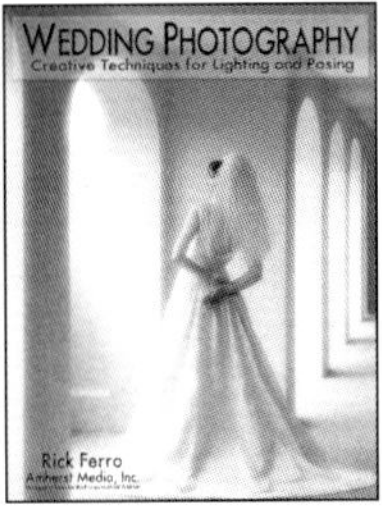

Wedding Photography: Creative Techniques for Lighting and Posing

Rick Ferro

Creative techniques for lighting and posing wedding portraits that will set your work apart from the competition. Covers every phase of wedding photography. $29.95 list, 8½x11, 128p, b&w and color photos, index, order no. 1649.

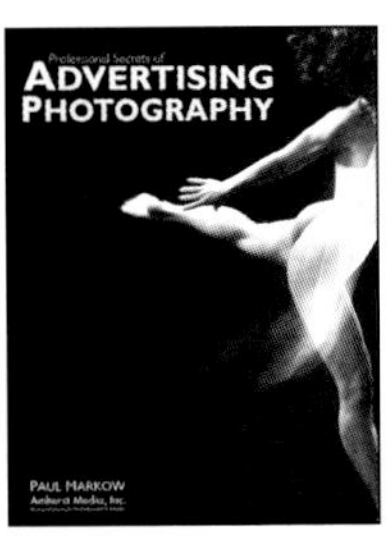

Professional Secrets of Advertising Photography

Paul Markow

No-nonsense information for those interested in the business of advertising photography. Includes: how to catch the attention of art directors, make the best bid, and produce the high-quality images your clients demand. $29.95 list, 8½x11, 128p, 80 photos, index, order no. 1638.

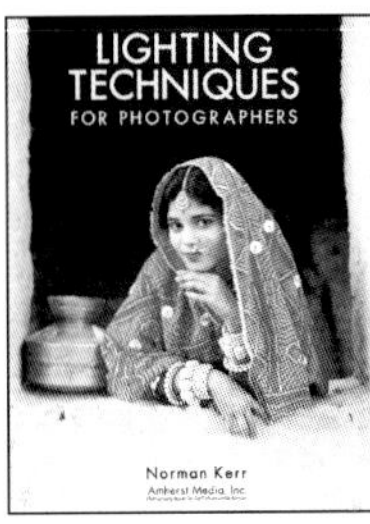

Lighting Techniques for Photographers

Norman Kerr

This book teaches you to predict the effects of light in the final image. It covers the interplay of light qualities, as well as color compensation and manipulation of light and shadow. $29.95 list, 8½x11, 120p, 150+ color and b&w photos, index, order no. 1564.

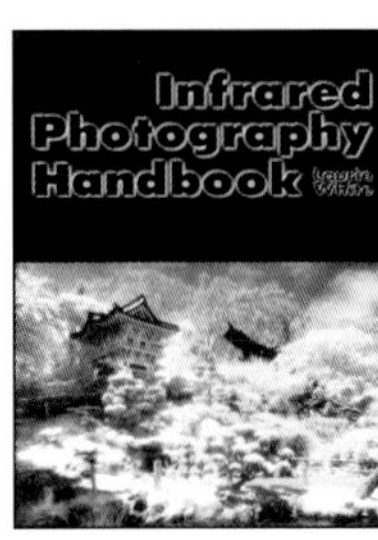

Infrared Photography Handbook

Laurie White

Covers black and white infrared photography: focus, lenses, film loading, film speed rating, batch testing, paper stocks, and filters. Black & white photos illustrate how IR film reacts. $29.95 list, 8½x11, 104p, 50 b&w photos, charts & diagrams, order no. 1419.

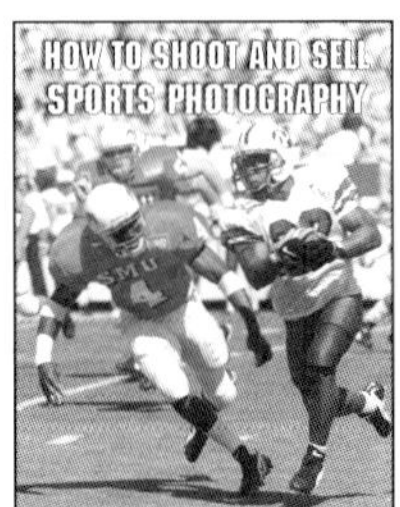

How to Shoot and Sell Sports Photography

David Arndt

A step-by-step guide for amateur photographers, photojournalism students and journalists seeking to develop the skills and knowledge necessary for success in the demanding field of sports photography. $29.95 list, 8½x11, 120p, 111 photos, index, order no. 1631.

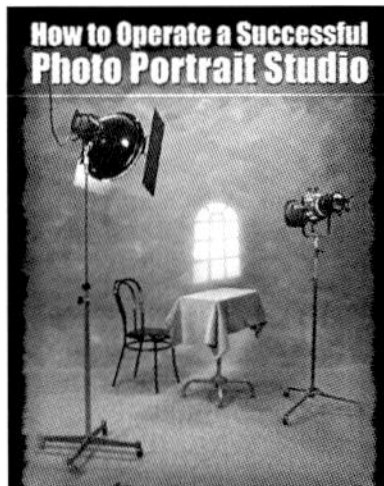

How to Operate a Successful Photo Portrait Studio

John Giolas

Combines photographic techniques with practical business information to create a complete guide book for anyone interested in developing a portrait photography business (or improving an existing business). $29.95 list, 8½x11, 120p, 120 photos, index, order no. 1579.

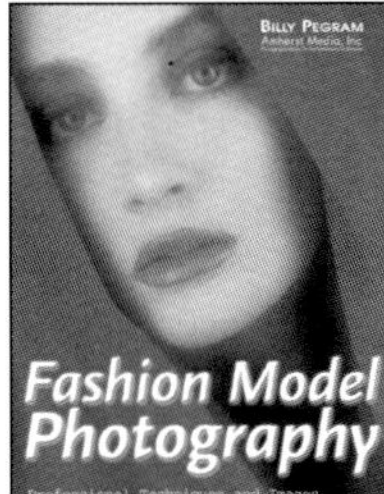

Fashion Model Photography

Billy Pegram

For the photographer interested in shooting commercial model assignments, or working with models to create portfolios. Includes techniques for dramatic composition, posing, selection of clothing, and more! $29.95 list, 8½x11, 120p, 58 photos, index, order no. 1640.

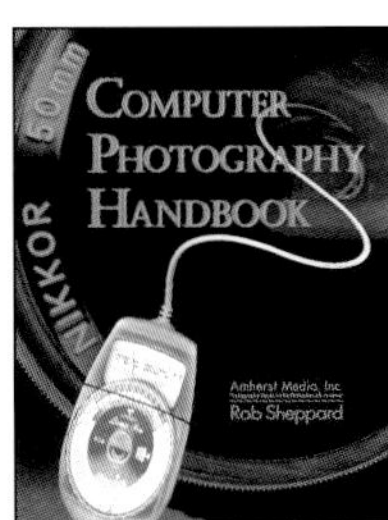

Computer Photography Handbook

Rob Sheppard

Learn to make the most of your photographs using computer technology! From creating images with digital cameras, to scanning prints and negatives, to manipulating images, you'll learn all the basics of digital imaging. $29.95 list, 8½x11, 128p, 150+ photos, index, order no. 1560.

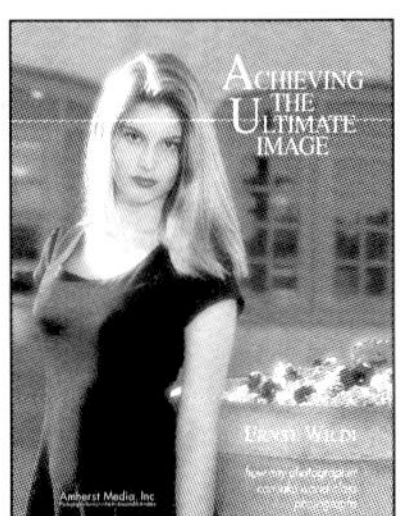

Achieving the Ultimate Image

Ernst Wildi

Ernst Wildi teaches the techniques required to take world class, technically flawless photos. Features: exposure, metering, the Zone System, composition, evaluating an image, and more! $29.95 list, 8½x11, 128p, 120 b&w and color photos, index, order no. 1628.

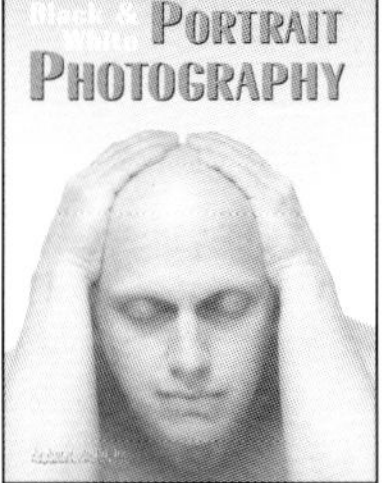

Black & White Portrait Photography

Helen T. Boursier

Make money with b&w portrait photography. Learn from top b&w shooters! Studio and location techniques, with tips on preparing your subjects, selecting settings and wardrobe, lab techniques, and more! $29.95 list, 8½x11, 128p, 130+ photos, index, order no. 1626

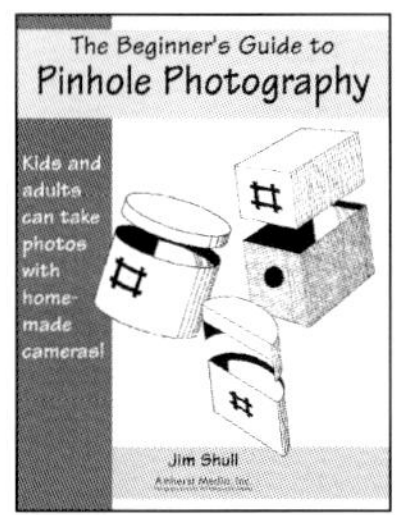

The Beginner's Guide to Pinhole Photography

Jim Shull

Take pictures with a camera you make from stuff you have around the house. Develop and print the results at home! Pinhole photography is fun, inexpensive, educational and challenging. $17.95 list, 8½x11, 80p, 55 photos, charts & diagrams, order no. 1578.

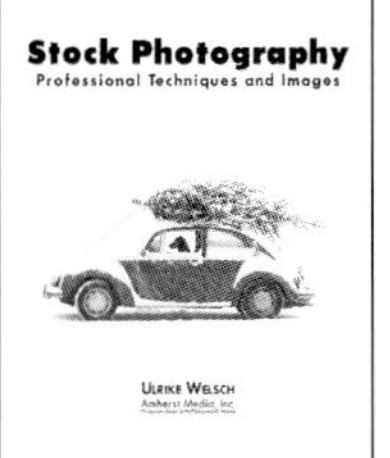

Stock Photography

Ulrike Welsh

This book provides an inside look at the business of stock photography. Explore photographic techniques and business methods that will lead to success shooting stock photos — creating both excellent images and business opportunities. $29.95 list, 8½x11, 120p, 58 photos, index, order no. 1634.

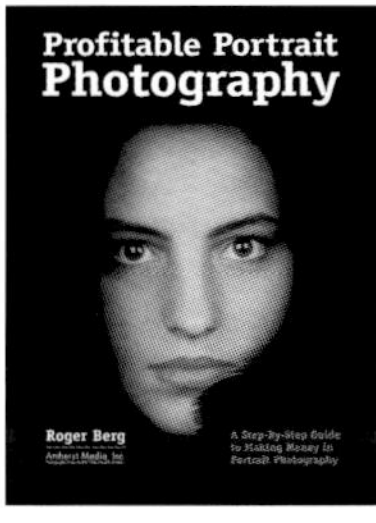

Profitable Portrait Photography

Roger Berg

A step-by-step guide to making money in portrait photography. Combines information on portrait photography with detailed business plans to form a comprehensive manual for starting or improving your business. $29.95 list, 81/2x11, 104p, 100 photos, index, order no. 1570

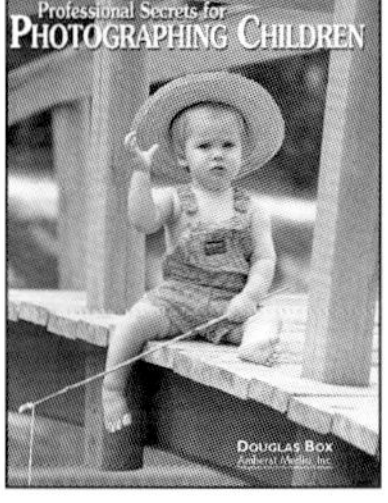

Professional Secrets for Photographing Children

Douglas Allen Box

Covers every aspect of photographing children on location and in the studio. Prepare children and parents for the shoot, select the right clothes capture a child's personality, and shoot story book themes. $29.95 list, 8½x11, 128p, 74 photos, index, order no. 1635.

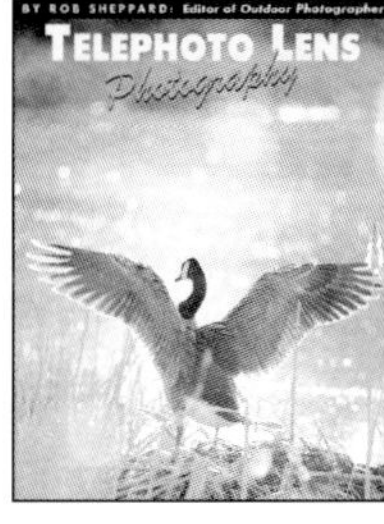

Telephoto Lens Photography

Rob Sheppard

A complete guide for telephoto lenses. Shows you how to take great wildlife photos, portraits, sports and action shots, travel pics, and much more! Features over 100 photographic examples. $17.95 list, 8½x11, 112p, b&w and color photos, index, glossary, appendices, order no. 1606.

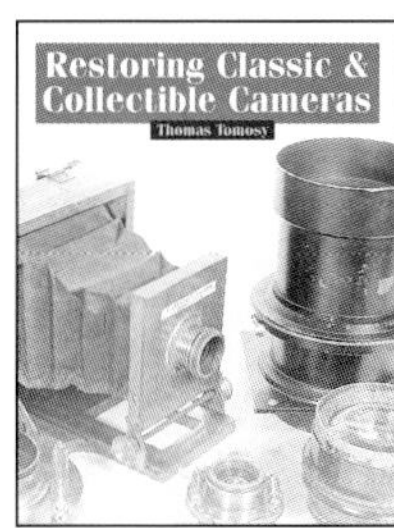

Restoring Classic & Collectible Cameras (Pre-1945)

Thomas Tomosy

Step-by-step instructions show how to restore a classic or vintage camera. Repair mechanical and cosmetic elements to restore your valuable collectibles. $34.95 list, 8½x11, 128p, b&w photos and illus., glossary, index, order no. 1613.

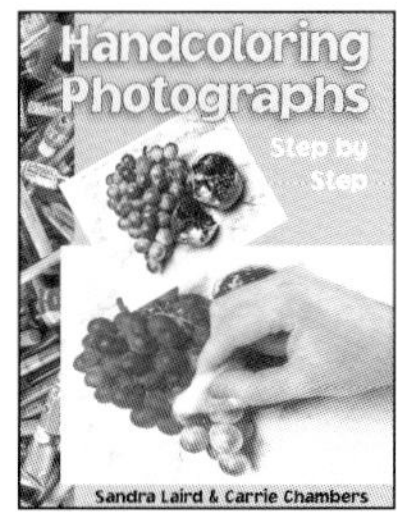

Handcoloring Photographs Step-by-Step

Sandra Laird & Carey Chambers

Learn to handcolor photographs step-by-step with the new standard in handcoloring reference books. Covers a variety of coloring media and techniques with plenty of colorful photographic examples. $29.95 list, 8½x11, 112p, 100+ color and b&w photos, order no. 1543.

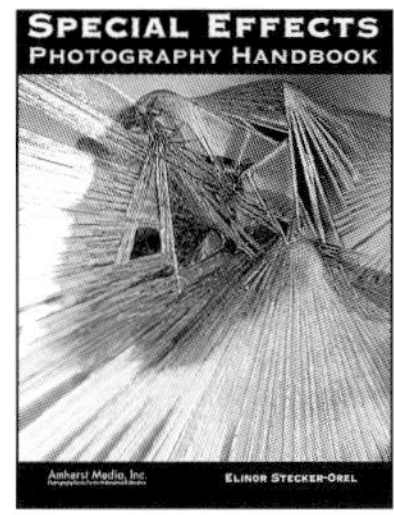

Special Effects Photography Handbook

Elinor Stecker-Orel

Create magic on film with special effects! Little or no additional equipment required, use things you probably have around the house. Step-by-step instructions guide you through each effect. $29.95 list, 8½x11, 112p, 80+ color and b&w photos, index, glossary, order no. 1614.

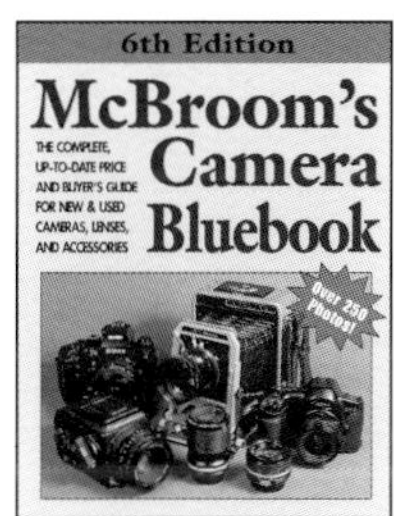

McBroom's Camera Bluebook, *6th Edition*

Mike McBroom

Comprehensive and fully illustrated, with price information on: 35mm, digital, APS, underwater, medium & large format cameras, exposure meters, strobes and accessories. Pricing info based on equipment condition. A must for any camera buyer, dealer, or collector! $29.95 list, 8½x11, 336p, 275+ photos, order no. 1553.

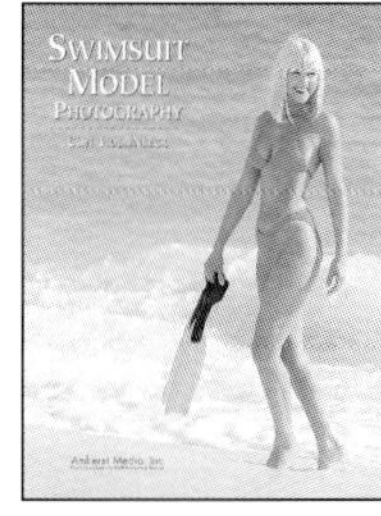

Swimsuit Model Photography

Cliff Hollenbeck

The complete guide to the business of swimsuit model photography. Includes: finding and working with models, selecting equipment, posing, using props and backgrounds, and more! $29.95 list, 8½x11, 112p, over 100 b&w and color photos, index, order no. 1605.

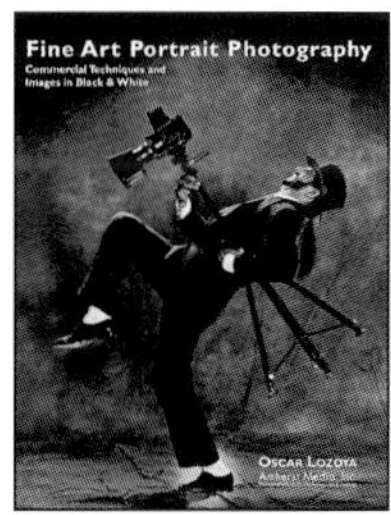

Fine Art Portrait Photography

Oscar Lozoya

The author examines a selection of his best photographs, and provides detailed technical information about how he created each. Lighting diagrams accompany each photograph. $29.95 list, 8½x11, 128p, 58 photos, index, order no. 1630.

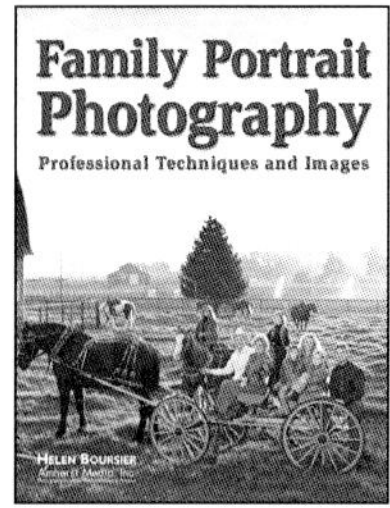

Family Portrait Photography

Helen Boursier

Learn from professionals how to operate a successful portrait studio. Includes: marketing family portraits, advertising, working with clients, posing, lighting, and selection of equipment. Includes images from a variety of top portrait shooters. $29.95 list, 8½x11, 120p, 123 photos, index, order no. 1629.

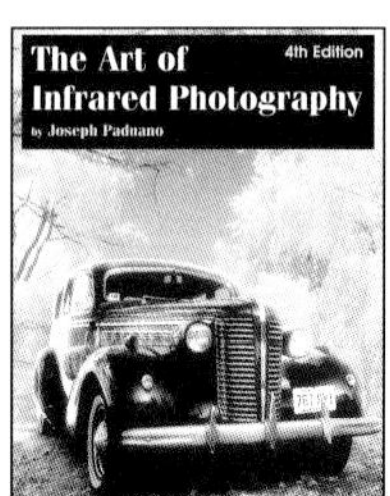

The Art of Infrared Photography, *4th Edition*

Joe Paduano

A practical guide to the art of infrared photography. Tells what to expect and how to control results. Includes: anticipating effects, color infrared, digital infrared, using filters, focusing, developing, printing, handcoloring, toning, and more! $29.95 list, 8½x11, 112p, order no. 1052

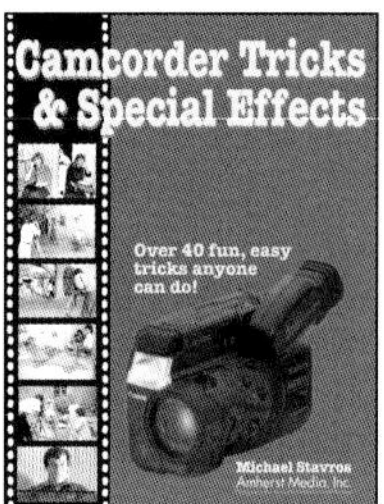

Camcorder Tricks and Special Effects, *revised*

Michael Stavros

Kids and adults can create home videos and mini-masterpieces that audiences will love! Use materials from around the house to simulate an inferno, make subjects transform, create exotic locations, and more. Works with any camcorder. $17.95 list, 8½x11, 80p, order no. 1482.

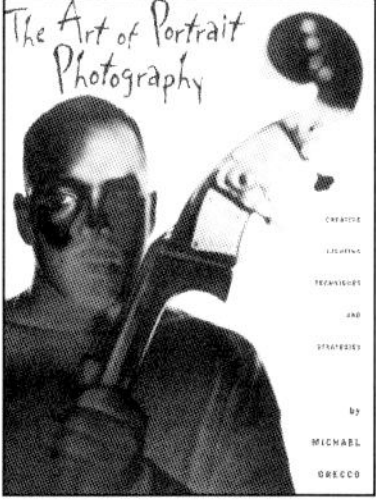

The Art of Portrait Photography

Michael Grecco

Michael Grecco reveals the secrets behind his dramatic portraits which have appeared in magazines such as *Rolling Stone* and *Entertainment Weekly*. Includes: lighting, posing, creative development, and more! $29.95 list, 8½x11, 128p, order no. 1651.

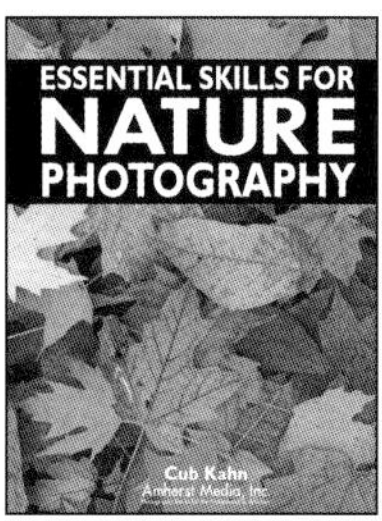

Essential Skills for Nature Photography

Cub Kahn

Learn all the skills you need to capture landscapes, animals, flowers and the entire natural world on film. Includes: selecting equipment, choosing locations, evaluating compositions, filters, and much more! $29.95 list, 8½x11, 128p, order no. 1652.

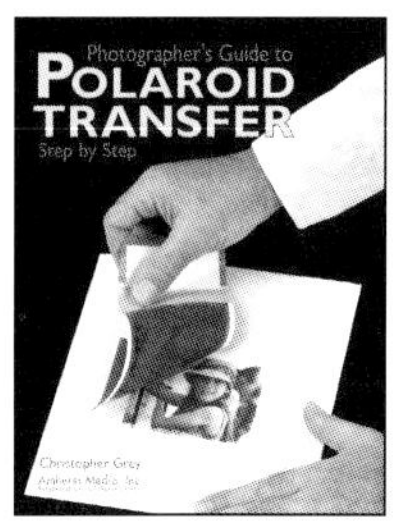

Photographer's Guide to Polaroid Transfer

Christopher Grey

Step-by-step instructions make it easy to master Polaroid transfer and emulsion lift-off techniques and add new dimensions to your photographic imaging. Fully illustrated every step of the way to ensure good results the very first time! $29.95 list, 8½x11, 128p, order no. 1653.

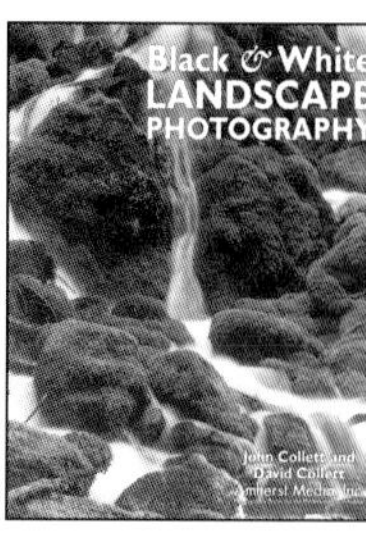

Black & White Landscape Photography

John Collett and David Collett

Master the art of b&w landscape photography. Includes: selecting equipment (cameras, lenses, filters, etc.) for landscape photography, shooting in the field, using the Zone System, and printing your images for professional results. $29.95 list, 8½x11, 128p, order no. 1654.

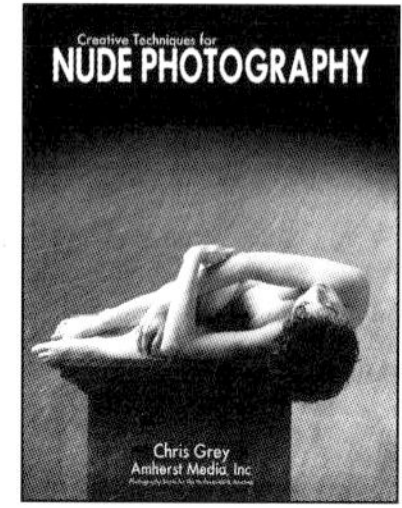

Creative Techniques for Nude Photography

Christopher Grey

Create dramatic fine art portraits of the human figure in black & white. Features studio techniques for posing, lighting, working with models, creative props and backdrops. Also includes ideas for shooting outdoors. $29.95 list, 8½x11, 128p, order no. 1655.

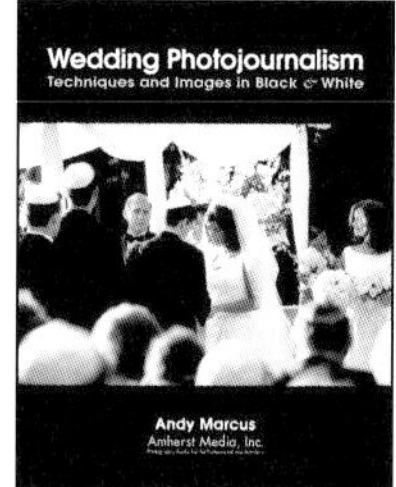

Wedding Photojournalism

Andy Marcus

Learn the art of creating dramatic unposed wedding portraits. Working through the wedding from start to finish you'll learn where to be, what to look for and how to capture it on film. A hot technique for contemporary wedding albums! $29.95 list, 8½x11, 128p, order no. 1656.

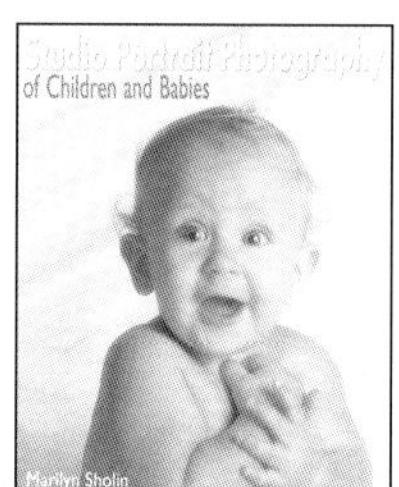

Studio Portrait Photography of Children and Babies

Marilyn Sholin

Learn to work with the youngest portrait clients to create images that will be treasured for years to come. Includes tips for working with kids at every developmental stage, from infant to pre-schooler. Features: lighting, posing and much more! $29.95 list, 8½x11, 128p, order no. 1657.

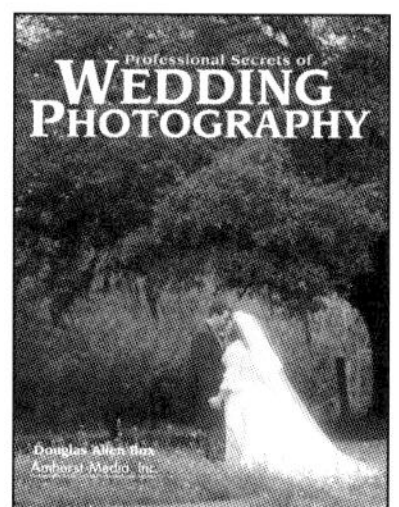

Professional Secrets of Wedding Photography

Douglas Allen Box

Over fifty top-quality portraits are individually analyzed to teach you the art of professional wedding portraiture. Lighting diagrams, posing information and technical specs are included for every image. $29.95 list, 8½x11, 128p, order no. 1658.

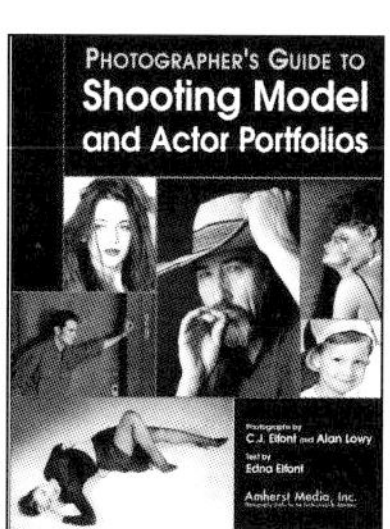

Photographer's Guide to Shooting Model & Actor Portfolios

CJ Elfont, Edna Elfont and Alan Lowy

Learn to create outstanding images for actors and models looking for work in fashion, theater, television, or the big screen. Includes the business, photographic and professional information you need to succeed! $29.95 list, 8½x11, 128p, order no. 1659.

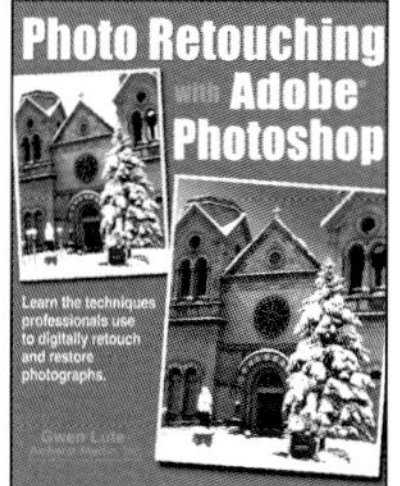

Photo Retouching with Adobe® Photoshop®

Gwen Lute

Designed for photographers, this manual teaches every phase of the process, from scanning to final output. Learn to restore damaged photos, correct imperfections, create realistic composite images and correct for dazzling color. $29.95 list, 8½x11, 120p, order no. 1660.

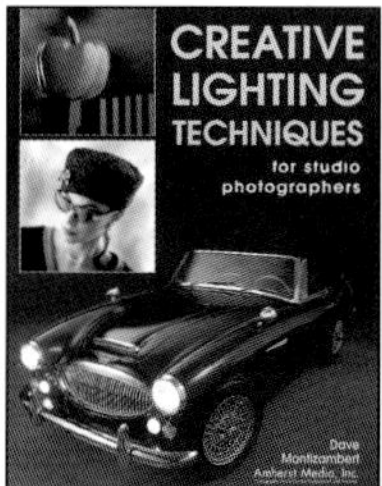

Creative Lighting Techniques for Studio Photographers

Dave Montizambert

Master studio lighting and gain complete creative control over your images. Whether you are shooting portraits, cars, table-top or any other subject, Dave Montizambert teaches you the skills you need to confidently create with light. $29.95 list, 8½x11, 120p, order no. 1666.

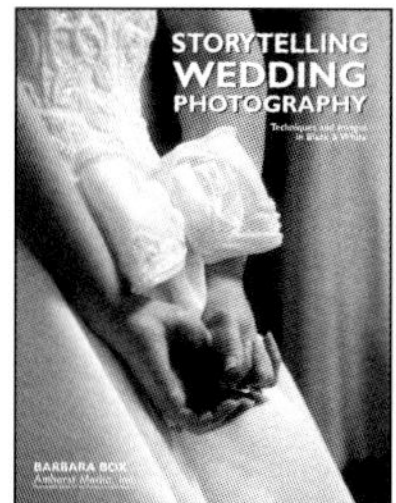

Storytelling Wedding Photography

Barbara Box

Barbara and her husband shoot as a team at weddings. Here, she shows you how to create outstanding candids (which are her specialty), and combine them with formal portraits (her husband's specialty) to create a unique wedding album. $29.95 list, 8½x11, 128p, order no. 1667.

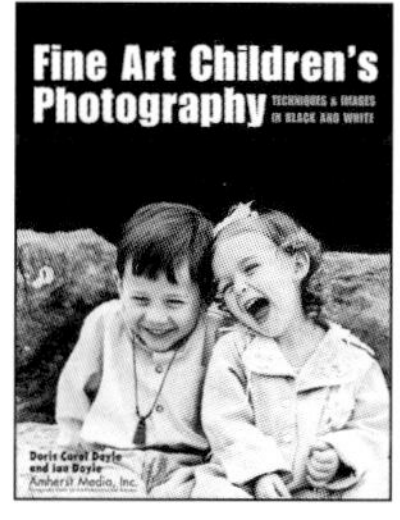

Fine Art Children's Photography

Doris Carol Doyle and Ian Doyle

Learn to create fine art portraits of children in black & white. Included is information on: posing, lighting for studio portraits, shooting on location, clothing selection, working with kids and parents, and much more! $29.95 list, 8½x11, 128p, order no. 1668.

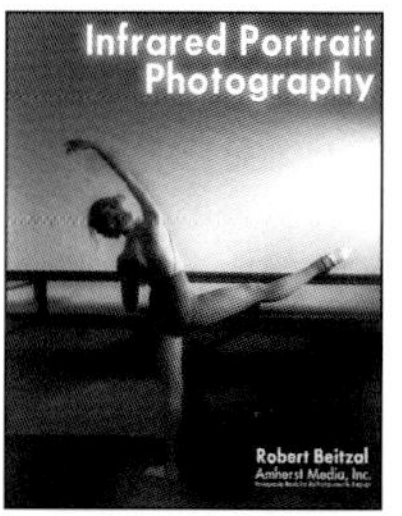

Infrared Portrait Photography

Richard Beitzel

Discover the unique beauty of infrared portraits, and learn to create them yourself. Included is information on: shooting with infrared, selecting subjects and settings, filtration, lighting, and much more! $29.95 list, 8½x11, 128p, order no. 1669.

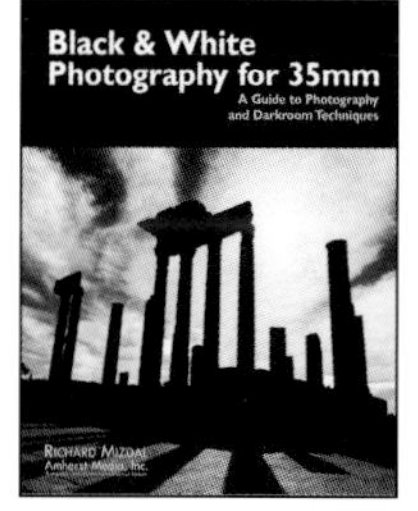

Black & White Photography for 35mm

Richard Mizdal

A guide to shooting and darkroom techniques! Perfect for beginning or intermediate photographers who wants to improve their skills. Features helpful illustrations and exercises to make every concept clear and easy to follow. $29.95 list, 8½x11, 128p, order no. 1670.

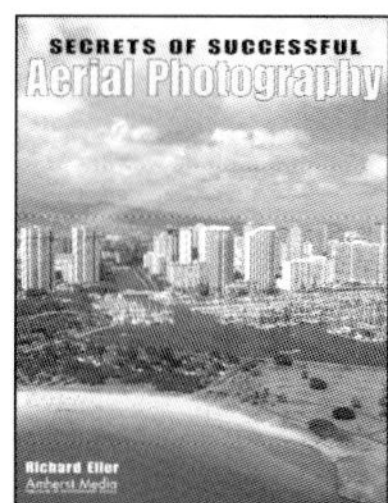

Secrets of Successful Aerial Photography

Richard Eller

Learn how to plan for every aspect of a shoot and take the best possible images from the air. Discover how to control camera movement, compensate for environmental conditions and compose outstanding aerial images. $29.95 list, 8½x11, 120p, order no. 1679.

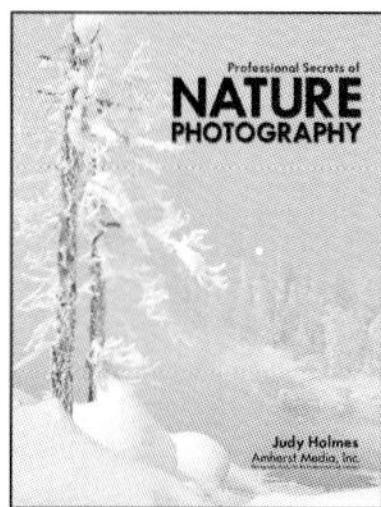

Professional Secrets of Nature Photography

Judy Holmes

Improve your nature photography with this must-have, full color book. Covers every aspect of making top-quality images, from selecting the right equipment, to choosing the best subjects, to shooting techniques for professional results every time.$29.95 list, 8½x11, 120p, order no. 1682.

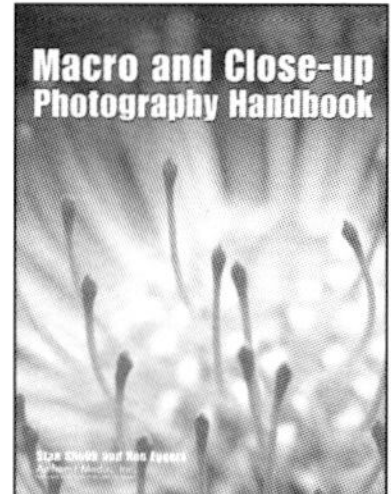

Macro and Close-up Photography Handbook

Stan Sholik and Ron Eggers

Learn to get close and capture breathtaking images of small subjects – flowers, stamps, jewelry, insects, etc. Designed with the 35mm shooter in mind, this is a comprehensive manual full of step-by-step techniques. $29.95 list, 8½x11, 120p, order no. 1686.

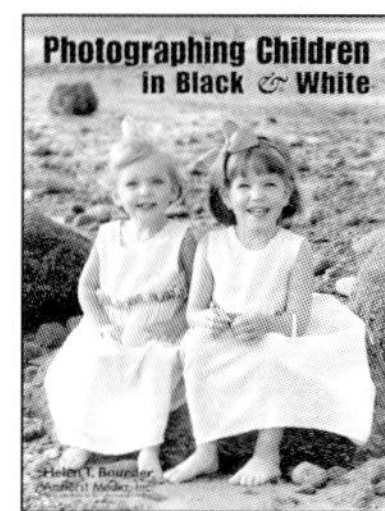

Photographing Children in Black & White

Helen T. Boursier

Learn the techniques professionals use to capture classic portraits of children (of all ages) in black & white. Discover posing, shooting, lighting and marketing techniques for black & white portraiture in the studio or on location. $29.95 list, 8½x11, 128p, order no. 1676.

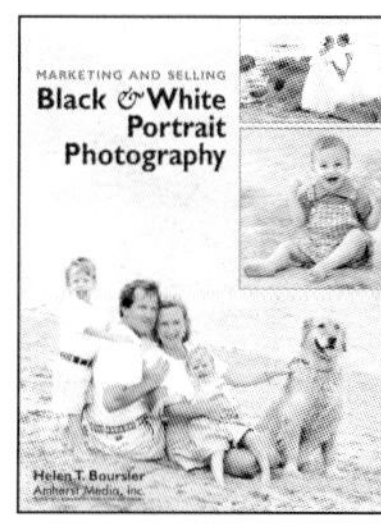

Marketing and Selling Black & White Portrait Photography

Helen T. Boursier

A complete manual for adding b&w portraits to the products you offer clients (or offering exclusively b&w photography). Learn how to attract clients and deliver the portraits that will keep them coming back. $29.95 list, 8½x11, 128p, order no. 1677.

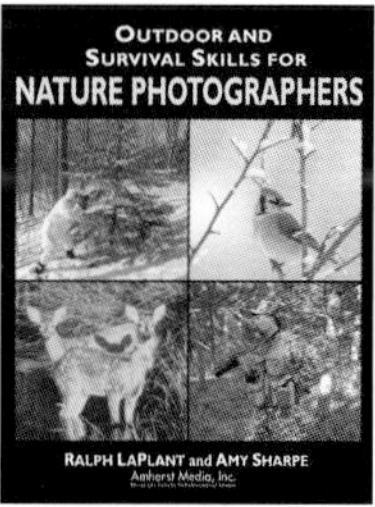

Outdoor and Survival Skills for Nature Photographers

Ralph LaPlant and Amy Sharpe

An essential guide for photographing outdoors. Learn all the skills you need to have a safe and productive shoot – from selecting equipment, to finding subjects, to preventing (or dealing with) injury and accidents. $17.95 list, 8½x11, 80p, order no. 1678.

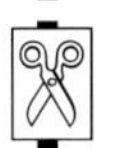

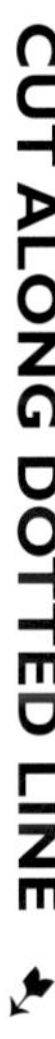

AMHERST MEDIA'S CUSTOMER REGISTRATION FORM

Please fill out this sheet and send or fax to receive free information about future publications from Amherst Media.

CUSTOMER INFORMATION

DATE

NAME

STREET OR BOX #

CITY STATE

ZIP CODE

PHONE ( )

OPTIONAL INFORMATION

I BOUGHT *DRAMATIC BLACK AND WHITE PHOTOGRAPHY* BECAUSE

I FOUND THESE CHAPTERS TO BE MOST USEFUL

I PURCHASED THE BOOK FROM

CITY STATE

I WOULD LIKE TO SEE MORE BOOKS ABOUT

I PURCHASE BOOKS PER YEAR

ADDITIONAL COMMENTS

FAX to: 1-800-622-3298

if mailing, fold in number order along dashed lines.

①

②

Name________________________________
Address______________________________
City________________________State_____
Zip__________________ — __________

Place
Postage
Here

Amherst Media, Inc.
PO Box 586
Amherst, NY 14226

③

if mailing, paste underside of flap, or tape here.